TREATISE

UPON THE

Estate and Rights of the Corporation

OF THE

CITY OF NEW YORK,

AS PROPRIETORS:

By MURRAY HOFFMAN, Esq.

Volume II.

APPENDIX,

CONTAINING

NOTES AND DIAGRAMS.

SECOND REVISED EDITION.

NEW YORK:
EDMUND JONES & CO., PRINTERS TO THE CORPORATION,
No. 26 John Street.
1862.

APPENDIX.

NOTES.

Note 1.—Page 16.

Appointment of a Representative Council, in 1647.—*Gov. Stuyvesant.*

"*Whereas*, we desire nothing more than that the government of New Netherlands, entrusted to our care, and principally New Amsterdam, our capital and residence, might continue and increase in good order, justice, police, population, prosperity, and mutual harmony, and be provided with strong fortifications, a church, a school and reading-place, harbor and similar necessary public edifices and improvements, for which we are desirous of obtaining the assistance of our whole community. Being unwilling, however, to vex and harass our dear subjects in any way with exactions, impositions and burthens, but rather to induce and solicit them voluntarily to assist in such honest and highly necessary work; and

"*Whereas*, it is difficult to cover so many heads with a single cap, or to reduce so many different opinions into one, so did we, with the advice of our Council, heretofore propose to the Commonalty, that the inhabitants should nominate a double number of persons from the most notable, reasonable, honest and respectable of our subjects, from which we might select a single number of nine men, to confer with us and our Council, as their tribunes, on all means to promote the welfare of the Commonalty, as well as that of the country ; wherefore a double number of our good and lawful subjects having been proposed, we with our Council did select from said nomination nine men to wit: (*three from the merchants, three from the citizens, and three from the farmers, all named,)* as interlocutors on behalf of the Commonalty."

Then follow provisions as to their powers and duties most jealously guarded, and reserving almost entire control to the Director and Council.

Note 2.—Page 18.

Burgher-recht.—February 1, 1657.

Dr. O'Callaghan (vol. 2, p. 338) says, "The exclusive right to trade was confined, almost from the beginning of the city of Amsterdam, to the Burghers. These were constituted by birth, purchase, intermarriage, or a vote of the city." Very important privileges, commercial, political, and legal, resulted from the possession of this right; which the learned author states in detail. The Burgomasters, however, pursuaded the Council to divide the Burghery into two classes, the greater and small citizens ; "giving to those who should pay the sum of five hundred guilders the privilege of enrolling their names on the list of the great, who alone were to be invested with the monopoly of offices. The lessor citizenship conveyed only freedom of trade, and the privilege of being received into the respective guilds."

This law was received with very little favor, and was abolished by an edict of the 25th of March, 1668. "Unfortunately for New Amsterdam, it was after the establishment of these unwise distinctions at home, that Burgher right was conferred upon her. Governor Stuyvesant divided the citizens into two castes—the great and the small burghers. The members of the Council—all burgomasters and schepens, all ministers of the gospel and officers of militia, with their descendants in the male line—were enrolled in the first class, and all others could obtain the same on payment to the city treasury of fifty guilders, Holland currency."

It may reasonably be concluded, that after the example of Amsterdam, the chief officers were exclusively given to the higher class.

Note 3.—Page 19.

Charter of Nicolls, 12th of June, 1665.

This charter is set forth in the records of the Burgomasters and Schepens, of 1665. On the 14th of June, of that year, the Governer Nicolls appeared in the Assembly, and delivered to the clerk his act of revocation, dated the 12th of June, of the form of the old government of Schout, Burgomasters and Schepens; and declared that a commission should be instituted for the city government, "to consist of the Mayor, Aldermen, and Sheriff, according to the custom of England, in other his Majesty's corporations."

This was followed by his new charter, also dated the 12th of June, 1665, which is as follows: "Whereas, upon mature deliberation and advice, I have found it necessary to discharge the form of government late in practice within this his Majesty's town of New Yorke, under the name and style of Schout, Burgomasters, and Schepens, which are not known or customary in any of his Majesty's dominions —To the end that the course of justice may be legally, equally, and impartially administered for the future, to all his Majesty's subjects, as well inhabitants as strangers.— Know all men by these presents, that I, Richard Nicolls, Deputy-Governor of his Royal Highness, the Duke of York, by virtue of his Majesty's Letters Patent, dated the 12th day of March, in the sixteenth year of his reign, do ordain, constitute and declare that the inhabitants of New York, New Harlem, and all other his Majesty's subjects, inhabitants upon the island, commonly called and known by the name of Manhattan Island, are and forever shall be accounted, nominated and established, as one body politique and corporate, under the government of a Mayor, Aldermen and Sheriff; and I do by these presents constitute and appoint, for one whole year, commencing from the date hereof, Mr. Thomas Willet, to be Mayor; Mr. Thomas De La Vall, Mr. Oloff Stevenson, Mr. John Brugges, Mr. Cornelius Van Ruyven, and Mr. John Lawrence to be Aldermen; and Allard Anthony to be Sheriffe; giving and granting to them, *the said Mayor and Aldermen*, or any four of them, whereof the said Mayor or his Deputy shall be always one, and upon equal divisions of voyces, to have always the casting and decisive voyce, full power and authority to rule and governe as well all the inhabitants of this Corporation as any strangers, according to the general laws of this government, and such peculiar laws as are or shall be thought convenient or necessary for the good and welfare of this his Majesty's Corporation; as also to appoint such under officers as they shall judge necessary for the ordinary execution of justice. And I do hereby strictly charge and command all persons to obey and execute, from time to time, all such warrants, orders and constitutions as shall be made by the said Mayor and Aldermen, as they will answer the contrary at their utmost perill; and for the due administration of justice, according to the form and manner prescribed in this commission by the Mayor, Aldermen and Sheriffe, these presents shall be to them, and every of them, a sufficient warrant and discharge in that behalf.

"Given under my hand and seal, at Fort James, in New York, on Manhattan Island, this 12th day of June, 1665.

"RICHARD NICOLLS."

NOTE 4.—PAGE 19.

Acts of the Corporation under the Charter of 1665.

On the 9th of May, 1676, an ordinance was passed as follows: "Ordered, that all persons living within the street, called the Heer Graft (Broad street), shall fill up the Ditch, Graff, or Common Sewer, and make the same level with the street, and then pave and pitch the same before their doors with stones, as far as every inhabitant's house shall be front-ting towards the said Graff or Ditch, upon pain of having such fines inflicted upon them as the court shall see fit."—[English Records, Com. Council.]

On the 24th of July, 1677, a rate was laid upon the inhabitants' houses and vacant lands in the city. This was done by the authority of the Mayor and Aldermen. It is stated to be laid for defraying the city debt, and was to be paid one half immediately, and the other half by the 26th of October ensuing.

The names of probably all the principal inhabitants may be found in this document. We find also the names of the following streets, &c.:

The Heer Graft, the Stone street, Marvelt street, Winkle street (Broadway), Marketfield street, The Wall, the High street, Mill street lane, Smith street lane, Beavers Graft, Field street, and the water side.

February 16, 1676. It was ordered that the several persons named build wells in certain streets, of which they were inhabitants.

And on the 23d of February, 1683, a committee, before appointed to search the records for ordinances, laws, &c., for the government of the city, made a report; and a committee was appointed to draw up orders relating to the several heads of such report. On the 15th of March, 1683, a large body of ordinances was adopted.

They comprehended a great variety of subjects—the observance of the Lord's day—the registering of strangers—the regulation of cartmen, their number, fees and various rules for their conduct, among them, that they were not to ride upon their carts in the streets—that freemen only should keep shops—the licensing of public houses—appointment of surveyors, without whose sanction no building should be erected—relating to markets, fire-wood, and many other particulars.

Note 5.—Page 20.

Petition for the Charter of 1686.

"To the Honorable Thomas Dongan, Esquire, Lieutenant-Governor and Vice Admiral under His Royal Highness, James, Duke of York, &c.

"The humble petition of the Mayor, Aldermen, and Commonalty of the city of New York, sheweth,—

"That this city hath had and enjoyed several ancient customs, privileges and immunities, which were confirmed and granted to them by Colonel Richard Nicolls, late Governor of this Province, by authority of His Royal Highness, A. D., 1665, who incorporated the inhabitants thereof, New Harlem and others inhabiting on the Island Manhattan, whereon this city standeth, as one body politic and corporate, under the government of a Mayor, Aldermen and Sheriff, in which manner it hath continued in practice ever since, and hath had and enjoyed the custom, liberties and privileges following, viz.:

'1st. That all the inhabitants on the Island Manhattan were under the government of the city of New York.

'2d. That the government of said city was by seven magistrates and a schout, formerly called burgomasters and schepens, now one Mayor, six Aldermen and one Sheriff.

'3d. These magistrates had power to appoint all inferior

officers, as constables and overseers, under-sheriffs, cryers and marshals throughout the whole island; and also to make such peculiar orders as they judged convenient for the well governing the inhabitants of said corporation, and held once in fourteen days (or oftener, on special desire or occasion) a Court of Judicature, at the City Hall, where they did hear and determine all causes and matters whatsoever brought before them, by jury or in equity, as the case required. The Mayor or chief magistrate had power to determine all matters that came before him under forty shillings, without appeal, or any other process than a verbal hearing thereof.

'4th. The sheriff served all writs, and summons, and attachments within the limits of the corporation, and acted as water bailiff on the water.

'5th. They had their own clerk, and kept the records of the city distinctly.

'6th. This city was the staple port of the whole province, where all the merchandise was shipped and enrolled.

'7th. None were to be esteemed freemen of the city but such as are admitted by the magistrates aforesaid, and none before such admission are to sell by retail, or exercise any handicraft trade or occupation; and every merchant or shop-keeper was to pay for the public use of the city £3 12s.; every handy craftman, £1 4s. on being made free.

'8th. No freemen of the city were to be arrested, or have their goods attached, unless it was made to appear that they were departing, or conveying away their estates to defraud their creditors.

'9th. No person was admitted to trade up the North river, except he was a freeman, and had been an actual inhabitant of this city for the space of three years; and if any freeman shall be absent out of the city the space of twelve month, and not keep fire and candle, and pay scot and lot, he should lose his freedom.

'All the inhabitants up Hudson river were forbid to trade over sea.

'10th. No flour was to be bolted or packed, or biscuit made for exportation, but in the city of New York; it being for the encouragement of trade, and keeping up the reputation of New York flour, which is in great request in the West Indies, and the only support and maintenance of the inhabitants of this city, and if not confirmed to them, will ruin and depopulate the same.

'12th. That the said city had a common seal, to serve for the sealing of all and singular their affairs, matters and business touching the said corporation.'

"All which said ancient customs, privileges and liberties, the said Mayor and Aldermen, in behalf of themselves and the citizens of said city, humbly present and make known to your honor, humbly beseeching your honor in their behalf to intercede and procure that the same be confirmed to them by charter from his Royal Highness, with the additions following."

The petition then asks for certain specified additions to their powers and organization, which were generally granted, and which it is needless here to state in detail. The Governor and Council asked for an explanation of certain points of the petition, and in reply the Common Council, among other things, stated as follows:

"The town of Harlem is a village belonging to this city and corporation. For the more easy administration and dispatch of justice, officers have been annually appointed by the Mayor and Aldermen, to hold courts, and determine matters not exceeding 40*s*. both for Harlem and the Bowery, and shall do the like for the future, as it is intended to be one of the six wards."

"The whole island being one corporation, the inhabitants are all members of one body, and conceive no need of distinction."—[Minutes of C. C., 9th and 27th Nov., 1683.]

Note 6.—Page 20.

Preamble to the Charter of 1686.

"I, Thomas Dongan, Lieutenant-Governor and Vice Admiral of New York and its dependencies, under his Majesty, James the Second, by the Grace of God, of England, Scotland, France and Ireland, King, Defender of the Faith, Supreme Lord and proprietor of the colony and province of New York, and its dependencies in America. To all to whom these presents shall come, Greeting. *Whereas*, the city of New York is an ancient city within the said province, and the said city has anciently been a body politic and corporate, and the citizens of the said city have held, used, and enjoyed, as well within the same as elsewhere in the said province, divers and sundry rights, liberties, privileges, emoluments, &c., as well by prescription as by charter, letters patent, and grants, and confirmations, not only of divers governors and commanders-in-chief of the Nether Dutch Nation, while the same was under their power and subjection.

"*And whereas*, divers lands, tenements and hereditaments, jurisdiction, liberties and privileges have heretofore been given or granted, or intended to be given or granted to the citizens and inhabitants of the said city, sometimes by the name of the Mayor and Aldermen and Sheriff of the city of New York, and sometimes by the name of the Mayor and Aldermen of the city of New York—and by divers other names, as by their several letters patent, charters, grants, writings, records and muniments, amongst other things, may more fully appear.

"*And whereas*, the citizens and inhabitants of the said city have erected, built and appropriated, at their own proper costs and charges, several public buildings, accommodations and conveniences for the said city, that is to say, the City Hall, or State House, with the ground thereunto belonging; two market-houses; the bridge into the dock; the wharves or docks, with their appurtenances, and the new burial-place without the gate of the city: and have established and settled one ferry from the said city of New York to Long Island, for the accommodation and conveniences of passengers, the said citizens and travelers."—

The preamble also recites the holding and enjoying, by several the inhabitants of the city, of lands, privileges, &c., under prior grants, charters and conveyances. The attestation is—"In witness whereof I have caused these presents to be entered in the Secretary's office, and the seal of the said province to be hereunto affixed, this 27th day of April, in the second year of the reign of his sacred Majesty aforesaid, and in the year of our Lord, 1686."

NOTE 7.—PAGE 25.

Minute of statutes under the charter of 1686.

The principal statutes passed after 1686, the date of Dongan's charter, to 1730, that of Montgomerie, which affected the powers of the Corporation of New York, were the following:

The act for confirming the charters of cities, of May, 1691, is before fully stated.

The act for regulating buildings, streets, wharves, lanes, docks and alleys in the city of New York, passed Oct. 1, 1691, S. & L., p. 8.

This important statute is quoted particularly under the head of wharves, and also streets, &c. It is sufficient here to observe that the Common Council was empowered to make all laws and regulations for the laying out of streets and wharves, as should be found convenient; and if, in laying out any streets or wharves, it should be found necessary to take any person's lands, and the amount to be paid cannot be agreed upon, a jury was to be impanneled to assess it.

The third section contained the principle of imposing the charge for paving of streets, pitching and cleaning sewers, drains, &c., upon the houses within the city, in proportion to the benefit they shall receive thereby.

July 3, 1695, an act (the first of a long series) to enable the city of New York to relieve their poor, and to defray the necessary and public charges. (Ibid., p. 2.)

May 16, 1699.—"An act to enable the city of New York to pay their debts, and repair their public buildings."

Oct. 18, 1701.—"An act for encouraging the city of

New York." Part of this expired in three years, and the residue, relating to ferriages, was provided for by the ferry act of October 14, 1732.

Act 17th October, 1701, § 9.—" *Whereas*, the cities of New York and Albany, by their several charters, differ in the ways and means for their defraying their public charge and maintaining their poor from the several counties within this province—

" Be it therefore enacted, that the said Common Councils of such cities respectively are hereby authorized to follow their former methods in the premises. And they were empowered to raise, by annual tax, such sum as should be necessary to pay their representatives, bellmen or watchmen, or such other necessary public charge as should be requisite. Not to exceed, however, £300 per annum for their public charge."

May 1, 1702.—" An act for declaring, confirming and explaining the liberties of the city of New York, relating to the election of their magistrates." Repealed by Queen Anne, Dec. 31, 1702.

Nov. 20, 1702.—" An act for the better support of the poor in the city of New York." Expired Nov. 12, 1704.

Nov. 25, 1702.—" An act to enable the Mayor, &c., to raise money upon the freeholders and inhabitants thereof, and for defraying their public and necessary charges annually." Expired Nov. 25, 1704.

Nov. 27, 1702.—" An act to enable the city of New York to supply the vacancy of such public elective magistrates and officers as may die, remove, or be incapacitated before the time of the annual election." Expired Nov. 27, 1705.

June 19, 1703.—" An act for prohibiting the distilling

of rum, or burning of oyster-shells into lime, within the city of New York, or within a half mile's distance of the said City Hall." Expired 1710.

June 27, 1706.—"An act to enable the Mayor, Aldermen, and Common Council of the city of New York, to carry on the fortifications of said city." Ibid., p. 69.

Oct. 24, 1706, another act to raise £3,000 for the same purpose.

Oct. 16, 1708.—"An act to enable the Mayor, Aldermen, and Commonalty of the city of New York to raise £600, in two years, for the uses therein mentioned." Repealed by Queen Anne, Dec. 17, 1709.

Nov. 11, 1709.—"An act to regulate the sale of goods by public outcry, auction, or vendue, in the city of New York." Renewed or provided for until the act of Nov. 19, 1720, which expired July 1, 1726.

July 21, 1705.—"An act to oblige the inhabitants of each particular ward within the city of New York to make good their respective quotas of all public taxes."

By this act, "if any collector or constable of any ward proved insolvent, or withdrew with the public money, the inhabitants of the ward who elected him should make good the loss by a new levy, and not the city at large, as had been formerly."

May 14, 1717.—"An act to enable the Mayor, Aldermen, &c., to raise the sum of £500 for altering the course of the Common Sewer, at the end of Broad street, and for cleansing the dock of the city." It was recited that the public and annual income of the city was so small, that they would not defray the necessary and public charge thereof. (Law in the office of Secretary of State.)

Sept. 20, 1782.—"An act to raise the sum of £268, in

the city and county of New York, for discharging the debts therein mentioned."

Sept. 20, 1728.—" An act for raising or levying £200 for repairing the barrack in his Majesty's Fort George, in the city of New York."—

In 1713, an act was passed for amending and keeping the Post road, from New York to King's Bridge. It was successively renewed until 1741, when it was materially altered. Its chief provision was, that the portions of the street, from the dwelling house of Joachim Anderson, should be repaired and amended by the inhabitants of all the wards of the city except the Out Ward; and all that part of the road from Joachim Anderson's to the limits of Harlem patent shall be amended and repaired by the inhabitants of the Bowery division of the Out Ward.

In 1717, an act was passed as to Ferries. This was to last for seven years. It was renewed in 1724, again in 1726, and finally in 1732, when the law was passed which remained in force down to the Revolution, and which will be particularly noticed under the head of Ferries. By the act of 1717, the rates of ferriage were established, the times of running, and number of boats prescribed, and other regulations imposed.

NOTE 8.—PAGE 25.

Acts of the Corporation under the charter of 1686.

On the 24th of April, 1686, there was the following proceeding:

" Adrian Waterhouse, making application for satisfaction of his ground that was taken away to make the New street, did consent to convey his right and title therein to the city; and in consideration thereof to be free from all public taxes for the use of the city for a term of years, and also from payment of what has been already taxed."

On the 8th of August, 1687, an ordinance was passed, directing the inhabitants to pave the portions of the streets opposite their lots, and imposing a fine for neglect.

On the 15th of October, 1691, several ordinances were adopted. Two markets were established—the sale of butcher's meat and fish was regulated—the duties of carmen were prescribed—two persons were appointed city surveyors, to lay out lots—and the assize of bread was settled.

Dec. 4th, 1691.—A committee was appointed to lay out streets, and highways, and lots of ground, with power to treat with claimants for their rights, and to sell lots.

January 21, 1692.—The inhabitants from the widow Lewis to the water gate were summoned to produce their patents, to show what claim they had to the ground before their doors unto low water mark. Upon perusal of the patents exhibited, it appeared that they had no title or pretense to such ground.

N. B. Several of the inhabitants did not appear. Daniel Van Vost produced his patent, laying claim to certain ground. Eight days given him to make his defense.

Feb. 5th, 1692.—" Upon perusal of Daniel Van Vost, his patent, the Common Council are of opinion that all the land, without the wall, belongs to the city." This means, it is supposed, the land which Van Vost claimed under his patent, and lying outside the wall.

The wall was first erected in 1653, being an entrenchment and line of palisades, running through Wall street, to Broadway, and to the North River. In 1699, the Common Council petitioned the governor to have it demolished, and the materials to be employed in building the City Hall. (Valentine's Manual, 1852, p. 353.)

On the 11th of February, 1692, an ordinance was adopted, directing the inhabitants in the streets and lanes, called Bridge street, Broad street, Church street, Broadway, Beaver street, Pearl street, and others not named, to pave so much thereof as shall front their respective buildings and lots, according to the dimensions and proportions specified. This ordinance was enforced by a penalty of 20*s*. for every neglect, to be levied by distress of goods and chattels. An Alderman and Assistant Alderman in each ward were to levy of the goods and chattels of the defaulters, until the same should be done. (Published at the City Hall after the ringing of three bells.)

October 6th, 1722.—Ordered that Alderman Cortlandt and Mr. Roosevelt be a committee to fence in the land belonging to the Corporation, from high water to low water mark, from the west side of the slip near the house of Andrews Hartenbrook, and that they take the affidavits of such ancient and honest inhabitants as can best inform them, where the high water mark was about twenty or twenty-two years ago.

2

NOTE 9.—PAGE 26.

Proceedings and Petition of the Common Council for the Charter of 1730, and acts of the King's Council.

At a meeting of the Common Council, held on the 23d of March, 1729, it was

"*Resolved,* That this Corporation do make application to his Excellency the Governor, for his Majesty's grant of confirmation of the charter of the Corporation in the Royal style, and of all their ancient rights and privileges thereunto belonging, and for such additions, grants, emoluments and privileges as can be obtained."

A committee was appointed to consider what things it would be needful to be petitioned for by this Corporation. The committee made their report "as to what may be thought necessary to ask and petition for, in order to obtain a new charter in the Royal style, to confirm and grant unto this city their present grant and charter."

They reported eighteen different subjects to be asked for. The report was approved of.

A committee was appointed to wait upon the Governor in relation to the matter. They did so, and were informed that he would refer any such petition to his Majesty's Council for their advice, as he was bound to do by his instructions. (Minutes C. C., Board of Assistants, 1729.)

A petition was then drawn, and on the 3d of August, 1729, was approved and directed to be presented to the Governor.

"*To his Excellency, &c.:*

"The humble petition of the Mayor, Aldermen, and Commonalty of the city of New York, sheweth:

"That the city of New York is an ancient city, and the citizens thereof have anciently held and used, and still do hold and use divers rights, liberties, privileges, franchises, jurisdictions and emoluments, lands, tenements, heredita-ments, and public buildings, as well by the name of the Mayor, Aldermen, and Commonalty of the city of New York, as otherwise, as well to the great improvement of his Majesty's revenue, and the sensible increase of naviga-tion, trade, and commerce, as to the advancement of the said city in the number of buildings and inhabitants, whereby the said city is become a considerable seaport, and exceedingly necessary and useful to Great Britain in supplying his Majesty's government in the West Indies with bread, flour, and other provisions.

"That the said Corporation and citizens have been stren-uous assertors of the Protestant religion, and upon all occa-sions shewed an earnest and hearty zeal for the Protestant suc-cession in his Majesty's illustrious house, and ever demon-strated their sincere loyalty and affection to the crown of Great Britian, by an unfeigned readiness and alacrity in paying all due regard to the support of the honor and dignity of his Majesty's government, and in the cheerful payment of those duties and taxes for that purpose raised and layed, and of which they bear a voluntary, though very great part.

"And as this city, under the influence of his Majesty's just, mild, and gracious government, as well as that of the royal predecessors, is grown large and populous, and under your Excellency's wise and prudent administration hath the fair prospect of a numerous accession of inhabitants, the same grows daily sensible of a want of sufficient power and authority, so to regulate and improve these great advantages, as might render it of further use and service to the crown, to the advancement of morality and true religion, to their trade and navigation, to the better order, rule and government thereof, and to the general good of the whole body of people in this his Majesty's colony of New York.

"*Wherefore* your Excellency's petitioners most humbly pray, that your Excellency and the Honorable Council of this colony will be favorably pleased to direct and order his Majesty's Letters Patent, under the great seal of the colony, to pass in the Royal style, confirming and granting to this city and Corporation, by the name, style, and title of Mayor, Aldermen, and Commonalty of the city of New York, all their lands, tenements, public buildings, and hereditaments, wharves, docks, bridges, slips, ferries, cranes, grants, charters, liberties, franchises, free customs, jurisdictions, emoluments and immunities, now and heretofore by them held and enjoyed; *and that*, for the greater ease and encouragement of trade, the bounds and limits of this city be enlarged, and do hereafter extend to and comprehend four hundred feet beyond low water mark on Hudson's river, from the certain creek or kill, called Bestaver's Killitjie, southward to the Fort, and from thence the same number of feet beyond low water mark around the Fort and along the East river, as far as the north side of a certain hill call Corlear's Hook; and that they may have the soil thereof at a reasonable quit rent.

"That the Corporation may have the sole power and authority of appointing ferries around this island, with the profits, benefits, and advantages arising therefrom, with such fees as shall be regulated by the act of Assembly.

"That they should have all the market-houses, slips,

wharves, docks, cranage and wharfage, and profits which may arise therefrom."

Various other powers, of a municipal or judicial nature, are then sought for, which it is needless to particularize. They also pray that the Corporation may have a confirmation and grant of the lands they held on Nassau Island, the ferry houses and appurtenances thereunto.

Mr. Recorder (Aug. 10, 1729) presented to this court a draft of a new charter and confirmation, &c., which was read; and it was ordered that a Committee examine the same, and advise with Mr. Murray and such other counsel as they think needful thereupon.

Proceedings of the King's Council.

Upon the charter being submitted to the Governor in Council, it was referred to Mr. Van Dam, Mr. Clark, Mr. Harrison, Mr. Alexander, Mr. Provost, Mr. Kennedy and Mr. Philip Van Cortlandt to examine and report upon.—[Minutes of Council, 1730—Albany Records.]

The Committee made a most elaborate report to the Council, passing separately upon every clause, and sanctioning or modifying each successively. Among the important changes was one stopping the grant of the four hundred feet at the Fort, and recommencing at Whitehall. They also added a clause, providing that the wharves towards the rivers should be forty feet wide, for the convenience of trade and for defense. This provision is in the charter.

The report being concurred in by the Council, it was unanimously

"*Resolved*, That the Governor be advised to grant the charter."—Ibid.

It was issued accordingly; and on the 11th of February, 1730, was presented to the Mayor by the Governor, with much ceremony.—[Ibid., and Minutes of Common Council, New York, of that date.]

NOTE 10.—PAGE 26.

Recital in Montgomerie's Charter, 1730.

(After stating the charter of Dongan, &c., Queen Anne, it proceeds :)

"By virtue, or under pretext thereof, the said inhabitants and citizens of the city of New York have held and enjoyed, or have claimed to hold and enjoy, and still do claim to hold and enjoy, the ferry, vacant land, profits, privileges, and others the premises in the before-recite letters patent mentioned and intended to be granted.

"*And whereas*, besides all the aforesaid particulars in the said grant or instrument of the year 1686, and in the before-recited letters patent of Queen Anne, mentioned or intended to be thereby granted, the citizens and inhabitants of the said city of New York have anciently held, or claimed to hold, use and enjoy divers other rights, privileges, franchises, powers, profits, lands, tenements and hereditaments, as well by prescription as by divers grants and confirmations of and from divers governors, lieutenant-governors, by the name of Mayor, Aldermen, and Commonalty of the city of New York, and by divers other names, styles and titles, and otherwise.

"*And whereas*, divers questions, doubts and opinions, ambiguities, controversies and debates have arisen and been made, as well upon and concerning the validity and force of the said recited grant or writing, dated in the year of our Lord 1686, and the before-recited letters patent of Queen Anne, as upon all and every other grant and confirmation of divers governors, lieutenant-governors, and commanders-in-chief, made to our city of New York as aforesaid, by reason of the variety of names, styles, titles and incorporations aforesaid, and by reason that the before-mentioned grant or instrument, dated in the year of our Lord 1686, and the other grants and confirmations, were made in the Governor's own name respectively, when they should have been made in the respective names, styles and titles of former kings and queens, our royal predecessor, under whom they were governors, &c.

"*And* by reason, as some suggest and say, that the said city, or inhabitants or citizens thereof, never were well, regularly or legally incorporated, and for want thereof, none of the said grants, confirmations and writings hereinbefore mentioned, could take effect or operate; and for divers other defects in all or some of the aforesaid grants, confirmations and writings.

"*And whereas*, the said," (the petition of the Corporation is then recited.) "*And we*, considering that the strength and increase of this our province of New York does in a great measure depend upon the welfare and prosperity of our said city, wherein the trade and navigation thereof are principally carried on, promoted and encouraged, and we are desirous to give encouragement to the said city, inhabitants and citizens, and to remove, utterly abolish, and wholly take away all and all manner of causes, occasions, and matters, whereupon such questions, doubts, opinions, ambiguities, controversies and debates as aforesaid, or any other questions or doubt may or can arise, in order thereunto," &c.

Note 11.—Page 27.

Act confirming the Charter, October 14th, 1732.

"An act of confirming unto the city of New York its rights and privileges, passed October 14, 1732.

"1st. Be it declared and enacted by the Governor, the Council and the General Assembly of the colony of New York, and it is hereby enacted by the authority of the same, that the Mayor, Aldermen and Commonalty of the city of New York shall and may forever hereafter continue and remain *and* a body corporate and politic *in re facto et nomine*, by the name of the Mayor, Aldermen, and Commonalty of the city of New York; and by that name to sue, plead, and be impleaded, and to answer and be answered, without any seizure or forejudger for or upon any pretence of any forfeiture or misdemeanor at any time heretofore done, committed, or suffered.

"2d. And be it enacted by the authority aforesaid, that all and singular letters patent, charters, gifts, and grants, sealed under the great seal of the colony of New York, heretofore made and granted unto the Mayor, Aldermen, and Commonalty of the city of New York, be, and are hereby declared to be, and shall be, good, valid, authentic and effectual in the law, against the king's Majesty, his heirs and successors, and all and every person and persons whomsoever, according to the tenor and effect of the said letters patent, grants, charters and gifts.

"3d. And be it enacted by the authority aforesaid, that all and singular letters patent, grants, charters and gifts, sealed under the great seal of the colony of New York, heretofore made and granted to the Mayor, Aldermen, and Commonalty of the city of New York, be, and are to all intents and purposes, hereby ratified and confirmed.

"And be it enacted by the authority aforesaid, that the Mayor, Aldermen, and Commonalty of the city of New York, and their successors, shall and may forever hereafter peaceably have, hold, use and enjoy all and every the rights, gifts, charters, grants, powers, liberties and hereditaments which have heretofore been given or granted unto the Mayor, Aldermen, and Commonalty of the city of New York, by any letters patent, charter, grant or gift, under the seal of the colony of New York.

"5th. And be it enacted by the authority aforesaid, that this present act shall be taken, accepted and reputed, to be a general and public act, of which all and every the judges and justices of the colony in all courts, and all other persons, shall take notice on all occasions whatsoever, as if it were a public act of Assembly relating to the whole colony; any thing herein contained to the contrary thereof in anywise notwithstanding."

Note 12.—Page 27.

Minute of Colonial Statutes passed after the Charter of 1730.

The statute of 1732, respecting ferries, is hereafter noticed.

It is sufficient here to observe, that there is not a clause in it, except one, which could not have been made the subject of an ordinance, under a just construction of the powers of the Corporation.

October, 1730.—An act was passed to prevent damages arising from the running at large of swine; which gave authority to impound, and, if not redeemed within a limited time, to sell them at auction.

This was made perpetual by an act of the 14th September, 1739.

But on the 27th of February, 1751, it was enacted, that it should be lawful for the Mayor, &c., in Common Council convened, to make and establish such laws and ordinances as they may deem expedient, for the purpose of preventing swine from running at large in any of the streets, lanes or public places of the said city, and for impounding or forfeiting all swine which shall be found so running at large in said city, for such uses and purposes as the said Mayor, &c., shall direct.

Certain acts were passed for the better extinguishment of fires, which conferred new powers upon the Corporation. (Act of December 16, 1737; of December 31, 1751; of December 31, 1768; of December 30, 1769, and of April 1, 1774.)

A series of statutes was adopted respecting wells and pumps (act 27th November, 1741; of December 12, 1753;

of December 24, 1759; of October 20, 1764, and of January 26, 1770). Another class of statutes related to the Post road, and other roads within the limits of the city. (Act of 1738; of November 7, 1741; of November 25, 1751; of October 39, 1764, and of March 9, 1774. As to wharves and slips, see act of September 21, 1744; of January 27, 1770, and of February 16, 1771.)

As to bridges, see the act of March 10, 1774.

Various statutes were also passed in relation to streets. Most of these acts will be noticed more particularly, and commented upon when their subjects are discussed. I shall then endeavor to point out where they appear to have been superfluous, where necessary, and where merely auxiliary.

Note 13.—Page 28.

The letter of Governor Cosby is to be found in the London Documents of Mr. Broadhead, vol. 24. There is an entry in the minutes of the Board of Trade, dated 22d of August, 1734, in which they say, that the charter of Montgomerie is referred to in the act of 1732, but not transmitted; without which they could not properly judge of the act. They direct the Governor to transmit a copy.—(London Doc., vol. 25.) No further notice of the statute, nor of any act respecting it, can be found.

Note 14.—Page 28.

Extract from the Commission to Sir Danvers Osborne.

"And you, Sir Danvers Osborne, by and with the consent of our said Council and Assembly, or the major part of them, shall have full power and authority to make, constitute and ordain laws, statutes and ordinances for the public peace, welfare and good government of our said province; which said laws, statutes and ordinances are not to be repugnant, but as near as may be agreeable to the laws and statutes of this our kingdom of Great Britain; provided that all such laws, statutes and ordinances be within three months or sooner, after the making thereof, transmitted to us under our seal of New York, for our approbation or disallowance; and in case any or all of the said laws, statutes or ordinances, being not before confirmed by us, shall at any time be disallowed and not approved, *and so signified by us, our heirs or successors, under our or their Privy Seal,* unto you the said Danvers Osborne, or to the commander-in-chief of our said provinces for the time being; then so much and so many of the said laws, statutes and ordinances as shall be so disallowed and not approved of, shall *from thenceforth* cease, determine, and become utterly void."

Dr. O'Callaghan has been so kind as to examine the Commissions of Slaughter, Fletcher, Belmont, Hunter and Montgomerie, and they all contain the above clause in the same words.

NOTE 15.—PAGE 36.

The pamphlet in question is entitled "An Examination of the Validity of the pretended Charters of the Cities of New York, Brooklyn, 1852."

The following are the writer's objections and difficulties:

1st. He asks how the charter was delivered to the Mayor on the 15th of February, 1730, when it is dated the 15th of January, 1732?

The charter is attested as of the 15th of January, in the fourth year of his Majesty's reign, George the Second, which the writer will find was 1730, and the certificate of Bradley is of the same date.

2d. That it did not pass the Council, or was submitted to that Body, or that there is no indorsement on the instrument to that effect.

It *was* submitted to the Council, most thoroughly sifted by them, ratified and unanimously approved. The want of an indorsement to that effect is really an objection not worth refuting.

3d. That there is no indorsement upon it that Montgomerie consented to it, or proof that he did consent.

The seal of the province could not be affixed without the Governor's consent; and, as he never sought to break the charter, on the ground of its being surreptitiously obtained, or on any other ground, it is no very extravagant presumption that he did consent. It cannot be imagined that the writer means that the consent must have been indorsed on the document.

4th. It is objected that Montgomerie did not sign it.

Perhaps the judicial decision of Assistant Vice Chancellor Sandford, that the signature of the king or governor, to a patent or grant emanating from the crown, was not necessary to its validity, is equal in weight to the writer's opinion. (Bogardus *vs.* Trinity Church, 4 Sandford's Ch. R.)

5th. It is next said, " that the consent of the Assembly is wanting."

No man, before this, ever doubted that the king could grant a charter, and empower his governors to do so. No one has ever before imagined that the assent of a colonial assembly was requisite for this purpose. If the king had agreed to abridge his prerogative in this particular, it seems reasonable to ask for some proof of it. The character of Charles and James makes such a concession rather improbable.

6th. Again it is urged, that the charter was not sent to the Board of Trade, submitted to the king, or received his sanction.

It has been shown that such sanction was not necessary for the passage of binding statutes. They were valid until the king disaffirmed them. Much less could the royal approval be necessary for charters and patents. The unrestricted power to issue them passed to the Duke of York, and from him to his governors.

7th. The only glimmer of argument in the publication, is that part of it which relates to the repealing act of 1828.

In a previous part of this work, many considerations have been urged to show that this act could not repeal either the statute of 1691 or that of 1732. These considerations appear to the author to be unanswerable ; but if untenable, then the charters are left as they were before the acts; and, as nothing yet urged against them shakes them in the most trivial degree, they were valid grants of the kings of Great Britain, and are saved by the Constitution.

NOTE 16.—PAGE 78.

Boundaries of the Wards, October 6, 1683.

At a meeting of the Mayor and Aldermen, at the City Hall, the 8th day of December, 1683, the division of the city and Corporation of New York, into six wards, is agreed upon to be as follows:

THE SOUTH WARD.—"To begin at the corner house of James Mathews, by the water side, and so northwards along the Heer Graft (Broad street) to the house of Simon Johnson Romaine; and from thence westward up the Beaver Graft to the corner house of Barent Coursen; and from thence southward by the fort to the water-side, including the Pearl street; and so to the house of James Mathews, again."

THE DOCK WARD.—"To begin at the house of Mr. Stephen Van Cortlandt, by the water side, and so northwards to the corner house of Gusie Denys, from thence eastward to the house of Tryntie Clox; and so westward to Mr. Van Cortlandt's again."

THE EAST WARD.—"To begin at the house of Thomas Lewis, and from thence northward to the house of Lawrence Keys; then along the wall to the corner house of Miriam Levy, and so to Thomas Lewis' again, with all the houses in the Smith's Fly, and without the gate on the south side of fresh water."

The North Ward.—" To begin at the house of Arian Jansen Lagener; thence eastward along the Beaver Graft and Princes street to the house of Christian Lawrence; and so northwards to the house of Garet Hendrix, and from thence westward to the corner of New street, and thence southward to Arian Jansen, again."

The West Ward.—" To begin at the house of Thomas Coker, so northward to the gate, and from thence eastward along the wall to the corner of New street; and from thence southward to the house of Peter Bestrede, and from thence westward to the widow of John Johnson Bestrede, and so to Thomas Coker, again."

The Out Ward.—" To contain the town of Harlem, with all the farms, plantations and settlements on this Island Manhattan's, from the north side of the fresh water."

Mem. on these Boundaries.

The Heer Graft is now Broad street. The Beaver Graft is Beaver street. Pearl street was that part of the present Pearl street which lay west of Broad street, and the part east of the same was Hoogh straat, or High street. At least this was the case under the ordinance as to streets of 1656. New street appears to have been the same as it is at present. The house of Thomas Coker is mentioned in the charter of 1686, " as a messuage by the Fort," and was reserved out of that grant.

NOTE 17.—PAGE 78.

Boundaries of County of New York, in Act, Nov. 1, 1683.

"The city and county of New York to contain all the islands commonly called Manhattan's Island, Manning's Island, and the two Barn Islands; the city to be called as it is, New York, and the islands above specified, the county thereof."—Copied from original act in the office of Secretary of State.

Boundary of New York by Act of October 1, 1691.

"For as much as mistakes arise about the limits and bounds of the respective counties, within this province, for the prevention thereof—

1. "Be it enacted by the commander-in-chief and Council and Representatives, and by the authority of the same, that the said province be divided into twelve counties, as followeth:

2. "The county of New York to contain all the islands, commonly called Manhattan's Island, Manning's Island, the two Barn Islands, and the three Oyster Islands; Manhattan's Island to be called the city of New York, and the rest of the islands the county."

Boundaries of the City in the Charters of 1730, § 2.

"To begin at the river, creek or run of water, called Spuyten Duyvel, over which King's Bridge is built, where the said river or creek empties itself into the North river, on the Westchester side thereof, at low water mark, and so to run along the said creek, river, or run at low water mark on the Westchester side, unto the East river or Sound; and from thence to cross over to Nassau Island, to low water mark there, including Great Barn Island, Little Barn Island, and Manning's Island; and from thence all along Nassau Island shore at low water mark, unto the south side of Red Hook, and from thence to run a line across the North river so as to include Nutten Island, Bedlow's Island, Bucking Island, and Oyster Island, to low water mark on the west side of the North river, or so far as the limits of our said province extend there, and so to run up the west side of the said river at low water mark, or along the limits of our said province, until it comes directly opposite to the first-mentioned river or creek, and thence to the place of beginning."

NOTES 18 and 19.—PAGES 79 and 80.

Boundary of the County of New York, Act March 7th, 1788.

The county of New York to contain the islands called Manhattan's Island, Great Barn Island, Little Barn Island, Manning's Island, Nutten Island, Bedlow's Island, Bucking Island, and the Oyster Islands, and all the land under water within the following bounds:

"Beginning at Spuyten Duyvel creek, where the same empties itself into Hudson's river, on the Westchester side thereof, at low water mark, wherever the same now is or hereafter may be, and so running along the said creek at low water mark as aforesaid, on the Westchester side thereof, unto the East river or sound, and from thence to cross over to Nassau Island to low water mark there *as aforesaid*, including Great Barn Island, Little Barn Island, and Manning's Island, and from thence along Nassau Island shore, at low water mark, as aforesaid, unto the south side of Red Hook; and from thence across the North river so as to include Nutten Island, Bedlow's Island, Bucking Island and the Oyster Islands, *to low water mark on the west side of Hudson's river, or so far as the bounds of this State extend there, and so up along the west side of Hudson's river, at low water mark, or along the limits of this State*, until it comes directly opposite the first-mentioned creek; and thence to the place where the said boundaries first began."

[The boundary of New York, in the act of 1813, is precisely the same as the foregoing.]

Boundary in Revised Statutes, 1830, 3 *R. S.*, *p.* 2.

"The county of New York shall contain the islands called Manhattan's Island, Great Barn Island, Little Barn Island, Manning's Island, Nutten Island, Bedlow's Island, Bucking Island, and the Oyster Islands, and all the land under water within the following bounds:

"Beginning at Spuyten Duyvel creek, where the same empties itself into Hudson river, on the Westchester side thereof, at low water mark, and running thence along the said creek, at low water mark, on the Westchester side thereof, to the East river or sound; then to cross over to Nassau or Long Island, to low water mark; there, including Great Barn Island, Little Barn Island, and Manning's Island; then along Nassau or Long Island shore, at low water mark, to the south side of Red Hook; then across the North river so as to include Nutten Island, Bedlow's

Island, Bucking Island, and the Oyster Islands to the west bounds of the State, until it comes directly opposite the first-mentioned creek, and then to the place where the said boundaries began."

[The variations are shown by the clauses in italics, in the act of 1788, which are omitted in that of 1830. The description on the New Jersey side adapts itself to the boundary as settled by the Commissioners of the two States in 1833. The material change seems to be in respect to low water, omitting the clause "wherever the same now is, or hereafter may be," and the word "aforesaid," which implies the same.]

Note 20.—Pages 80, 81, 82.

Boundary of Kings County, November 1, 1683.

"Kings county to contain the several towns of Boshwyck, Bedford, Brooklyn, Flatbush, New Utrecht, and Gravesend, with the several settlements and plantations adjacent."—[Copied from the original act in office of Secretary of State.]

Boundary of Kings County, October 1, 1691.

"Kings county to contain the several towns of Boshwych, Bedford, Brooklyn, Flatbush, Flatlands, New Utrecht, and Gravesend, with the settlements and plantations adjacent."

Boundary of Kings County, October, 1788.

"The county of Kings to contain all that part of this State, bounded easterly by Queens county, northerly by the county of New York, westerly, partly by Hudson's river and partly by the ocean, and southerly by the Atlantic Ocean, including Coney Island."

Boundary of Kings County—Act of 1813.

"The county of Kings to contain all that part of this State bounded easterly by Queens county, northerly by the county of New York, westerly, partly by Hudson's river and partly by the ocean, and southerly by the Atlantic Ocean, including Coney Island and Barren Island; and that the island on which the said three counties last mentioned are situated, shall continue to be called and known by the name of Nassau Island."—[Kings, Queens, and Suffolk.]

Boundary of Kings County—R. S., 1830.

"The county of Kings shall contain all that part of the State, bounded easterly by Queens county, northerly by the county of New York, westerly by the middle of the main channel of the Hudson's river, from the southern boundary of the county of New York to the ocean, and southerly by the Atlantic Ocean, including Coney Island and Barren Island, together with all the islands south of the town of Gravesend."

Description of Fire District in Act of April 2, 1801.

All, &c., comprised "within a line to begin at the East river, opposite to, and to be drawn up the road that leads from the still-house, late the property of Philip Livingston, deceased, and including the said still-house and the other buildings on the south side of the said road, to and across the road leading from Bedford, south of the house now or late of John B. Johnson, and from thence north-easterly, including all the houses on the east side of the road last mentioned, to and including the house and mills of John Jackson, at the East river aforesaid; and from thence down the East river to the place of beginning."

Description of Fire District of Brooklyn, in Act of April 12, 1816.

That section of the town of Brooklyn, commonly known by the name of the Fire District, and contained within the following bounds, viz.:

"Beginning at the public landing, south of Pierpont's distillery, formerly the property of Philip Livingston, deceased, on the East river, thence running along the public road leading from said landing to its intersection with Red Hook lane; thence along said Red Hook lane to where it intersects the Jamaica Turnpike road; thence a north-east course to the head of the Wallabought mill-pond; thence through the centre of said mill-pond to the East river to the place of beginning, shall continue to be known and distinguished by the name of the village of Brooklyn."

Charter of Brooklyn, 1834.

Brooklyn was incorporated as a city by the act of April 8, 1834. (Sess. Laws, 1834.) The city was divided into nine wards. The five districts of the village, as before established, were declared to be the first five wards. The limits of the other wards are defined. Whenever they come to the water side, the description is, "along the Gowannus bay," "along the Wallabout bay," "along the East river," "to the bay or river," or similar words.

The first six wards of Brooklyn were defined by an act of the Legislature, of the 9th of April, 1840. Where the lines reach the water, they are described as running "to the river."

Note 21.—Page 83.

Act settling the boundary between New York and New Jersey, Feb. 5, 1834.

The act recited a certain agreement made between the Commissioners of the State, and declared it ratified on the part of the State of New York. It is as follows:

Article First.—"The boundary line between the two States of New York and New Jersey, from a point in the middle of Hudson river, opposite the point on the west shore thereof, in the forty-first degree of north latitude, as heretofore ascertained and marked, to the mean sea, shall be the middle of said river, of the bay of New York, of the waters between Staten Island and New Jersey, and of Raritan bay, to the main sea, except as hereinafter otherwise particularly mentioned.

Article Second.—"The State of New York shall retain its present jurisdiction of and over Bedlow's and Ellis' Islands, and shall also retain exclusive jurisdiction of and over the other islands lying in the waters above mentioned, and now under the jurisdiction of that State.

Article Third.—"The State of New York shall have and enjoy exclusive jurisdiction of and over all the waters of the bay of New York, and of and over all the waters of the Hudson river, lying west of Manhattan Island, and to the south of the mouth of Spuyten Duyvel creek, and of and over the land covered by the said waters to the low water mark on the westerly or New Jersey side thereof; subject to the following rights of property and of jurisdiction of the State of New Jersey, that is to say:

1st. "The State of New Jersey shall have the exclusive right of property in and to the land under water lying west of the bay of New York, and west of the middle of that part of the Hudson river, which lies between Manhattan Island and New Jersey.

2d. "The State of New Jersey shall have the exclusive jurisdiction of and over the wharves, docks and improvements made and to be made on the shore, or fastened to any such wharf or dock, except that the said vessels shall be subject to the quarantine or health laws, and laws in relation to passengers of the State of New York, which now exist, or may hereafter be passed.

3d. "The State of New Jersey shall have the exclusive right of the fisheries on the westerly side of the middle of the said waters, provided that the navigation be not obstructed or hindered.

Article Fourth.—"The State of New York shall have the exclusive jurisdiction over the waters of Kill Van Kull, between Staten Island and New Jersey, to the westernmost end of Shooter's Island, in respect to such quarantine laws, and laws relating to passengers as now exist, or may hereafter be passed under the authority of that State, shall also have exclusive jurisdiction for the like purposes of and over the waters of the Sound, from the westernmost end of Shooter's Island to Woodbridge Creek, as to all vessels bound into any port in the said State of New York.

ARTICLE FIFTH.—" The State of New Jersey shall have and enjoy jurisdiction of and over all the waters of the Sound, between Staten Island and New Jersey, lying south of Woodbridge creek, and of and over all the waters of Raritan bay, lying westward of a line drawn from the lighthouse, at Prince's Bay, to the mouth of Mattawan Creek, subject to the following rights of property, and of jurisdiction of the State of New York:

1st. " The State of New York shall have the exclusive right of property in and to the land under water lying between the middle of the said waters and Staten Island.

2d. " The State of New York shall have the exclusive jurisdiction of and over the wharves, docks, and improvements made and to be made on the shore of Staten Island, and of and over all vessels aground on said shore, or fastened to any such wharf or dock, except that the said vessel shall be subject to quarantine or health laws, and laws in relation to passengers of the State of New Jersey, which now exist, or may hereafter be passed.

3d. " The State of New York shall have the exclusive right of regulating the fisheries between the shores of Staten Island and the middle of the said waters, provided that the navigation of the said waters be not obstructed or hindered.

ARTICLE SIXTH.—" Criminal process, issued under the

authority of the State of New Jersey, against any person accused of an offense committed within that State, or committed on board of any vessel being under the jurisdiction of that State, as aforesaid, or committed against the regulations made or to be made by that State in relation to the fisheries mentioned in the third article; and also civil process, issued under the authority of the State of New Jersey, against any person domiciled in that State, o.r against property taken out of that State to evade the laws thereof, may be served upon any of the said waters within the exclusive jurisdiction of the State of New York, unless such person or property shall be on board of a vessel aground upon, or fastened to, the shore of the State of New York, or fastened to a wharf adjoining thereto, or unless such persons shall be under arrest, or such property shall be under seizure, by virtue of process or authority of the State of New York.

ARTICLE SEVENTH.—" Criminal process, issued under the authority of the State of New York, against any person accused of an offense committed within that State, or committed on board of any vessel being under the exclusive jurisdiction of that State, as aforesaid, or committed against the regulations made or to be made by that State in relation to the fisheries mentioned in the fifth article; and, also, civil process, issued under the authority of the State of New York, against any person domiciled in that State, or against property taken out of that State to evade the laws thereof, may be served upon any of the said waters within the exclusive jurisdiction of the State of New Jersey, unless the person or property shall be on board a vessel aground upon, or fastened to, the shore of the State of New Jersey, or fastened to a wharf adjoining thereto, or unless such person shall be under arrest, or such property shall be under seizure, by virtue of process or authority of the State of New Jersey.

ARTICLE EIGHTH.—"This agreement shall become binding on the two States when confirmed by the Legislatures thereof respectively, and when approved by the Congress of the United States."

NOTE 22.—PAGE 83.

Relative to the Controversy with New Jersey.

In a note of the revisers of 1830 (vol. 3, R. S., 425), a reference is made to the history of this controversy, as detailed by Smith, in his History of New York, p. 228, and to various acts of the Colonial Assembly, passed to obtain a settlement of the boundary.

In the Journal of the Assembly (vol. 2, p. 393) is a document, showing the violence with which this dispute was carried on, and containing much interesting historical matter.

In the year 1806, an attempt was made to adjust the difficulty. New Jersey passed an act appointing commissioners, which was followed by New York. The attempt failed, each party insisting upon their respective claims—New Jersey that her territory extended to the middle of the Hudson River, and New York that it was only to low water mark, on the western shore. [See the report of the Commissioners to the Governor, Senate Journal of 1808, p. 51.]

On the 6th of April, 1808 (1 R. S., 1813, p. 238), an act of our Legislature was passed relating to this subject. It recited the statute of New Jersey, of the 2d of November, 1806, appointing commissioners for the adjustment of the line, as also the act of our own Legislature for the same purpose. That the Commissioners had met without coming to any agreement, and that it appeared by the report of the New York Commissioners, that the State of New Jersey claimed, as comprehended in the grant from the Duke of York to Carteret and Berkeley, the Hudson River, *ad filum aquæ*, as far down as Sandy Hook; but that New York had, coeval with the commencement of the colonial government of the two States, hitherto actually exercised or possessed the jurisdiction over the Hudson River and Staten Island, and the bay between it and Long Island, as a portion of her rightful territory. The act then proceeded to declare, that it was the duty of the Governor to sustain the jurisdiction of the State over the said territory until the State should be evicted thereof by due course of law; and also, that the whole of Hudson River, southward of the northern boundary of the city of New York, and the whole of the bay between Staten Island and Long or Nassau Island, should henceforth be deemed to be within the jurisdiction of the city and county of New York, and that all the offenses against the act should be cognizable in the courts held in and for such city and county."

Note 23.—Page 94.

Form of a Ground Brief.

We, William Kieft, Director General, and the Counsellors, in behalf of the High and Mighty Lords, the States

General of the United Netherlands, His Highness (the Prince) of Orange, and the Noble Lords the Managers of the Incorporated West India Company in New Netherland residing, make known, that we on this day, the date underwritten, have awarded and granted unto *Tymen Jansen*, a certain piece of land lying and bordering on the Marsh (valley), with the condition that the said *Tymen* shall, in connection with the aforesaid land, possess in his own right the marsh lying behind and before his land, which are separated by Kils (creeks), and all this with the express condition and terms that the said *Tymen Jansen*, or those who, by virtue of these presents, shall obtain his action, shall acknowledge the Noble Lords and States General, the managers aforesaid, for their Lords and Patroons, under the sovereignty of the High and Mighty Lords, the States General, and to their Directors and Counsellors here, shall in all things be conformed as all good citizens are in duty bound; provided, also, that the said Tymen shall submit to all such burdens and imposts as by the Noble Lords already have been directed, or hereafter shall be directed; constituting over the same, the said *Tymen Jansen*, in our stead, in the real and actual possession of the aforesaid piece of land and marsh thereunto appertaining; giving him by these presents, full right, authority, and special permission, the above described parcel of land to enter, cultivate, and use in like manner as he has the right to do, with other his patrimonial lands and effects, without our, the Grantors, in our quality as aforesaid, thereof, any longer having, reserving, or saving any part, action, or control whatever; but to the behoof as aforesaid therefrom desisting, from this time forth and forever; Promising this Transport firmly, inviolably, irrevocably, to maintain, fulfill and execute, and to do all that in equity we are bound to do, without fraud or deceit. These presents have been by us undersigned and confirmed, with our seal of red wax, here underneath suspended. Done at Fort Amsterdam, this —— day of A. D. 1642, was undersigned,

WILLIAM KIEFT.

Lower down:

By order of the Noble Lords, the Director General and Counsellors of New Netherlands, and was signed,

CORNELIUS VAN TIENHOVEN, *Sec'y.*

Confirmation of a Ground Brief.

RICHARD NICOLLS, Esquire, Governor, &c.

Whereas, there was heretofore a Patent, or ground brief, granted by the Dutch Governor, William Kieft, to Govert Lockerman and C. Lockerman, for a house and lot upon the Island, towards the East river, (description.) The said Patent, or ground brief, bearing date the 26th day of March, 1642. Now, for a confirmation unto the said Govert Lockerman in his possession and enjoyment of so much of the premises as remains untransported, Know Ye, that by virtue of the Commission, &c., I have ratified, confirmed, and granted, and do hereby ratify, confirm, and grant unto said Govert Lockerman, the parcels untransported, and to all persons unto whom transports have been made, their several parcels. To Have and Hold to them, their heirs and assigns, forever.

The patent dated 18th April, 1667.

No. 24, see end of volume.

Note 25.—Page 160.

Petition of 1702, *for land under water on Long Island.*

To his Excellency, Lord Viscount Cornbury, &c., &c.

The humble petition of the Mayor, Aldermen and Commonalty of the city of New York, most humbly showeth unto your Excellency :

That your petitioners, by their charter, having a right and interest in the ferry from this city across the river to Nassau Island, and from the said island to this city again, and to all the perquisites, profits, and advantages thereof, which your petitioners perceive to fall much short of what they might reasonably expect from the same, if the bounds and limits of the said ferry were something extended on the said island side, whereby to hinder and prevent that privilege and liberty, which divers persons now take, of transporting themselves and goods to and from the said Island of Nassau over the said river, without coming to or landing at the usual and accustomed place, where the said ferry is kept and appointed, to the great loss and damage of your petitioners, whose farmer of the said ferry complains he cannot live upon, nor longer hold the same, though at a moderate and very easy rent; which mischief and inconvenience your petitioners know not better how to remedy than by gaining a further interest on the shore adjoining to the said island, so as to oblige persons to pay the rate and duty of the ferry who pass and repass the said river with themselves or goods, to or from any other part of the said island, within the bounds and compass hereby prayed for, than that where the said ferry is now kept; which being in your Lordship's power alone to enable your petitioners to do,

We, your said petitioners, do most humbly beg of your Excellency, that you would be pleased to grant unto us and our successors, for the use and behoof of this city and Corporation, under the seal of this province, all the vacant land from high water to low water mark, fronting the harbor of this city, from the east side of the Red Hook, upon Nassau Island aforesaid, to the east side of Wallabout, upon the said island, for the better and more convenient taking in and loading of passengers, corn, and other goods and things bound to and from this city.

And your petitioners, as in duty bound, will ever pray. (Read in Council, 11th March, 1702.)

The trustees for the town of Brookland, in Kings county, on Nassau Island, whose names are hereunder written, for and on behalf of themselves and said town, enter a caveat against the city of New York, or any particular person, for having a patent for any land between high water and low water mark, from Kickout and the Wallabout to Red Hook in said township, till they be heard, &c. March 16, 1702-3.

No further action appears to have been taken.

Note 26.—Page 164.

Grants of Land under water on Long Island.

On the 15th of August, 1764, a grant was made by the Corporation of New York to Philip Livingston, of a parcel of ground between high and low water, near Jeroleman street. December 4, 1801, a grant to Ebenezer Pierpont;

and another grant was made to him on the 23d of September, 1823. These were for strips in front of the land known as the Pierpont property.

Between 1809 and 1817, a large number of grants were made ; and indeed the principal part of the strip from Atlantic street to a point on the north, near the Fulton Ferry, is held under the grants of the Corporation.

On the 10th of April, 1850, a release and quit-claim was given by the Corporation to W. F. Havemeyer and others, in consideration of six hundred and fifty dollars, for a strip near Baltic street, of about one hundred and thirty feet in breadth, and extending about three hundred and sixty-nine feet from high to low water mark.

NOTE 27.—PAGE 185.

Documents as to the space between high and low water mark around New York.

January 21, 1691–2.—Upon summoning the inhabitants, from the widow Lewis's house to the water gate, to produce their patents to show what claim they had to the ground before their doors to low water mark, upon perusal of their patents it is found that Mr. Lawrence, Mr. Carsen, and Mr. Dusen, and the late widow of Abraham Leversen, and Jabobus D——, had no right by their patents, to any ground before their houses ; and Captain De Ray, on behalf of his father-in-law, doth declare, that he hath no pretense to any ground before his house.

Daniel Van Vort, his patent being produced, eight days

time is given him to make his defense, according to his request.

The rest of the inhabitants did not appear.

February 5, 1691–2.—Upon the perusal of Daniel Van Vort, his patent, the Common Council are of opinion that all the land without the wall belongs to the city.

The wall was first established in 1653, being an entrenchment and line of palisade running through Wall street, to Broadway, thence diagonally to near the river. In the year 1699, the Common Council petitioned the Governor to have it demolished, and the materials applied in building the new City Hall.

In 1691 it was ordered that all the ground by the water side, from the block-house to the hill, next to Mr. Beekman's, be sold.

The block-house was on the north-west corner of Wall and Pearl streets, projecting beyond the wall of the city The possession of Beekman was of a farm near Beekman street, and appears to have vested in him as early as 1656.

Again, the proceedings with respect to what were known as the extravagant grants of Governor Fletcher, throw light upon this subject. In the year 1696–7, that governor had made various grants, among which was one to Colonel Heathcote, of a portion of the King's Garden, "running to low water mark." That garden was known in Dongan's charter as a piece of ground by the gate, called the Governor's Garden, and was especially excepted out of the grant to the Corporation. By the statute of 1699, this patent to Heathcote was, with several others, vacated and annulled; and it was provided, that no governor should devise or grant the King's Garden, the Swamp, &c., for a period longer than his own continuance in office; saving, however, to the city of New York all their *right to the Swamp, and to the ground behind the Queen's Garden to low water mark.* Queen Ann was then on the throne. In the grant of Queen Ann, of 1705, to Trinity Church, the Queen's Garden was included. After giving the King's Farm, bounded on the west by Hudson's river, it proceeds—" And also all our piece or parcel of land situate on the south side of the church-yard of Trinity Church, aforesaid, commonly called and known by the name of the Queen's Garden, fronting the Broadway on the east, and extending to low water mark upon Hudson River, on the west." Trinity Church, by a series of conveyances, became seized of the property (three hundred and ten feet on Broadway), being the northern portion of its possession, and the Queen's Garden constituted the southern portion of its possession, probably commencing at a point about opposite the centre of Wall street. The northern part is marked on the map of 1695 as the burial-ground, and undoubtedly is the parcel spoken of in the charter of Dongan as the new burial-place without the gate of the city, erected by it at its proper cost. It ran to Hudson River. Then on the 21st of May, 1751, Trinity Church received from the Corporation a grant of water lots extending along the whole line of their property, acquired either as the burial-place or the Queen's Garden, described as adjoining to the rear of their church-yard, and extending from each side or corner of the rear of their ground, two hundred feet into the river below low water mark ; being of breadth on the east side at high water mark four hundred and thirty-eight feet, and at low water mark four hundred and forty-eight feet.

It may be useful to advert to the title to the burial-ground in Trinity Church, as connected with this subject.

The charter of 1697, to Trinity Church, recited a peti tion of the church for a grant of a piece of ground without the north gate of the city, in or near to a street called the Broadway, in breadth on the east side as the said street rangeth northward three hundred and ten feet, until you come to the land of Thomas Lloyd; and from thence toward the west by the said land until you come to Hudson River, and thence southward along the Hudson River, three hundred and ninety-five feet, and from thence by the line of our garden, eastward, unto the place of the said street or the Broadway where it first begun.

This charter made no express grant of this piece of land. In truth, it appears to operate only as a sanction or permission on the part of the Crown, so far as it had any power remaining, to use the land as a cemetery. The ground itself, as before observed, was the new burial-ground erected at the cost of the city, and confirmed to it by Dongan's charter; and in 1703 the Corporation made a conveyance of the land to Trinity Church, describing it as all the burying-place of the said city.

There is also a recital in the colonial act of the 27th of June, 1704, that the church was in possession of this ground, describing it nearly as it is described in the charter of 1697, except that the northern boundary line is made to run along the north side of the burying-place continued to low water mark of Hudsǒn River. The grant from the city is recognized in this act. Then in May, 1751, as before observed, the church accepted the grant of the water lots from high water along this piece of ground, as well as the Queen's.Garden.

Thus, as to the Queen's Garden, we find a right in the Corporation to low water mark recognized in the statute of 1699. Clearly this was the space between high and low water, for the garden itself extended to the river, and was expressly reserved out of Dongan's grant. The patent of Queen Ann professed to convey it, and yet Trinity Church accepts a conveyance from the Corporation of this intermediate strip, as well as of a certain depth into the river beyond it.

It would not be warrantable to press this circumstance as decisive of the right, but it is a striking instance of the claim of title of the Corporation to this strip, even in the case of a piece of upland expressly reserved.

So as to the northern portion of the Trinity Church possession, the recital in the charter of 1697 only carried the boundary to the river. That charter probably did not pass any title. The city had the title, and conveyed it in 1703. The colonial act of 1704 recognized the title of the church, and perfected it, if it needed any aid. The recital does indeed carry the line to low water. It is but a recital. The true source of the ownership, viz.: the deed of the Corporation, did not, it is supposed, go so far. If it did, the right came from that body; and if it did not, still the right came from it under the grant of 1751.

Again, the grant of the King's Farm, by Queen Ann, in 1705, extended only to the river, being bounded on the west by Hudson River, and the church or its assigns has received grants of water lots in various places running from high water. In 1773, November 18, for example, a grant was made of a strip, six hundred and twenty-four feet in length, beginning on the north side of Vesey street, at high water mark, and so extending to the land granted to the Governors of the College, adjoining Barclay street, and from the north side thereof to the north side of Chambers street to low water mark, and the soil under water from thence the whole breadth thereof, two hundred feet into the Hudson River.

Again, on the 23d of April, 1686, William Dyre conveyed to Thomas Lloyd a piece of land thus described: "Beginning at the corner of the way or passage that leads to the mill of Peter J. Mesier, and running southerly along the highway to the church-yard or burial-place, as the fence of said Dyre now standeth, four hundred and sixty-eight feet; from thence westerly upon a direct line as the fence of the said church-yard or burial-place now standeth, to the water side of Hudson river, six hundred and thirty-six feet, and so along the water side, four hundred and sixty-eight feet, thence along," &c.

In October, 1694, Lloyd conveyed to John Rodman a portion of this land. In May, 1695, he conveyed a part of it to John Hutchins. Lloyd and his grantees had therefore a right to upland acquired before April, 1686. And it is also clear that P. J. Mesier had acquired his title before that time. Yet we find that in 1699, Huddlestone, Hutchins and Rodman applied to the Corporation, stating that upon surveying their land, with a view to make wharves, &c., there was found a strip belonging to the Corporation, which they petition may be granted to them. They describe their land as fronting the Hudson River, and the strip in question prayed to be given them, as extending to low water mark.

In the case of Mesier's petition (April 15, 1701), he expressly asks for a grant from high to low water, and the grant was for eighteen rods in length, at high water mark.

In fact, I have ascertained that the soil, below high water, in the North river, from Battery place to the northern limit of the King's Farm, with only one exception, is derived from the Corporation.

That exception is of the land at the corner of Battery place and Broadway. It appears that in 1729, this property, of fifty-four feet by one hundred and twelve, on the south, and one hundred and thirty feet on the north side, belonged to Charles Sleigh. He, it will be noticed, is mentioned in the description of the westward boundaries in Montgomorie's charter, as owning a lot of ground, between which and a house and lot of Thomas Edes, the street from the parade ran before the fort to the river. This lot was mortgaged to A. De Peyster, in 1729. The equity of redemption was released, and De Peyster conveyed it to Archibald Kennedy, in August, 1756. The mortgage of 1729 shows that Sleigh had then a right to three hundred and ninety-two feet from the corner of Broadway, westward, or two hundred and seventy feet from high water mark, into the river. (See records, 1729, Register's office, New York.) That brought his land to near the east side of Washington street. Then, in 1770, the Corporation made a grant of another one hundred feet to Archibald Kennedy.

NOTE 28.—PAGE 186.

Grant of the four hundred feet in Charter of 1730, *section* 38.

"All the space of ground and soil of Hudson river, lying and being under the water of said river, to begin at a certain place near high water mark, at the south end of a piece of upland, which lies between the said river and a piece of meadow ground or marsh, being the first piece of meadow ground or marsh near Hudson river, to the southward of Greenwich, and from whence the above-named run of water, called Bestaver's Killitjie or rivulet, runs into Hudson river; from which place of beginning to extend or run to the south side of the street which runs from our parade before our fort in New York, to Hudson's river, south eighteen degrees thirty minutes west, on a straight line, the distance being one hundred and twenty-five chains; from which line to run a perpendicular breadth of, and to comprehend four hundred feet from low water mark into the Hudson river; the same containing eighty-two acres and one half of an acre of land, or thereabouts. *Also all* that space of ground and soil of the East river, from the north side of Corlaers Hook to Whitehall, beginning at two large stones set on the south side of a small creek in a marsh on the north side of Corlaers Hook, from whence to the easternmost point of Corlaers Hook, the distance on a straight line running south fifteen degrees thirty minutes east, is forty chains and two rods; from thence to Whitehall, on a straight line running south, seventy-eight degrees thirty minutes west, the distance is one hundred and fifty-two chains; from which two lines to run a perpendicular breadth of, and to comprehend four hundred feet from low water mark into the East river, the same containing one hundred and twenty-seven acres or thereabouts, together with all benefits, easements, wharfs, ways, hereditaments and appurtenances to the same belonging; with full power and authority at any time or times thereafter, to fill, make up, wharf and lay out, all and every part thereof, and the same to build upon and make use of, in such manner as they and their successors shall see fit; and all our estate, right, title and interest in and to the same. To have and to hold all and singular the premises unto the said Mayor, Aldermen and Commonalty, and their successors, to their own proper use, benefit and behoof forever. *Provided* that nothing therein shall be construed to empower the Mayor, &c., to wharf out before any persons who have prior grants from us or some one of our predecessors, of quays or wharfs beyond low water mark, without the actual agreement of such persons, their heirs or assigns, owners of such quays or wharfs; and also that of the wharves to be built or run out, there should be left toward the East and North rivers, forty feet broad, as well for the greater convenience of trade, as to plant batteries thereon in case of necessity."

Note 29.—Page 188.

Ordinances of 1795 *and* 1796, *as to South and West streets.*

"Whereas, the unlimited exclusion of this city into the East River, by making further grants to the proprietor of water lots, hath long been conceived injurious, if not ruinous to the internal and lower parts of the city, through want of the necessary descent for carrying off the water out of the streets into the river; and the Board judging that a wide and spacious street along the front of the city would tend very much to its ornament, convenience, and safety, directed their Street Committee to cause a survey and chart of the front of the city along the East River, with the line of such street marked thereon, to be made and reported to the Board; and the said committee accordingly having reported the said chart, with the lines of the said street, which is to be of the breadth of seventy feet, and beyond which no further grants into the river are to be made, or any buildings or wharves erected or made, excepting such as the Board from time to time shall hereafter deem necessary for the safety of the shipping, and the convenience of trade and navigation; and the Board having frequently had the said chart with the lines of the street run out and marked thereon, under consideration, did this day, after making some alterations as to the course of the lines of said street, agree to the same according to the following description thereof, viz.: Beginning at a point or station in the river, opposite the east side of the Whitehall slip, two hundred and twenty-nine feet six inches (229 ft. 6 in.), from the corner of the south side of Water street; thence in a direct line to a point or station opposite the west side of Coenties slip, two hundred and twenty-eight feet six inches (228 ft. 6 in.), from the corner at the south side of Water street; then beginning at a point or station opposite to the east side of Coenties slip, one hundred and sixty feet (160 ft.), from the corner at the south side of Front street; thence on a direct line to a point or station opposite the western range of the Crane wharf, three hundred and thirty-one feet nine inches (331 ft. 9 in.), from the corner at the south side of Water street; thence on a direct line to a point or station opposite the western boundary line of the grant to Thomas Barnes, now belonging to Samuel Ackerly, three hundred and fifty feet (350 ft.), from the south side of Water street; thence on a direct line to a point or station opposite the west side of Rutgers' slip, four hundred (400) feet from the south side of Cherry street; thence on a direct line to a station or point at the east part of Corlears Hook, one hundred and sixty (160) feet perpendicular from the south side of Crown point street, at high water mark; which said line is the inner side of the intended street of seventy feet wide."

On the 10th of February, 1796, the same Committee reported an alteration in the permanent line of the outer street in front of the city on the East river, as was agreed to on the 7th of April, 1795, which was also approved of by the Board, and is as follows: "Beginning at a point as laid down on the map, at the angle opposite Alderman Beekman's house, which said point is from the south side of Water street at the continuation of the south-western-most boundary line of the grant to Thomas Barnes, and now belonging to Samuel Ackerly, four hundred and twenty (420) feet into the East river; thence running on a course, as it appears on the map, N. 83° 36' east, to a point at the west range of Rutgers street, on the estate of Henry Rutgers, deceased, which said point is from the south side of Cherry street, on a course south 3° 15' east, as said Rutgers street now runs, five hundred and ninety (590) feet into said East river; thence running on a course as it appears on the map, north 87° 15' east, to a point into the East river at Corlaers Hook, which point is (after measuring on a course of north 87° 30' east) eight hundred and seventy (870) feet from the east side of Ferry street along Crown Point street; thence running at the extent of said distance south 2° 30' east, three hundred and sixty (360) feet from the south range of said Crown Point street into the river, to the said last-mentioned point."

Ordinance as to West street, 10th February, 1796.—"The Street Committee reported to the Board a description, from an actual survey, made of an outer street, along the west side of the city, which is to be of the breadth of seventy (70) feet, and beyond which no grants ought to be made, and no buildings erected; which was read and approved of by the Board. Beginning at the centre of the arched bridge over the run of water called the Bestaver's Killitjie or rivulet, and running from thence in the present range of Greenwich street, north 11° and 30′ east, one hundred and fifty (150) feet, to the south end of a piece of meadow ground, or marsh (being the first piece of meadow ground, or marsh, near the Hudson river, to the south of Greenwich), and running thence along the said point of upland, from the west side of Greenwich street, north seventy-eight degrees thirty minutes (78° 30′) west, four hundred and twenty (420) feet into Hudson's River; thence running on a course, as it appears on the map, south, eleven degrees forty-five minutes (11° 45′) west, to a point on the southern range of Duane street, which said point is from the west side of Greenwich street, along Duane street, on a course, as the said Duane street now runs north, seventy-six degrees forty minutes (76° 40′), four hundred and forty (440) feet into the Hudson's River; thence running from the said point, on a course southward, seventeen degrees thirty minutes (17° 30′) west, to a point at the north-easternmost range of the street or lane, between Kennedy's corner house and the Battery; which said point is from the west side of Greenwich street, on a course of north, sixty-eight degrees fifty minutes (68° 50′) west, at the extent of three hundred and sixty (360) feet into the Hudson River."

On the 11th of July, 1808, the Street Commissioner reported to the Common Council, that by a survey made by himself and Mr. Loss, along the Hudson River, for the purpose of directing the sinking the blocks for the piers at the foot of Partition street, he finds that the line prolonged by the survey of Mr. Magnin, as the west line of West street, is not far enough into the water by near forty (40) feet, if the line of West street be continued as it ought to be, straight from Cortlandt street to Harrison street; so that the pier to be built would be two hundred and ten (210) feet in length, instead of two hundred and fifty (250) feet, as stipulated. A resolution was adopted accordingly, making a straight line from Cortlandt to Harrison street.

Note 30.—Page 188.

Petition for the Act of 1798.

The petition of the Mayor, Aldermen and Commonalty of the city of New York, in Common Council convened, respectfully showeth: That as well for the ornament and improvement of the city, as for the encouragement of the trade and commerce of the State, and the safety of the shipping at the wharves of the city, your petitioners have lately directed a permanent street, of seventy feet wide, to be laid out and completed, at and on the extremity of their grants already made, and hereafter to be made, to individuals, on the East river, called South street, and on the North or Hudson river, called West street, south and west of which no buildings of any description are to be permitted to be erected, so that vessels lying at the wharves may be secured from fires.

That by reason of the curves and otherwise irregular state of the shore at low water mark, in the East and North rivers, at the time of the making of the grants of the predecessors of your petitioners (a general map of which, if ever made, cannot now be found), such grants are deemed to extend to unequal distances in both rivers, which occasions difficulties in making the permanent streets aforesaid, regular; and that in many instances also, your petitioners are willing, gratuitously, to give the soil, under the water, on which those streets of seventy feet are to be made, yet doubts are entertained whether your petitioners can compel any of the proprietors of the lots, fronting thereon (and who may be unwilling), to make those streets for public use, in any given reasonable time to be appointed by the Common Council.

And your petitioners further show that part of their plan aforesaid was to extend piers at right angles from the said permanent streets into the rivers, at proper distances from each other, with suitable bridges; but doubts have also arisen, whether your petitioners can compel the individual proprietors of the wharves to sink and lay out those piers, or, if they shall refuse, whether your petitioners will be authorized to sink and build those piers at the expense of the city, and receive the wharfage, without incurring a breach of the conditions and covenants contained in their grants to individuals.

The petition prayed that such powers should be conferred as should be proper to remove the difficulties and doubts stated, or for such other provisions as should seem meet.

Note 31.—Page 188.

Act of April 3, 1798.

"*Whereas*, it would conduce to health and improvement of the said city, as well as to the safety of such ships or vessels as may be employed in the trade or commerce thereof, that regular streets or wharves, of the width of seventy feet, should be laid out and completed in front of those parts of the said city which adjoin to the East river or sound, and to the North river or Hudson's river, and that piers should be extended from the said streets into the said rivers respectively, at convenient distances from each other, with suitable bridges for the accommodation of sea vessels, and upon such a construction as to admit the currents of the said rivers at both ebb and flood, to wash away all dirt and impurities. And whereas, the said Mayor, Aldermen and Commonalty, by petition to the Legislature under their common seal, have represented that they are disposed to make the said improvement, but that from the curvings and irregularities of the shores of the said rivers in their original state—from the grants made by their predecessors being deemed to extend to unequal distances into the said rivers—and from other causes, difficulties have arisen as to the execution of a proper plan, and doubts have been entertained whether they could compel the proprietors of lots fronting on said rivers to make those streets within a reasonable period, or to sink and build those piers; and whether the petitioners could, without a breach of the conditions and covenants contained in their grants to individuals, upon the refusal or neglect of such proprietors, sink, build, and make those piers, streets or wharves at their own expense, and receive wharfage as a compensation for the same; which doubts and difficulties can only be removed by the aid of the Legislature."

Therefore, Be it enacted by, &c.,

§ 1. That it shall be lawful for the Mayor, Aldermen and Commonalty to lay out, according to such plans as they shall or may agree upon or determine, such streets or wharves as are hereinbefore mentioned, in front of those parts of the said city which adjoin the said rivers, and of such extent along those rivers respectively as they may think proper; and that as the buildings of the said city shall be further extended along the said rivers, it shall be lawful for the said Mayor, &c., from time to time, to lengthen and extend the said streets and wharves.

§ 2. That the said streets and wharves shall be made and completed according to the said plan, by and at the expense of the proprietors of land adjoining, or nearest and opposite to the said streets or wharves, in proportion to the breadth of their several lots, by certain days, to be for that purpose fixed by the said Mayor, Aldermen and Commonalty, and that the respective owners of such of the said lots as may not be adjoining to said streets or wharves, shall also fill up and level at their own expense, according to such plan, and by such days respectively, the space lying between their said several lots and the said streets and wharves, and shall, upon so filling up and levelling the same, be respectively entitled to, and become the owners of the said intermediate spaces of ground in fee simple.

§ 3. If either of such proprietors should neglect or refuse to fill up and level such intermediate spaces of ground by the times appointed, the Mayor, Aldermen and Commonalty may cause the same to be done on behalf of the proprietors, and charge them with the expense ; and it was provided that if the said expense was not paid within a time fixed in the act, with interest, the same might be recovered by distress and sales, or by an action of debt.

The 4th section provided, that the sums so to be expended on behalf of the proprietors, and all sums of money which might be assessed under the act for regulating the buildings, wharves, and slips in the city of New York, should be a real encumbrance and charge upon the houses and lots in respect of which such assessment shall have been made, and shall bear lawful interest until paid, and shall be entitled to a preference above all other encumbrances upon the same ; and the same with interest and costs may be sued for and recovered in like manner as if the said house and lots were mortgaged to the said Mayor, Aldermen and Commonalty for the payment thereof.

The 5th section authorized the erection of piers in front of the said streets or wharves. It will be particularly cited under the head of Wharves and Piers, *post* sect.

NOTE 32.—PAGE 189.

Law of 1798, *as amended, and now in force.*

SECTION 220 OF LAW OF APRIL 9, 1813.—" And be it further enacted, that it shall be lawful for the said Mayor, Aldermen and Commonalty to lay out, as far as the same has not been already done, and according to the plan agreed upon for that purpose, regular streets or wharves, of the width of seventy feet in front of those parts of the city which adjoin to the East river or sound, and to the North or Hudson's river, and of such extent along the said rivers respectively as they may think proper ; and as the building of the said city shall be further extended along the said rivers, it shall be lawful for the Mayor, Aldermen and Commonalty, from time to time, to lengthen and extend the said streets or wharves."

SEC. 221 OF THE LAW OF 1813, is precisely the same as section 2, of the act of 1798, which is transcribed in Note 31.

SECTION 1 OF THE ACT OF APRIL 7, 1820.—Be it enacted, &c., "That if the proprietors of the lots of land, or land under water adjoining, or nearest and opposite to the East river or sound, and to the North or Hudson's river, in the city of New York, shall not respectively make and complete, in proportion to the breadth of the said lots of land, at their own expense, regular streets or wharves, of the width of seventy feet, *according to the plan which has been agreed upon* for that purpose, by the Mayor, Aldermen and Commonalty, and also fill up and level, at their own expense, according to such plan, the spaces lying and being between the said streets and wharves, called South street and West street, and on a level therewith, that then it shall be lawful for the said Mayor, &c., to cause the said streets or wharves, and the said intermediate lots or pieces of land, or land under water, or any part thereof, to be executed and done, for and on account of the said proprietors respectively, and if such proprietors shall not forthwith repay the said expense, with lawful interest therein, from the time of the expenditure, that then it shall be lawful for the said Mayor, Aldermen and Commonalty to levy the same, together with the interest thereof, and all the reasonable costs and charges attending such proceedings, by distress and sale of the goods and chattels of such proprietors respectively, or by action of debt, in the Supreme Court of this State, wherein it shall be sufficient to allege generally that the defendants respectively are indebted to the said Mayor, Aldermen and Commonalty in a certain sum of money expended on their account by virtue of this act, and in such action any less sum than the one declared for may be recovered, and full costs shall be given in their favor.

§ 2. And be it further enacted, that whenever such sums of money, or any part thereof, shall not be collected, and the person to whom said warrant shall be directed shall make affidavit of this, demanding the same two several times of the respective proprietors of such lots of land, or of land under water, as may reside in said city, and that they have neglected or refused to pay the same, or shall make affidavit that the proprietor or proprietors of such lots of land cannot be found in the said city, then and in such case it shall and may be lawful for the Mayor, Aldermen and Commonalty of New York to take order for advertising and selling the said lots of land, or any of them, together with all the rights and privileges thereunto appertaining or belonging, in pursuance of the second section of the act entitled "An act for the more effectual collection of taxes and assessments in the city of New York," and the said second section of the said act shall have the same application, and the like force to all intents and purposes relative to the premises, which it has relative to the premises therein mentioned.

§ 3. And be it further enacted, that every clause, covenant and condition in the several grants of the Mayor, Aldermen and Commonalty of the said city, to the said proprietors respectively, and their assigns, shall, notwithstanding this act, retain their full force and validity, and shall be in no manner affected by the same, or by anything to be done or performed in consequence thereof; and the said Mayor, Aldermen and Commonalty shall have, possess and be entitled unto the like payments, rights and remedies by virtue of the said grants, as they might or could have had, or would have been entitled to, if this act had not been passed, and shall not, by the performance of anything herein contained, be deemed to have broken or infringed any of the covenants or conditions on their part contained in the said grants.

Note 33.—Page 190.

Act of February 25, 1826.

It shall be lawful for the Commissioners of the Land Office, and they are hereby directed, to issue letters patent, granting to the Mayor, Aldermen and Commonalty of the city of New York, and their successors, all the right and title of the people of this State to the lands covered with water along the easterly shore of the North or Hudson's river, contiguous to and adjoining the lands of the said Mayor, Aldermen and Commonalty within the said city of New York, at and from low water mark, and running four hundred feet into the said river, from a point on the easterly shore of said river to Spuyten Duyvel Creek, otherwise called King's Bridge Creek or Harlem river; and also all the land covered with water along the westerly shore of the East river or sound, contiguous to and adjoining the lands of the said Mayor, Aldermen and Commonalty, at and from low water mark, and extending four hundred feet into the said East river or sound to Spuyten Duyvel creek, otherwise called Harlem river. Provided always that the proprietor or proprietors of the lands adjacent shall have the pre-emptive right in all grants made by the Corporation of the city of any lands under water granted to the said Corporation by this act.

Note 34.—Page 191.

Act of March 31, 1828, *Session Laws, p.* 163.—*Extension of West street to Great Kill Road.*

West street, along the North or Hudson river, as laid out and approved by the Mayor, Aldermen and Commonalty of the city of New York, shall be the permanent exterior street on the North or Hudson river, from the present northerly termination of West street to its intersection with a continuation of the Great Kill Road; and all grants made or to be made by the said Mayor, Aldermen and Commonalty, shall be construed as rightfully made to extend thereto; and all the provisions of an act to reduce several laws relating to the city of New York into one act, passed April 9, 1813, and the several acts amendatory thereof and in addition thereto, shall be construed to apply to said West street, herein and hereby made the permanent exterior street as aforesaid.

Note 35.—Page 191.

Act of January 18, 1830.—*Battery to Albany Basin.*

January 18, 1830.—It was provided " that it should be lawful for the Mayor, &c., of New York, whenever West street should be made between the Albany basin and Battery place (late Marketfield street) in the said city, to alter the plan or direction thereof, as heretofore laid out, approved or agreed upon, in such manner that the line thereof shall run parallel with the line of Washington street; and that the easterly side thereof shall be one hundred and eighty (180) feet distant from the westerly side of Washington street, at the termination of the said streets or Battery place, late Marketfield street, in the said city."

Note 36.—Page 191.

Act of April 12, 1837, *establishing Thirteenth avenue.*

The Thirteenth avenue, as laid out on a map made by George B. Smith, City Surveyor, bearing date March tenth, eighteen hundred and thirty-seven, and approved by the Mayor, Aldermen and Commonalty of the city of New York, by a resolution passed in Common Council, on the twenty-eighth day of March, eighteen hundred and thirty-seven (which map is filed in the office of the Street Commissioner of the city of New York), shall be the permanent exterior street or avenue in the said city, along the easterly shore of the North or Hudson's river, between the southerly line of Hammond street and the northerly line of One Hundred and Thirty-fifth street.

"The several streets of the said city, as laid out on the map or plan, made by the Commissioners appointed by the act entitled 'An act relative to improvements, touching the laying out of streets and roads in the city of New York, and for other purposes," passed April 3, 1807, or as subsequently established by law, southerly of, and including One Hundred and Thirty-fifth street, shall be continued and extended westerly along the present lines thereof, from their present terminations on the said map or plan respectively, to the said Thirteenth avenue. Also, the Eleventh avenue shall be continued and extended on the said map or plan along the present line thereof, from Thirty-sixth street to One Hundred and Thirty-fifth street.

"The Mayor, Aldermen and Commonalty of the city of New York shall be, and they are hereby, vested with all the right and title of the people of this State, to the lands covered with water along the easterly shore of the North or Hudson's river, between Hammond street and One Hundred and Thirty-fifth street, and extending from the westerly side of the lands under water heretofore granted to the said Mayor, Aldermen and Commonalty of the city of New York, by letters patent, in pursuance of the act entitled 'An act relative to improvements in the city of New York,' passed February 25th, 1826, to the westerly side of Thirteenth avenue. And the said letters patent shall be construed so as to grant to the said Mayor, Aldermen and Commonalty, forever, the said lands under water, easterly of the westerly line of the said Thirteenth avenue.

"The proprietors of all grants of land under water or of water lots heretofore made by the said Mayor, Aldermen and Commonalty of the city of New York, on the easterly shore of the North river, shall have the pre-emptive right in all grants to be made by the said Mayor, Aldermen and Commonalty of the city of New York, of any lands under water granted to them by this act, adjacent to and in front of the said lands under water so heretofore granted; and the proprietors of lands having a pre-emptive right to grants of land under water by virtue of the said act entitled 'An act relative to improvements in the city of New York,' passed February 25, 1826, shall have the same pre-emptive right in all grants made by the said Mayor, Aldermen and Commonalty of the city of New York, of any lands under water granted to them by this act."

NOTE 37.—PAGE 191

Act of May 13, 1846—*Eleventh avenue.*

By the second section, the proprietors of all former grants of land, under water, or of water lots adjacent to and fronting on the Eleventh avenue, between Seventeenth and Nineteenth streets, shall have the pre-emptive right in all grants to be made by the said Mayor, Aldermen and Commonalty of the city of New York, of any lands lying under water, or water lots lying between Eighteenth and Nineteenth streets, and the Eleventh and Thirteenth avenues, as laid down on said map, on paying the following sums, in gross, as a consideration for the same, to wit: For the grant of land under water, or water lots lying between Eighteenth and Nineteenth streets, and the Eleventh and Thirteenth avenues, three hundred and sixty-eight dollars; for the grant of land under water, or water lots lying between Eighteenth street and the line of the centre of the block between Seventeenth and Eighteenth streets and the Eleventh and Thirteenth avenues, one hundred and thirty-one dollars and thirty-three cents; and for the grant of land under water, or water lots lying between Seventeenth street and the said centre line, and the Eleventh and Thirteenth avenues, one hundred and six dollars and sixty-four cents.

NOTE 38.—PAGE 204.

Abstract of opinion of Judge Talmage, 1837.

The learned counsel shows conclusively, that the claims of owners of the upland lots is wholly untenable, as the line of the streets never touched such a lot, and that water lots only could have been referred to by the Legislature. He then states that it is obvious, from an inspection of the plan, for South street, as it was in 1801, and the plan of 1804, for West street, in the Street Commissioner's office, and from the several plans of West and South streets, as since altered, that most of West street, on the North river, and of South street, on the East river, were laid out further than four hundred feet from low water mark. Hence most of these streets are upon lands which were, at the time the plans were adopted, the property of the State. (The learned counsel, as I understand, means that West street and South street, for the most part of their respective lengths, were upon such land.) In the language of the statute, then, there were spaces lying and being between the lots and the said streets and wharves. Such a law was necessary to enable the Corporation to build a street beyond the four hundred feet grant. The law then authorized the street to be formed on the lands of the State; and to provide the means of building it in those cases where the water lots had been granted away, it was provided that the owners thereof might be compelled to fill up the street and any space between their lots and the street.

The act makes no provision for those cases where the Corporation continue to own the water lots. It would be absurd to apply the present provisions to lots owned by the Corporation. Such an application would empower the Corporation to compel themselves to fill up a street adjoining to or opposite their own property. The act was passed to reach two classes of cases only; the one where the street or wharf was laid out within or contiguous to the four hundred feet grant to the Corporation; the other where the street was laid out beyond the four hundred feet grant, and the water lot did not reach the street, but, in the language of the act, left a space lying and being between the lots and the streets or wharves.

"In the other, it empowered them to compel the owner of the water lot, not contiguous but opposite to the street or wharf, to fill up the street; and also to fill the space between this lot and the street or wharf. This statute, therefore, has no reference to upland lots whatever."

He concludes—"The statute relates entirely to the manner in which the boundary streets of the city are to be made, and its provisions are limited to this. If the water lots reach the street to be constructed, and are granted away by the Corporation, the proprietor thereof must make the street opposite and adjoining his lot. If such lot does not extend to the street, then the proprietor must make such street, and in addition fill up the intermediate space; and upon so doing the fee of such intermediate space shall pass to such proprietors."

The counsel refers to the case of Bergh *vs.* The Corporation, not reported. The case was this: In 1809 or 1810, Christian Bergh was in possession of several water lots, on the East river, south of Corlaers Hook, having no grant from the Corporation, but he was the owner of the adjoining upland to the water lots. He filled in such lots and made a wharf, insisting that, by the operation of the statute of 1807, re-enacting that of 1798, he had become entitled to the lands filled in. Upon a case made in an ejectment suit, brought by the Corporation, and after argument, the court decided against his claim. Bergh brought a bill in Chancery, but before hearing, the suit was settled, and he took a grant of the water lots. Goerck's map of 1793 is marked in this cause as produced before an Examiner.

Note 39.—Page 210.

Line of West street, under Ordinance of 1796.

The ordinance of 1796, laying out West street, fixes three points—

1st. A point of upland on the west side of Greenwich street, one hundred and fifty (150) feet north and along Greenwich street, from the centre of the arch or bridge over Bestaver's Killitjie, from which point of upland there is to be run (on a course north 78° 30′ west,) four hundred (400) feet into the river.

The Bestaver's Killitjie was afterward known as the Minetta Brook, and crossed Greenwich street in the vicinity of Charlton street. (See Loss's shore map, 1807, in the Street Commissioner's office.)

By the map of Loss, of June, 1807, in the possession of Trinity Church, and much relied upon by our surveyors, the line of even high water is to the west of Greenwich street. And in a grant with a map annexed, made to J. J. Astor, in 1807, of water lots, in the vicinity of Charlton street, it appears that from low water mark to the west side of West street, as then set down, is two hundred and ninety-eight (298) feet. The map of Loss, before mentioned, makes the distance from the west side of Greenwich to the west side of West street about five hundred and sixty feet.

2d. The next point established in the ordinance of 1796, is at the foot of Duane street. The line is from a point on the southern range of Duane street, four hundred and forty (440) feet into the Hudson river. By Magnin's map of 1804, the distance from the west side of Greenwich street to the west side of West is four hundred and eighty (480) feet. The change under the ordinance of 1808 (*ante*, p. 47) will account for the difference. The present line is as follows: West street, seventy feet; Washington to West, two hundred and sixty-two feet; Washington street, fifty; and Greenwich to Washington, one hundred and sixty feet; making five hundred and forty-two (542) feet.

Low water mark is here found to the west of Washington street, on Loss's map of 1807; of course, even including West street, there was less than 332 feet from low water occupied.

3d. The third point fixed in the ordinance of 1796 is at the foot of Marketfield street.

It is from the west side of Greenwich street (on a course west, 68° 50') 360 feet into the river, and on the northwesternmost range of the street, between Kennedy's corner house and the Battery. Everything is here plain and certain.

The title of Charles Sleigh, acquired before 1729, gave him, as before observed, 270 feet into the river, from high water mark. That mark was at the east side of First street, which was nine feet two inches (9 ft. 2 in.) east of the east side of Greenwich street. Then, in 1770, A. Kennedy acquired by grant one hundred feet more, which carried his line to the west side of Third street. This point was only two hundred feet below low water mark, and two hundred and fifty-seven feet three inches from the west side of Greenwich street. The ordinance made the west line of West street one hundred and two feet nine inches further, or three hundred and two feet nine inches from low water mark.

It appears by the maps, made in 1828, that the outer

line of West street was laid down thirty-three feet six inches further into the river, being three hundred and sixty feet three inches from low water mark, and the street being but sixty feet in width at this point, we have actually, even at the present time, only three hundred and ninety-six feet three inches from low water mark to the outer line of West street.

And this is independently of the operation of the act of 1826, by which, in making West street parallel with Washington, the block was increased by sixty feet, and of course West street pushed so much further into the river. Magnin's map, of 1804, shows that block to be one hundred and nineteen feet, and it is now one hundred and eighty. By the same map, the distance from Greenwich to West street, west side, is three hundred and fifty-eight feet.

It is then a clear demonstration that there was a space of thirty-two feet nine inches between the extremity of the grant to Kennedy, in 1770, and the east side of West street, as fixed in the ordinance. It is also clear that this space was within the four hundred feet belonging to the Corporation.

Again, a series of grants was made, from 1739 to 1770, from Marketfield street to Albany Basin. That to Oliver Delancey, in 1765, will illustrate and be sufficient, as it is similar to the others. The grant first conveys the soil between the high and low water mark ; then for two hundred feet beyond. Three streets were to be made by him, of forty feet each, to be called First, Second and Third streets.

The exterior line of Third street was the end of the two hundred feet, and of course the right of the city was but half exhausted.

These were the only grants along this line which had been made prior to 1798.

I have taken pains to make a diagram of the grants and the line of the ordinance from Marketfield street to Albany Basin. In no place does West street, even in its outer line, go beyond the four hundred feet.

There again it is manifest that there was an intervening space between the termination of the grants and the inner line of streets, and that space belonged to the Corporation.

I may advert to some other points on this river. Between Desbrosses street and Canal street, low water mark is laid down just on the eastern line of Washington street. This is less than three hundred feet from the outer line of West street. (Map in Lib. E, p. 422, Book of Grants. Comptroller's office, 16th Dec., 1807.)

Between Charlton and Hamersley streets, low water line is below Washington street.—(Map in Book E, p. 405.) And from Washington to West, at Hubert street, it was just about four hundred feet from low water to the outer side of West street; and at Beach street about three hundred and eighty feet. (Book E, p. 208.)

NOTE 40.—PAGE 210.

Line of South street, &c.

The ordinance of 1795, with the amendment of 1796, fixes four points on the line of South street, and I propose to show the extent of the grants and location of the street at these points, as well as at a few others of importance to understand the subject.

The first point was at Whitehall. The inner line of South was to be two hundred and twenty-nine feet six inches from the south side of Water street, now Front. Goerck's map, of 1793, makes the distance the same, and the present line, as measured, is two hundred and thirty feet two inches.

The grants at this place running along the line of Whitehall are as follows:

One to David Clarkson, of the 12th of May, 1732; another to Anthony Rutgers, also of the 12th of May, 1732; and a third to Anthony Rutgers, of the 11th of October, 1734.

The first conveys a lot of ground and croft (one of seven lots, lately sold), lying on the west side of the dock and weigh-house, between the Weigh House street and the street called the Broadway, fronting north on Custom House street; on the south fronting a street forty feet wide, called Whitehall street; west, by Broadway; east, by lot No. 2, and being one hundred and eight feet nine inches in depth on Broadway, and on the east side one hundred and seven feet nine inches.

The next grant (viz., to Rutgers) is for another of the lots sold as aforesaid (No. 7), described as a lot of ground fronting on Whitehall street to the north, bounded on the west by the street called the Broadway, on the south by a new street to be made, of forty-five feet wide; east by a lot sold R. Livingston; being one hundred and thirty-six feet deep on the street called the Broadway, and the same depth on the other side.

The third grant, that of 1734, was of a lot of ground, to be made land, and gained out of the East river, now being under water, between the Great Dock and Whitehall, being the corner lot on the east side of the street, to be continued, called the Broadway; contiguous to the south end of the lot No. 7, lately purchased by A. Rutgers; and which lot is to extend in length from the south end of the said lot number seven (7) two hundred and forty-five feet into the East river or harbor.

Rutgers covenanted to make a street or wharf of forty-five feet wide *on* the north end, or inward part of the water lot granted; and another *at* the outward part thereof, at the south end of the lot in the East river or harbor.

The Custom House street was the Dock street of Goerck's map of 1793, and, at present, part of Pearl street. On the map of 1728, we find the Custom House laid down on the north side of the street, but it is called, on that map, Dock street. The space of ground sold in 1732 is vacant on this map.

Whitehall street, of these grants, was the Dock street wharf of 1772; the Little Dock street of 1793, and is now Water street. The new street to be made is at present Front street.

The depth of these grants, from Pearl street, was, in the aggregate, five hundred and twenty-nine feet nine inches; the two hundred and forty-five feet including the inner street, now Front. The depth, by Goerck's map of 1793, was five hundred and fifty-nine feet eight inches to South street, and by present accurate maps it is five hundred and fifty-nine feet seven inches. The difference is twenty-nine feet four inches. The distance from the south side of Water street to South street is four hundred and eleven feet eight inches.

If we assume (as is generally considered the fact) that the south side of Water street generally represents low water mark in that vicinity, then we have the depth of the grants, from that point, three hundred and eighty-one feet (136 x 245), leaving nineteen feet, part of the four hundred not granted.

And then, as South street was laid down four hundred and eleven feet eight inches (411 8) from the south side of Water street, it follows, on this assumption, that there were eleven feet eight inches of land of the State to be filled up, and the street to be made of seventy feet, entirely on the State ground; the whole being four hundred and eighty-one feet eight inches.

The Corporation, however, undoubtedly construed the charter-grant to give them the power over four hundred and forty feet from low water mark—the forty feet to be kept open for public uses. In fact, then the Corporation sought here only forty-one feet eight inches extension beyond what they had a right to use.

A notice of the grants at the corner of Moore street will be useful in this particular.

The first was a grant to Stephen De Lancey, 12th of May, 1732, of three of the seven lots sold as before stated, viz., Nos. 1, 2, and 5, and bounding lots Nos. 1 and 2, north on Custom House street; in the rear on Whitehall street; east along Weigh House street one hundred and seven feet six inches; west by the lot sold Clarkson. No. 1 was the corner lot, running along Weigh House street one hundred and seven feet six inches.

The next is a grant to John Moore, of the 12th May, 1732, for lot No. 4, one of the seven lots before mentioned; bounded on the south by a new street, to be made, of forty-five feet wide, to run along East River or harbor; west by lot No. 5; north by Whitehall street, and east by the Weigh House street, being one hundred and thirty-six feet along Weigh House street. Weigh House street is now Moore street.

Next was a grant to John Moore, of the 11th October, 1734. This was of a water lot, to be made land, and gained out of the East River, on the west side of the street running along the west side of the Great Dock, commonly called the Weigh House street; and fronting and contiguous to a certain new house and tenement lately built by the said John Moore, on lot No. 4, lately purchased by him; which lot extends, in length, from the south side of such new house or tenement two hundred and forty-five feet into the East River or harbor, and is in breadth, on the north side, fronting and contiguous to such new house, thirty-one feet six inches, and in the rear, on the East River, thirty-two feet six inches. Northerly, by aforesaid new house and lot of ground; easterly, by part of a street or wharf of twenty feet at least, to be built by said John Moore; southerly by the East River or harbor, and westerly by the lot to be granted to S. De Lancey; with a covenant to make a street or wharf, forty-five feet wide, on the north end or inward part of the lot (this is the present Front street); and also to make a street or wharf *at* the south end of the lot, in the East River, at the outward part thereof, of forty feet wide.

Then there was a grant to Lambert Moore, October, 1796. After reciting the grant to John Moore, in October, 1734, extending from the new house or tenement lately built, two hundred and forty-five feet into the East River, with a covenant to make a street forty feet wide on the outer part, it proceeds: " And whereas, the Common Council, for improving the accommodation of shipping, have determined that a new street or wharf, to be called South street, of seventy feet in breadth, be made in the East River, in front of the water lots between Whitehall slip and Moore street, by reason whereof the said street, of forty feet in width, in the river at the south end of the water lot granted to the said John Moore, will become unnecessary; and have agreed to extend the lots of the said proprietors respectively between the Whitehall slip and Moore street, to the new street of seventy feet wide, to be called South street."

The grant is then made of sixty-four feet (64) from the south end of the former grant up to South street. The grantee covenants to make South street.

Thus, the Corporation give to Moore sixty-four feet, in order to bring him up to South street; or twenty-four feet beyond the exterior line of the street, to be made under his grants, and the forty feet intended for that street.

At this point, also, the grants prior to that of 1796 extended three hundred and eighty-one feet from the south side of Water street, leaving nineteen feet not granted. The Corporation, in 1796, granted this strip, with the forty feet reserved for the street and five feet more.

These statements have been made on the supposition of Water street representing low water mark.

But there are stronger reasons for thinking that low water mark, from Whitehall street east to Moore street, was at or about the north side of the present Front street.

1. In the year 1732, a division was made into lots by the Corporation, of all the space from the south side of Custom House street (Pearl) to the north side of a street to be made (now Front street). The ground was divided into

seven parcels and sold. Three of these lots ran from Custom House street to Whitehall street, near Water; and four of them from the latter street to "a street to be made of forty-five feet along the East River." All these lots are bounded "on Broadway," or "Broadway continued," on the west; and by Weigh House street on the east.

The lots are described as "all that certain lot or parcel of land," in the same manner as upland lots are described.

Now, although the soil between high and low water is sometimes described as a water lot, or soil under water, yet the soil beyond low water is never described except as 'land under water,' 'soil to be gained out of the river,' 'a water lot,' &c. In the grants to Eve Provost and others, in 1772, for example, the grant is first, "of a piece or parcel of land to low water mark, and then of land under water, two hundred feet into the East river." And yet a resolution of the Corporation, passed the 16th day of September, 1733, a grant of land running to low water mark is expressly stated to be a water lot. (Minutes of Common Council of that year.)

In the year 1724, the Corporation divided the same parcel of land (as I consider it) into lots, with a view of selling it. It appears, from a memorial to the Governor, that his interference had been requested by some owners of land in the vicinity.

The Corporation in this document assert their undoubted right to the property, admitting their error in not applying for a designation of such spots as would be suitable for forts, &c. Of course, in 1724, their right extended to low water only.

In the grant to John Moore, of 1734, the line is "from the new house or tenement then lately built, two hundred and forty-five feet in the East river." This new house must have been on the northerly side of Front street, and it is extremely improbable that between 1732, when Moore got the land, and 1734, he built a house below low water mark.

Every map of the city, and of these localities, will, I think, confirm this conclusion. On that of 1728, we find the space called Whitehall much wider than afterward; while on that of 1755, we see the three blocks formed out of this space, from Moore street, west, and sold in 1732 and 1734. The west and east docks, as they were termed, lay further east. On the map of the Battery (Atlas No. 7, Street Commissioner's office) we find, in 1774, the water line at the eastern end of the Battery, nearly opposite to Front street. The surveyors, whom I have consulted, consider this line not as designating precisely either high or low water, but the general or average course of the flow. The upland of the Battery clearly ran as low as Front street, and there is nothing to warrant the supposition that from that point to Moore street the shore so receded as to make a material change in the line, although further east, toward Broad street and Coenties slip, the tide did trench deeper into the land.

The next point of the ordinance is at the west side of Coenties slip. The inner side of the intended street is to be two hundred and twenty-eight feet six inches from the corner of the south side of Water street. Goerck's map, of 1793, makes the distance the same. The map in the Book of Quit Rents makes it two hundred and twenty-eight feet eight inches.

The present distances from Water street are as follows: From Water to Front street, one hundred and fifty-two feet four inches; Front street, forty-five feet; and Front to South street, two hundred and twenty-eight feet six inches; in all four hundred and twenty-five feet ten inches. From Pearl to Water street is one hundred and five feet five inches.

In 1772 a grant was made to A. & F. Van Cortlandt, by the following description: "All that certain ground and water lot opposite two dwelling-houses fronting the street commonly called the Dock street wharf, belonging to them; the said street lying between such houses and the lot hereby granted; bounded northerly by said Dock street wharf, which is to be enlarged and made of the breadth of forty feet, easterly by the pier of the said Mayor, Aldermen and Commonalty, southerly *as far into the river as the right of the Corporation extends*, westerly by the lot granted to Peter Jay."

In the previous part of the grant it is recited, that the Corporation mean to convey "as far into the river as the pier on the east side" (of the lot granted), "belonging to the Mayor, &c., doth extend."

There is a covenant to build a street of forty-five feet wide, at the distance of one hundred and fifty-two (152) feet from Dock street wharf; and also to build a street forty feet wide "*at* the extreme end of the water lot, being so far in the river as the right of the Mayor, &c., extends."

The pier referred to in this grant was erected by the Corporation between 1728 and 1755. It does not appear on the map of the former year, but is laid down in that of the latter. It is also upon the map of Rutzer, of 1766, and Hills, in 1782. It was called the Albany pier.

It was before shown that the depth from the present south side of Water street is four hundred and twenty-five feet ten inches; but from Water street, as it was in 1770, four hundred and forty feet ten inches. Therefore, if the south side of Water street, in 1770, represented low water mark, the ordinance extended forty feet beyond the right. But if low water was forty feet south of this point, then the ordinance lays out the street just at the end of the right.

Now it is a striking circumstance that on the map of Rutzen, of 1766, and on the excellent map of Hills, of 1782, the boundary line of the Dock Ward and South Ward is given, and the line of the Dock Ward is some distance beyond the extremity of the pier. That boundary was clearly intended to follow the description of the Wards in Montgomerie's charter, and therefore shows the extent of the four hundred feet as given by the 38th section of such charter. On the map of 1782, especially the end of the pier is within the limit of the four hundred feet by at least forty feet.

The Corporation pier, therefore, would, on this supposition, run three hundred and sixty feet below low water, whatever was its length from high to low water.

The pier was built about the year 1750. A resolution was adopted on the 22d of April, of that year, directing it to be made according to a draft then submitted.

All these considerations warrant the conclusion, that the street under the ordinance was laid down just about the extremity of the four hundred feet, and was so intended. The grant was to the whole extent of the right, and the street was therefore *at* its extremity. And the Corporation seem to have assumed that they could lay out the street, not only of forty, but seventy feet wide beyond this limit.

There is also a series of grants made in 1772, between

Broad street and Coenties slip, which deserve attention. None other of the same class are to be found.

That to William Milliner, on the east side of Broad street, may be taken as a sample. It is bounded northerly by a street called Dock street wharf, easterly by the lot granted to ; *southerly*, as far into the river as the right of the Mayor, Aldermen and Commonalty extends; *westerly* by Broad street. There is a covenant to make a street or wharf along the side, and another to make a street *on the extreme end of the lot granted*, to be forty-five feet wide, at the end of twenty years.

The next point of the ordinance is at the eastern side of Coenties slip. It is one hundred and sixty (160) feet from the corner of Walker street. The distance upon Goerck's map, of 1793, is the same, and by late measurements it is one hundred and fifty-nine feet five inches. The distances from Pearl to South street are as follows: Pearl to Water street, one hundred and twenty-six feet; Water street, forty-five feet; Water to Front, one hundred and seventy-five feet; Front street, fifty feet; and Front to South street, one hundred and fifty-nine feet five inches, being in all five hundred and fifty-five feet five inches. From the south side of Water to South street is three hundred and eighty-four feet five inches.

Grants.

1. To Conrad Ten Eyck, in 1687, for ninety-five feet from the Dock street; on the south, the boundary was the East river—doubtless high water.

2. To Conrad Ten Eyck, in 1697, bounded northerly by the house and ground of Ten Eyck; southerly by the

wharf or street fronting the East river, being in depth thirty-one feet nine inches. It is described as at low water, meaning, I apprehend, about low water, because, among other reasons, there was a covenant to make a street or wharf, of thirty feet, at the end of the premises granted, fronting the river.

Now at this period the Corporation could not authorize the erection of a wharf below low water. It is a fair conclusion that they did not exceed their power, until clear proof of the fact is produced. Therefore the outer end of this wharf was either at low water, exactly, or within low water mark.

Next, there was a grant made in 1750, to Samuel Ten Eyck, of a water lot of ground No. 1, to be made land and gained out of the East river, opposite to the south side of a certain messuage or tenement, and lot of ground of his the said Samuel Ten Eyck, which fronts the east side of the slip, commonly called Coenties slip, the street commonly called the Dock street wharf, lying between the said messuage and lot of land and the water lot hereby to be granted, to extend in length from the south side of the Dock street wharf, two hundred feet into the East river, bounded northerly by the street commonly called the Dock street wharf (which is to remain a public street and highway, of forty-five feet in breadth); southerly by the East river harbor of the city, and westerly by a pier, wharf or street, of twenty-five feet in breadth, to be made by said Samuel Ten Eyck, and fronting to the aforesaid slip or dock, called Coenties dock. There was a covenant by Ten Eyck, to make a street or wharf of fifteen feet wide in the inward part of the ground, granted to him contiguous to and adjoining the street called the Dock street wharf, so as to make the said street more spacious by adding fifteen feet thereto (which would make it forty-five feet). Also that he could make another street, of forty feet wide, "at the distance of two hundred feet from Dock street wharf, as it now is at the outward part thereof in the East river."

"Grant to Mary Ten Eyck, 1772, all that water lot, No. 16, to be made land out of the East river, opposite to a certain house fronting the street or wharf, called Cruger's wharf, belonging to the said Mary Ten Eyck, to extend in length from the south side of the said street, called Cruger's wharf, two hundred feet into said East river or harbor, and is in breadth twenty-four feet. Northerly by the street called Cruger's wharf, easterly by water lot No. 17, granted to John Moore, southerly by the East river or harbor, and westerly by the pier to be built by said Mary Ten Eyck."

A covenant to add five feet on the inward part of the lot granted, adjoining the present wharf or street, of forty feet, so as to make it five feet wider, and a covenant to make a street or wharf, of forty feet, *on* the outward part of the lot granted next to the East river or harbor.

The grants then give an extent of line from the south side of Water street, as it was in 1750, of four hundred and forty feet. The present line, as before shown, is three hundred and eighty-four feet five inches. Add fifteen feet, which was taken off the grant of 1750, to widen Water street, and we have three hundred and ninety-nine feet five inches, or, in other words, we have four hundred feet (less a few inches) from the outer side of the wharf to South street of the ordinance, as it now is. And then, if the extremity of that wharf may be taken as low water mark (as it scarcely can admit of a doubt, it may be) we have the exact four hundred feet granted up to South street. Forty feet more are granted, but it is to be made a street; and that street was entirely *on* the extremity of the grants.

If it is asked how the Corporation came, then, to grant four hundred and forty feet from low water (as in other cases it did), I answer, that the more the examination I have made extends, the more strong becomes my belief that they acted on the assumption that they were entitled to use, absolutely, the full four hundred feet; to build upon it, for example, leaving the forty feet open and unobstructed in front. This is a question of moment, and will be afterwards noticed more fully.

The line between Wall street and Maiden lane admits of a precise determination. I have found a diagram of Mr. Colden, Surveyor-General, made in 1721, which is very useful. It is in the Council minutes at Albany of that year. Garret Van Horne, Thomas Clarke, Rip Van Dam and others petitioned the Governor for patents to extend the wharves upon the shores of the East river, from Rip Van Dam's corner, at the lower end of Maiden lane, to the corner of Thomas Clarke, two hundred feet from the present wharf. (Jan. 18, 1721–2.)

The Common Council of New York opposed the grant.

February 1, 1721–2. The Surveyor-General laid before the Board a map of the soil of the river, petitioned for by E. Van Horne and others, describing the place of the wharves and that of low water mark.

November 1, 1722; it was ordered, with the advice of the council, that the prayer of Van Horne, &c., be granted; that the breadth of the street between the present houses and the improvements be forty feet; that the same be forever hereafter called Burnet's street; that the street called King street be continued on the same straight line on which it now is, at the common charge of the grantees.

The map of the Surveyor-General lays down Thomas Clarke's corner on the north-east corner of Wall street, and what is now Water street. The existing wharf was twenty-nine feet wide; and it is evident from that map, as well as the maps in the Street Commissioner's office, that the two hundred feet was to extend from the south side of Water street, as it then was, being sixteen feet further north than its present line; five more were subsequently added.

The grant is recited in Lib. D, p. 557 of Grants. The two hundred feet began on the south side of the wharf.

Upon the survey is the following memorandum: "N.B. The tide this day did not fall lower than the foundation of the present wharves. Jan'y 26, 1721–2."

Then Burnet's key was to be enlarged eleven feet, making it forty feet wide; and on the 28th of October, 1765, a grant was made to Cornelius P. Lowe: "Whereas, the said C. P. Lowe is possessed of a certain lot of ground on the southerly corner of Burnet's key, containing in breadth in front on said key thirty-five feet three inches in breadth, on the south-west side, fronting the street on the easterly side of the slip on Rotten row, thirty-three feet four inches—grant all that certain water lot, &c., opposite to a certain house and lot of ground belonging to said C. P. Lowe, to extend from the wharf or key into the river; two hundred feet in breadth towards the river, thirty-five feet nine inches.

To leave forty feet at the end of the water lot granted for a street, to be opened when deemed necessary.

Afterward, the ordinance of 1795–6 having been passed, and South street laid down, the Corporation made a grant to John Murray, Jr., dated the 10th May, 1797, before the act.

The grant recites that the Corporation had lately laid out a new street, to extend along the front of the south-east side of the city on the East river, and to be of the breadth of seventy feet; and had determined to grant to the proprietors of the water lots fronting on the said river all that vacant ground or soil under water, lying and being between the southern extent or bounds on the said river, of the water lots heretofore granted and the said new street on the river called South street.

That Murray was the proprietor of certain lots gained out of the river, between Front street and the river, bounded westerly by the wharf on the east side of Wall street slip, and had prayed a grant from the termination of his lots to the new street. The Corporation grant him a depth of sixty-six feet six inches. The northern or inner part of the said new street being along the street or pier on the east side of Wall street slip, at the distance of two hundred and twenty-one feet six inches from the south side of Front street.

The present distances are as follows: Water to Front street, one hundred and fifty-four feet; Front street, forty feet wide, and Front to South street, two hundred and twenty-one feet six inches; in all four hundred and fifteen feet six inches. Add the eleven feet—the enlarged width to Water street, under the grant of 1721—and we have four hundred and twenty-six feet and six inches.

It results that from low water, as it is stated to have been in 1721, there was granted into the river four hundred feet exactly, viz.: two hundred in 1721, and two hundred in 1763. The grantee in the last grant was to make the street of forty feet out of his two hundred feet, and at its extremity. Then, in 1797, the Corporation grant to Murray this forty feet, absolutely, and twenty-six feet six inches more.

At the corner of Maiden lane, the present distance to South street from Water is four hundred and forty-two feet, viz., one hundred and fifty-four feet, fifty-seven feet, and two hundred and thirty-one feet; add the eleven feet before mentioned, and we have four hundred and fifty-three feet. Here then there was a space of fifty-two feet on land of the State, between the limit of the grants and the inner side of the street.

At Crane Wharf.—A further point established in the ordinance, is at Crane Wharf. The line there is three hundred and thirty-one feet eight inches (331 8), from the south side of Water street to the inner line of South street.

Crane Wharf is laid down on Goerck's map, of 1793, about the foot of Beekman street, had it been continued in the course it then ran. When Beekman street was extended below Pearl, it took in the upper portion of Crane Wharf, all the ground granted to Robert Crommeline, in 1750, and to his executors in 1804, and a strip of about eleven feet from the soil granted to Robert Livingston, in 1750, and to Joanna Livingston, in 1804, leaving the residue of these grants bounded by the western side of Beekman street.

These latter grants will then sufficiently show the extent of the soil granted in the vicinity of Crane Wharf.

That to Robert Livingston, of the 12th of February,

1750, was for lot No. 7, being a water lot, and land to be gained out of the East river, bounded northerly by a certain street, formerly called Queen street Wharf, now Water street; easterly by R. Crommeline's lot (No. 8); southerly by the East river or harbor; westerly by lot No. 6, being, in front and rear, fifty-six feet nine inches (56 9), and in length on each side of the East river or harbor, two hundred (200) feet.

There was a covenant to add fifteen feet from the inward part of the premises granted, to Water street; so as to make it more spacious, adding fifteen feet to it.

There was another covenant to make a street or wharf on the outward part of the lot granted, of forty feet in width.

On the 4th of January, 1804, a grant was made to Joanna Livingston, of a water lot, or land under water, situate between Front and South streets, bounded north-westerly by Front street, south-westerly by a lot granted L. Lefferts, south-easterly by South street, and north-easterly by a lot granted to the executors of R. Crommeline. Being fifty-six feet nine inches (56 9) on Front and South streets, one hundred and fifty feet (150) in depth on the north-easterly side, and one hundred and forty-eight feet on the south-westerly side, as by a map of a piece of ground between Beekman and Peck slips, and Front and South streets, made July 6, 1803, by Joseph Tillagin, City Surveyor, and copied page 84 (Records of Grants), will appear.

There was a covenant to build South street seventy feet wide, in front of, and contiguous to, the premises granted.

The length under the ordinance, as before observed, was three hundred and thirty-one feet eight inches from Water street. By Goerck's map, of 1793, it is 331 feet 9 inches. On the assumption that low water was at the south side of Water street, as it was in 1750, we must add (15) fifteen feet to this amount, making three hundred and forty-six feet nine inches, the depth from low water.

As the extent of the grant, prior to 1798, was but two hundred feet, there was actually a space of one hundred and forty-six feet nine inches between the extremity of the grant, and the inner line of intended street, a space unquestionably belonging to the Corporation.

Again, the grant of 1804 purports to reach South street, and did so with a small variation, arising, no doubt, from the west side of Beekman street not corresponding exactly with Crane Wharf. It was for one hundred and forty-eight feet on one side, and one hundred and fifty feet on the other—an average of one hundred and forty-nine feet, making three hundred and forty-nine feet as the extent of all the grants from low water.

But the present line on the west side of Beekman street is three hundred and fifty feet ten inches from the present south side of Water street. The fifteen feet taken to widen Water street makes three hundred and sixty-five feet ten inches, thus leaving, at the present time, thirty-four feet two inches of the four hundred feet in South street, and the residue on the land of the State, viz.: thirty-five feet ten inches.

Again, the present distances are as follows: Water street to Front, one hundred and forty-four feet four inches; Front street, fifty feet six inches; and Front to South, one hundred and fifty-six feet, being three hundred and fifty feet ten inches. We find by Goerck's map, of 1793, that Front street was not then opened, but was laid down as fifty feet wide. The grants and the present distances correspond thus:

From Water to and including Front street was two hundred feet by the grant; but fifteen feet was to be taken to add to Water street, and forty feet to make Front street, leaving one hundred and forty-five feet. The present distance is one hundred and forty-four feet four inches. Front street was to be forty feet wide, and is fifty feet—an addition of ten feet. Front street to South was, by the grant, say one hundred and fifty feet, and is one hundred and fifty-six feet, so that sixteen feet was added at the extremity of the grant, the inner line carried so much further into the river when South street was finally made.

These observations and statements will in general apply to the whole line between Peck slip and Beekman slip.

The next point is at the south-westerly line of the grant to Thomas Barnes, now belonging to Samuel Ackerly, four hundred and twenty (420) feet from the south side of Water street, into the river. A grant was made to Thomas Barnes on the 1st of May, 1752, describing the water lot as bounded northerly by Water street; easterly, by another lot granted to John Beekman, being ninety-seven feet eight inches in front, eighty-nine feet four inches in the rear, and two hundred feet in length, into the East river.

There was a covenant to widen Water street fifteen feet, by taking so much from the inner side of the lot granted; and also to make a street or wharf of forty feet on the outward part of the lot.

This lot granted to Barnes was fifty feet seven inches westerly from the west side of what is now Roosevelt street, on Water street, and thirty-four feet from the same on Front street.

Various grants were made, at the same period, from what is now Roosevelt street, both to the eastward and westward; and there is no point along the line at which the grants come within a hundred feet of exhausting the four hundred feet.

The further grants in this vicinity, up to the line of South street, were generally made in 1817, and subsequently.

And lastly, the eastern point of the ordinance is at Corlaer's Hook. The ordinance of 1795, as amended in 1796, establishes South street at Corlaer's Hook, almost precisely as it now exists, viz.: three hundred and sixty (360) feet from the south side of Crown Point street, now Water street, at high water mark. By the maps used in the case of Furman *vs.* The Corporation, copied from those on file, it appears that the distance from the south side of Water street to the south side of South street is three hundred and ninety (390) feet, thus made up: Water to Front street, one hundred and thirty feet; Front street, fifty feet; Front to South street, one hundred and forty feet; and South street, seventy feet.

But high water mark appears to be about thirty feet south from the south-west corner of Water and Corlear's street, leaving about three hundred and sixty feet from high water. Goerck's map of 1793, although indistinct at this point, yet shows a line which I think corresponds with the ordinance. The conveyance of the adjoining soil was only to high water before 1793, and the Corporation had made no grant of land under water prior to that time.

Note 41.—Page 213.

Imposition for Improvement on particular Property.

On the 1st of January, 1658, it was made a subject of discussion, in the Court of Burgomasters, whether the paving of "The Brewer street" should be at the expense of the city, or whether the owners of the houses and lots should each pave before his own possession.

It was decided, on the 24th January, 1658, that the street should be paved with cobble-stones, under the oversight of certain persons, with the presiding Burgomasters, and after the completion of the work they were to assess the expense proportionately upon each house standing on the streets. (Records Burgomasters, N. Y.)

The Dutch annals abound with similar instances.

The thorough and learned examination which this subject underwent in the consummate argument of Mr. Spencer, and the opinion of the Court in the case of Adriance *vs.* The Mayor, &c., renders it unnecessary to enumerate instances under the Colonial government. I refer to one case which was not adverted to: In the statute of 1791, for improving John street, there was a provision that the Commissioners should assess so much of the damage, as they thought reasonable, upon the Corporation (the public at large), and the residue upon the owners assumed to be benefited. Theoretically, this, perhaps, is the true principle; and a relic of it is found in the present provision of assessing one-third of the value of buildings upon the Corporation.

Note 42.—Page 218.

Report of Ed. Taylor and Judge Ingraham, 1837.

That the petitioners are the proprietors of several water lots on the North or Hudson river, between the termination of Cedar street and Battery place, and they petition for a grant to them of the land under water between the front or westerly line of their grants and the line of West street, as now established by law. Along the whole line of West street, from Cedar street to Battery place, the line of the street is established to the westward of the line of all the water grants in that part of the city, but not at equal distances. In some cases the grants have been made after West street was laid out, but before the present lines were established; and, in others, the grants being made to the line of Third street, as originally laid out, leaving, thus, along the whole line, spaces of unequal width, between the exterior width of the water grants and the exterior line of the city.

These spaces would naturally be sought for by the owners of the water grants, and petitions to that effect have several times brought the subject before the Common Council. The difficulty seems to have been in settling the terms on which the grants should be made.

" In accordance with the practice heretofore pursued by the Corporation, the various committees to whom this subject has been heretofore referred, have recommended grants to be made to the proprietors, *instead of the Corporation taking the land to itself;* and have endeavored to fix the amount of compensation, either by way of quit-rents, or immediate payment, in some respects equivalent to the advantages derived. None of the plans recommended were ever adopted, and the matter has remained unsettled. As it will soon be necessary to complete the filling up and building of West street, your Committee, in fixing the terms, have inclined to place them so low that it is believed no dissatisfaction whatever can be felt by the proprietors, and have also fixed a period within which the grants shall be taken, so that, at the expiration of the period, no complaint can be made if the Corporation, on their own account, fill up and make those portions that may not be granted."

The Committee then recommended the rates, and period for the proprietors to take out the grants.

The report was adopted.

Note 43.—Page 222.

The Right of the Crown to the Soil under Water.

Selden's Mare Clausum, 256 ; 1 Roll. Ab., 168–4; Hale, De Portubus, 12. The third subdivision is—"What evidence is there of the king's property in the shore; that is, the ground between the ordinary high water and low water mark?

"For the third, it is admitted that, *de jure commune*, land between the high water and low water mark doth belong to the king" (5 Rep. 107, Constable's case, Dyer, 326), although it is true that such shore may be, and commonly is, parcel of the manor adjacent, and so may belong to a subject; yet, *prima facie*, it is the king's. So the shore of an arm of the sea belongs to him, as well as the shore of the sea."

The case cited by Lord Hale, Newcastle, and the Prior of Tinmouth, 20 Ed., 1, and that in the Exchequer, 8 Car., 1, are pertinent.

"The subject may acquire the right—1. By the king's charter or grant, he may grant a navigable river, that is, an arm of the sea, the water and port thereof. He may also grant a manor *cum litore maris eidem adjacente;* and the shore itself will pass, though in gross, and not parcel of the manor."

Other instances are mentioned of words in a grant sufficient to carry the soil.

"2. By prescription. The shore may belong to the subject, and not only belong to a subject in gross, which may possibly suppose a grant before time of memory, but may be parcel of a manor."

The case of the Royal Fishery. (Davies' Rep., 149.) "The king hath the same prerogative and interest in the branches and arms of the sea, and navigable rivers, so high as the sea ebbs and flows in them, which he has in *alto mare;* and this is manifest by several authorities and records." (Citing Selden Mare Clausum, 251; 1 Roll., 168.) "The letters patent to the Lord High Admiral (4 Inst., 142) grant the goods, &c., in the sea, and *infra fluxum et refluxum maris seu aquæ at plenitudinem.*" "The shore is that ground that is between ordinary high and low water mark. This doth, *prima facie,* and of common right, belong to the king, both in the shore of the sea, and the shore of the arm of the sea. It is certain that what the sea overflows, either at high spring tides, or at extraordinary tides, comes not, as to this purpose, under the denomination of *litus maris*, and consequently the king's title is not to that large extent, but only to land that is usually overflowed at ordinary tides. That, therefore, I call the shore that is between low and high water mark." (Hale, De Portubus, cap. 4.)

The Supreme Court, in Rogers *vs.* Jones (1 Wendell, 237), thus states the law: "The right of the king extends over all lands, as well such as are covered by water as such as are not. In England, it hath always been holden that the king is the lord of the whole shore. He has the property *tam aquæ quam soli*, and all profits of the sea, and all navigable rivers. So also he has the property of the soil in all rivers which have the flux and reflux of the sea, and not the lord of the manor adjoining, without grant or prescription; but by a grant or prescription a subject may have the interest in the water and soil of navigable rivers."

Judge Strong, in delivering the opinion of the court in Whitney *vs.* Corporation, quotes this, as well as other parts of the opinion, and adds: "In the case of Rogers *vs.* Jones, the patent from the Colonial government conveyed within the boundaries which it described, the whole of the harbor of Oyster Bay, which was a navigable water; and it was decided that it was a valid conveyance of the land under water, and vested the title in the patentee. A principle of the common law, laid down and sanctioned by such eminent jurists as Chief Justice Hale, Chief Baron Comyn and Judge Blackstone, should be considered as settled."

Chief Justice Hosmer, in East Haven *vs.* Hemingway (7 Conn., 196), explicitly lays down the law: "There is no doubt concerning the competency of Charles II. to convey the land in question to the Colony of Connecticut. A river, where the tide ebbs and flows, is an arm of the sea, and the shore is that space of ground which is between ordinary high water and low water mark. The title of the king, *prima facie*, to all ports and arms of the sea up to high water mark, and to the soil thereof, has long been established law; and, as an undoubted consequence, it is settled, that he may grant the property of the soil between high and low water mark to a subject or corporation."

Rex *vs.* Smith, Douglass, 425; Lansing *vs.* Smith, 4 Wendell, 20; Middleton *vs.* Prichard, 3 Scammon's Illinois Rep., 510; Middletown *vs.* Sage, 8 Conn. Rep., 221; Canal Comm. *vs.* The People, 5 Wendell, 423; Bell *vs.* Slack, 2 Wheaton, 508; Coles *vs.* Waddington, 2 McCord, 580; Cox *vs.* The State, 3 Blackford, 294; Ex-parte Jennings, 6 Cowen, 618.

Blundell *vs.* Catterall, 5 Barn. and Ald., 268, Bayley, J., says: "By the sea shore, I understand the shore between the high and low water mark, and the property of this is *prima facie* in the king. It may, indeed, by grant or prescription, belong to the subject; but, until the contrary is shown, the presumption is that it belongs to the king. See, also Lopez *vs.* Andrew, cited 3 Manning & Ryland, 474. In the London Law Magazine (vol. 45, p. 70) is a notice of Sergeant Merewether's argument in the case of The Attorney General *vs.* The Corporation of London in 1844. The information set forth, that by the royal prerogative the ground and soil of the coast and shores of the sea around the kingdom, and the ground and soil of every port, haven and arm of the sea, creek, pool, and navigable river thereof, into which the sea ebbs and flows, and also the shore lying between high and low water mark, belongs to her Majesty.

In 1849, December 8, the argument in question was addressed to the Lord Chancellor, and was afterward published.

The case is to be found in the 2d vol. of McNaughten and Gordon's Reports; but it came up merely on exceptions to a report of the insufficiency of the answer, and the Lord Chancellor observed that the question discussed did not then arise.

The writer cites the case of the Duke of Beaufort *vs.* The Mayor, &c., of Swansea, 3 Exch. Rep., 413 (1849), as incidentally settling the question against the right of the Crown.

The case was trespass for breaking into the plaintiff's close. The place was between high and low water. Several charters from King John, Edward I., II. and III., were produced, and evidence of many acts of ownership, in modern times, was produced to show that the *locus in quo* was part of the seignory of Gower. The judge told the jury that the question was whether the *locus* was part of the seignory of Gower; that the documentary evidence in law did not necessarily carry a right, and that they must look to all the evidence and say whether, by grant or prescription, the land had passed to those under whom the Duke claimed.

The jury, in answering a distinct question put to them, found, that the land between high and low water mark was part of the seignory of Gower.

The decision of the court is thus expressed—Pollock, C. B.: "In substance, the direction of the court is this—Here is a grant of the seignory of Gower. What is the seignory of Gower? The judge says, you cannot define the seignory merely from these words; you cannot say that the spot which the plaintiff claims is his, as being part of such seignory merely from such words. But if, by usage, which is of so long standing that we may presume it to be contemporaneous with the grant itself, the sea shore in question has always been considered to be part of the seignory, then you will take the grant and the usage together, and you are to form your own opinion. I think the direction perfectly right. Parke, B., noticed, "that the word 'terra,' used in the grant, was equivalent to the word 'manor.' That the authorities are clear that sea shore may be part of the manor. Lord Hale and Lord Coke affirm it, and modern usage was admissible to explain the meaning of an ancient grant."

Nothing can be more obvious than that this case supposes the title derived from the crown, and determines only that phraseology, incompetent of itself to pass the space, may be interpreted by long usage so as to comprehend it. If this is not a recognition, impliedly, of the right of the crown to grant, and that the crown is to be considered as having granted in that case, no words can be used which will contain the proposition.

Calmady *vs.* Rome (6 Comm. Bench Rep., 861, 1848) is also cited. It is a case of precisely the same character as that in the Exchequer. There was a grant of a manor, without words expressly conveying the *litus maris.* But there were words granting "the creek of the sea," "several fishery," and other rights of an extensive description. Acts of ownership by the lord of the manor on the sea shore adjoining, such as the exclusive taking of sand, sea weed, stones, &c., were admitted in evidence to show that the shore was parcel of the manor.

And Patterson, J., put the case to the jury thus: "It is for you to say, whether, from the evidence laid before you, you can satisfactorily arrive at the conclusion, that the sea shore was granted by the crown to the ancestors of Mr. Calmady—that is to say, that the sea shore was parcel of the manor."

The plaintiff had a verdict, and a new trial was refused.

"The right of wreck, according to Lord Hale, affords a strong presumption that the soil is intended to pass—and there was a considerable body of evidence to show that the plaintiffs were the owners of the soil."

The argument of the Reviewer in the London Magazine, before referred to, appears to amount to this, that Lord Hale was a believer in witches, and on some occasions held very high prerogative doctrines. This principle of reasoning would destroy Aristotle's logic, because he was a heathen.

NOTE 44.—PAGE 223.

Chancellor Walworth, in Lansing *vs.* Smith, 4 Wendell, says: "The king owned the soil under all the waters of navigable rivers and arms of the sea, including the shore or banks, to high water mark. He held the right, not for his own benefit, but for the benefit of his subjects at large, who were entitled to the free use of the sea, and of all tide waters, for the purposes of navigation, fishing, &c., subject to such restrictions and regulations as the crown or parliament might prescribe. By Magna Charta, and many subsequent statutes, the powers of the king are limited, and he cannot now deprive his subjects of those rights, by granting the public navigable waters to individuals. But there can be no doubt of the right of parliament in England, and of the legislature in this State, to make such grants, when they do not interfere with the vested rights of individuals. The right to navigate the public waters of the State, and to fish therein, and the right to use public highways, are all public rights, belonging to the people at large."

I am unable to reconcile this language, in its latitude, with the express decision in Rogers *vs.* Jones (1 Wendell, 237). The point of a right in the crown to grant a fishery in severalty was made and argued by counsel. The record presented it so distinctly, that if the court had supposed the crown disabled from making it, the judgment must have been different. The court distinctly examine the subject—distinctly pass upon the operation of Magna Charta, and explicitly decide that it had not impaired the prerogative in this particular.

But a difference may be pointed out, that although the right of fishing may be granted in severalty, this would not interfere with the free navigation of the waters, which a grant of a part of the soil covered by them for private purposes would do.

With reference to general principles, it is clear that it is essential, for the purposes of trade and navigation, that keys and docks should be erected. The common law did undoubtedly place the ownership of the soil for such purposes in the crown, to be exercised directly, or by grant or license to others. Of the expediency and extent of such grants or licenses, the crown was to judge, subject to the intervention of the judicial tribunals. I cite a single case among a multitude. Decree in a cause. Paschœ, 8 Car. 1—In Exchequer—Hale de Portubus. It was decreed that the soil and ground lying between Wapping Wall and the River Thames is parcel of the port of London, and therefore all the houses from, &c., to &c., belong to the king.

The title was thus laid in the bill or information:

1st. That the river Thames flowed and reflowed; 2d. That consequently it was an arm of the sea; 3d. That it was the king's port. And from all these it was concluded, that the land, between the high and low water mark, was the king's land, and accordingly so decreed.

Again. The court in Rogers *vs.* Jones pass upon this point also. They say, "It thus appears that by the common law the king was seized of all the lands under the navigable waters of the realm, and entitled to grant and convey them. It is argued, however, that the exercise of such a power was prohibited by *Magna Charta.* They proceed to examine and refute this proposition. They adopt the reasoning of the counsel (D. S. Jones, Esq.), that Sir Mathew Hale had explained the intent of Magna Charta in this particular. The king had been accustomed to put as well fresh as salt waters *in defenso,* for his private recreation, in fishing and fowling. And it was the intent of the statute to prevent this being done, except as to such rivers as were in defense in the time of Henry the Second.

Again, the decision of Whitney *vs.* The Mayor, &c., distinctly sanctions and recognizes the charter of Montgomerie as a valid source of title in the Corporation of New York to the four hundred feet below low water.

It is true, there are opinions of several judges (no decision) supporting the doctrine of an abridgment of the power of the crown by the statute referred to. See opinion of Judge Randolph, in Gough *vs.* Bell, 1 Zabriskie, 156; of Judge Green, Ibid., 2 Zabriskie; and of Ch. J. Taney, 16 Peters, 367. They cannot diminish the force of our own positive decisions. Besides the leading case of Rogers *vs.* Jones, upon the right to grant fisheries, see Davies' Rep., 511; Brinck *vs.* Ritchmeyer, 14 John. Rep., 355, and cases; Hooker *vs.* Cummings, 20 John. Rep., 90; Collins *vs.* Bunburg, Iredell, 277; Ibid., 5 Iredell, 118; Fleet *vs.* Hegerman, 14 Wendell, 42; Peck *vs.* Lockwood, 5 Day's Rep., 22.

Note 45.—Page 223.

Right of Bathing.

The case of Catterall *vs.* Blundell (5 Barn. and Ald., 268) settled, that there was no common right of bathing in front of the shore, where the shore, the *locus in quo*, had been actually granted to the lord of the manor. Justice Holroyd states this to be the question.

Note 46.—Page 224.

Absolute Right of Parliament and State.

It cannot be necessary, upon this point, to do more than refer to the cases before noticed, especially to Lansing *vs.* Smith, 4 Wendell, 20.

In the late English case of Abraham *vs.* The Northern Railroad Company, Queen's B., 1851 (Eng. case, Law and Eq., Phil. ed., vol. v., p. 255), the company had received authority, by an act of parliament, to run their road on the bank of the River Ause, a navigable stream ; and such right was not questioned, as legally conferred by the statute.

NOTE 47.—PAGE 224.

Cases on Rights of Riparian Owners.

In Lansing *vs.* Smith, Court of Errors, 4 Wendell, 9, J. Quackenboss was the original owner of a lot of upland, extending to the Hudson river. In 1814 the Commissioners of the Land Office granted to him a water lot adjoining his property, on which he built a wharf. The Chancellor says : "What were the rights of the owner of the land adjacent to this wharf before the patent was granted ? The bank of the Hudson river, between high and low water mark, belonged to the people of the State, and he had no better right to the use of it than any other person."

He distinctly recognizes the principle, that the State might make a grant of land under water without any regard to any supposed pre-emptive claim in an adjoining owner. The statutes had only restricted the Commissioners from doing so.

The statute referred to in the opinion expressly forbade the Commissioners from making a grant of land under water to any one but the proprietor of the adjacent land. (1 R. S,. 208.) The subject is forcibly argued by Judge

Mason, in Furman *vs.* The Mayor of New York, Superior Court, 1851. "It results from the nature of the estate to the crown, or the government in the property, that the riparian owner does not possess this right. There cannot be two owners to the same piece of land. Lord Hale quotes two decisions in which the claim of the riparian proprietors against the king was held to be invalid. (De Portubus, p. 13.) If the owner has the estate in fee, it follows that it can be granted. There is no such qualification in the books that the soil cannot be granted to any person but the riparian proprietor."

It is very true, a right to the soil, or a right to acquire it by occupation and improvement, are very distinct from a mere right to have the first offer when the owner decides to sell. Yet, even the latter is inconsistent with the entire power over a perfect absolute estate in fee. The preemptive right, as before stated, is expressly conferred in the statutes of 1807 and 1826, granting soil under water to the Corporation.

I have elsewhere observed, that even in the States (New Jersey and Pennsylvania), for example, where the right of docking, &c., is held to be in the shore owners, the fee of the soil is not considered to be in them ; but a right to acquire it upon making the improvement. This is well exemplified in a case in 26 Maine Reports, where, under the Massachusetts ordinance of 1661, giving a right to adjoining owners to a certain extent, the court held that until possession was actually taken, and the separate right asserted, the waters remained, for many purposes, in common.

In Gould *vs.* The Hudson River Railroad Company (Court of Appeals, 1852), it was definitely settled that there was no such riparian-right, in the adjoining owner of land upon a navigable water, as to prevent the State from making such use of the soil under water, for a railroad, or otherwise, as it should think fit.

In the case of the United States *vs.* Ruggles (United States Circuit Court, Nov., 1861), the bill was filed for an injunction to restrain the defendant from building a dock adjoining the Navy Yard, by which the free navigation of the East River was obstructed, and ingress and regress to and from the Navy Yard was interfered with.

The Government had purchased the site of the Navy Yard from the State sixty years before, and had made large improvements at the place. The defendant was the owner of a lot of land adjacent to and west of the Yard, and fronting also on the river, and had procured from the Commissioners of the Land Office of the State a deed of the land, in part covered with water, extending into the river between six and seven hundred feet.

The boundary line of the parties was not at right angles, but struck the shore in an oblique direction.

The general course of the river at this place is nearly east and west, and the course of the boundary line, and which is extended into the river, is north forty-two degrees and thirty minutes east, the effect of which is to carry the line thus extended into the water across a part of the water-frontage of the Navy Yard, which, as claimed, when the docks are erected, as contemplated by the defendant, will interfere with the free ingress and egress of vessels, and otherwise seriously impair the use of the yard, and will also have the effect to alter the channel of the river, and of the waters of the Wallabout Bay, by deposits of silt and sand, and render access to the yard difficult and hazardous.

The grant to the defendant by the Commissioners was made under an act of the State, passed April 10, 1850, which authorized them to grant land under waters of navigable rivers and lakes, as they may deem necessary to promote the commerce of the State, or proper for the beneficial enjoyment of the same by the adjacent owner; "but no such grant shall be made to any person other than the proprietor of the adjacent lands; and any such grant that shall be made to any other person shall be void."

Judge Nelson said: "In our judgment, the true construction of this statute is, that the grant of the water-lots, authorized to be made to the adjacent proprietor of the land, must be confined to a line starting at the intersection with the shore, and extending at a right angle with the thread of the stream, or at a right angle into the lake, without any regard to the course or direction of the line upon the land. It is apparent that this is the only construction upon which the intent and purpose of the statute can be carried into effect. The case in hand illustrates the practical difficulty attending any other construction. The Government, as well as the defendant, is an adjacent proprietor, within the meaning of the statute, and is entitled to the grant of water-lots in front, or, at least, no other party is entitled to it, according to its express terms. And yet, the grant to the defendant, if allowed, has already appropriated a considerable portion of this very water frontage. We shall, therefore, restrain the defendant from erecting his dock upon any portion of the water-lots granted, lying east of a line drawn from the intersection of his eastern line with the shore, in conformity with the interpretation given to the statute, as above explained.

"And even with this modification, we shall not at present interfere with the preliminary injunction, inasmuch as we are not sufficiently advised from the proofs in the case that, with the line drawn in conformity with the true meaning of the statute, as above given, and the docks to be erected confined to the remaining portion of the grant, the effect would not be to seriously interfere with the fair and full enjoyment of the rights and privileges belonging to the Government as proprietors of the Navy Yard. The large amount of money expended in its erection and improvements, as well as its great public importance and use, and the danger of imperiling them, lead to caution and hesitation upon a question involving all these considerations. A mistake might result in a public calamity. Before, therefore, we shall interfere with the preliminary injunction heretofore granted, the case must go before a Master *pro hac vice*, whom we shall appoint, to inquire into the effect of the dock to be erected, even with our modifications stated, upon the free ingress and egress of vessels to and from the Navy Yard."

NOTE 48.—PAGE 224.

Restrictions upon Powers of State.

The most important restriction upon the right of the crown consists in its inability to make a grant which shall impair the navigation of the river; in technical language, which shall be a purpresture. Whether the proposed erection is against the *jus publicum* or not, is a question of facts to be determined upon, an indictment for a nuisance, or upon a remedy, known in the English law as the writ *ad quod damnum*. In some cases an injunction may be obtained. The whole law is so most clearly stated by Sir Matthew Hale, that I have transcribed the passage with a statement of other leading cases.

De Portubus Maris, 1. He enumerates, among nuisances of ports, "the straitening of the port, by building too far into the water, where ships or vessels might have formerly ridden. It is to be observed, that nuisance or not nuisance, in such case, is a question of fact. It is not, therefore, every building below high water mark, nor every building below low water mark, that is *ipso facto*, in law, a nuisance; for this would destroy all the keys that are in all the ports of England. And it would be impossible for the king to license a new wharf, or key, whereof there are a thousand instances, if, *ipso facto*, it were a common nuisance. Indeed, when the soil is the king's, the building below high water mark is a purpresture, or encroachment or intrusion upon the king's soil; which he may either demolish, or seize, or arrest, at his pleasure; but it is not *ipso facto* a common nuisance, unless, indeed, it be a damage to the port and navigation. In the case, therefore, of building within the extent of a port in or near the water, whether it be a nuisance or not, *is questio facti*, and to be determined by a jury. See, also, Hind *vs.* Mansfield, Noy, 108.

The case of the Attorney General *vs.* Johnstone, in Ch. 1819, 2 Wilson's Rep., 95, is instructive upon this point. It was an information by the Attorney General and bill by the Relator, for an injunction against proceedings which, it was alleged, would be a purpresture in the river Thames. The defendant had been indicted for creating a nuisance, and that indictment was pending. The injunction was continued until the result of the indictment.

The city of London claimed the right of soil in the place in question, under various charters and acts of the crown.

The Lord Chancellor held, that whether the right of soi between high and low water mark was in the crown or in the city, was immaterial; or whether the city of London had the right of conservance merely. The questions were, whether the court had jurisdiction to prevent a nuisance being completed; and whether there was ground enough to treat the encroachment in question as such, at least, pending the indictment. If such was the case, the court would exercise the jurisdiction, whoever might have the right of soil.

"It is my present opinion, that the crown has not the right, either itself to use the title to the soil between high and low water mark as a nuisance, or to place upon that soil what will be a nuisance to the crown's subject. If the crown has not such a right, it could not give it to the city of London, nor could the city transfer it to any other person." On a subsequent day he renewed the statement that wherever the title was, it was clear that it could not be used as a nuisance to the king's subjects. "I take it to be clear that, *prima facie*, a grant includes the water between high and low water mark, when it covers the soil, and that those who think proper to inclose that soil are bound to show that they can take it away without injury to 'his majesty's subjects.'"

The indictment mentioned in this case was tried before

Lord Tenterden. (2 Starkie, 511.) His direction to the jury and the subsequent case of Rex *vs.* Russell (6 Barn. & Cres., 56) are fully stated in The King *vs.* Ward (4 Adol. & Ellis, 392). In the latter there was an indictment for a nuisance for erecting an embankment in a navigable river. Lord Denman adverted to the direction of the Judge, in Rex *vs.* Russell, which he states to have been this: "If you think this is placed in a reasonable part of the river—that it is not of any public benefit, or the benefit resulting from it is not equal to the public inconvenience which results from it, then you will find a verdict for the crown. If, on these points, you are of a different opinion, then you will find for the defendants." Lord Denman proceeds—"In substance, therefore, it would seem that they were to find the defendant not guilty, if his act, indicated as a nuisance, was productive, on the whole, of more public benefit than public inconvenience." It is this direction which Lord Denman criticises and objects to. His views are, that the advantages are to the navigation, to the very rights, the invasion of which is treated as a nuisance. "The advantage gained ought to be closely connected with the inconvenience resulting, or rather with that which would have been an inconvenience if it were not absorbed in the superior advantages. In the infinite variety of active operations always going forward in this industrious community, no greater evil can be conceived, than the encouragement of capitalists and adventurers to interfere with known public rights, from motives of personal interest, on the speculation that changes may be rendered lawful by ultimately being thought to supply the public with something better than what they actually enjoy."

The direction of Lord Denman, on the trial before him, was, that the jury should find, "whether the causeway, in its altered state, was a nuisance to the navigation of the river, and whether the public benefit was greater than the inconvenience, or was counterbalanced by the public benefit derived from it."

The jury found a verdict that the erection was a nuisance; but the public benefit exceeded the inconvenience. This was held to amount to a verdict of guilty upon the indictment.

Lord Tenterden, in Rex *vs.* Russell, expressed it to be his opinion, that the inquiry ought merely to be, whether the navigation and passage of vessels over this public and navigable river was injured by the erection.

The case of the Attorney General *vs.* Parmentier is one of great importance on this subject. It is to be found in the sixth volume of the Philadelphia edition of Exchequer Reports. Chief Baron McDonald there says: "It is perfectly clear, that all the soil under the salt water, between high and low water mark, belongs to the crown. Such property has certainly been, as it may be, transferred in a great many instances, to the subject; but that is always subservient to the public rights of the king's subjects generally. It is compared by Lord Hale to the case of a highway. The private rights of the crown may be disposed of, but not the public right of the subject.

Renwick vs. *Moore*, 3 Hill's Rep., 621.

The dam over the Harlem river called Macomb's Dam was built under an act of the legislature, passed the 8th of April, 1813. A section provided, that the dam should be so constructed as to admit the passage of boats and vessels accustomed to navigate the river; and a penalty was imposed for any obstruction or delay in such passage. There was evidence of frequent obstructions; that at high water, boats could not go through at all; and that, as there was no draw, vessels with masts could not go through. The dam had been built twenty years. The defendants removed the dam between three abutments, and took away one abutment. A verdict was found for the defendants.

Per Curiam. "The Harlem river being navigable, Macomb and his assigns would, independently of the statute, have been guilty of a public nuisance in building the dam. The only effect of the statute was to vest a power in him to build and maintain a dam in the manner prescribed by the legislature. It follows, that any excess or irregularity in the exercise of that power, by which the navigation became obstructed, was *pro tanto* a public nuisance."

The Court then decide, that the remedy, by abatement, was not gone by reason of a continuation of a nuisance more than twenty years; that there was no case denying that the remedy, by abatement, was in all respects concurrent with that by indictment. It was also held, that the addition of a penalty by a statute, for a common law offense, is merely cumulative, and, unless negative words were used, would detract nothing from the remedies before allowed.

The case of Hart *vs.* The Mayor, &c., of Albany, 9 Wendell, 607, is very instructive upon this as well as other topics. The power of a corporation, at least, of one charged with the conservation of a river, to abate a nuisance, is recognized. See also note 56, p. 201, Wetmore *vs.* Tracy, 14 Wendell, 255.

See some English cases in note 43; also, Wingfield *vs.*

Crenshaw, 1 Hen. & Munff., 474; 26 Maine Rep., 128; Bady *vs.* Weeks, 3 Barb. S. C. Rep., 158; Story, § 923–925.

See State of Pennsylvania *vs.* Wheeling Bridge Co., 18 Howard U. S. Rep., 421.

NOTE 49.—PAGE 225.

State Decisions.

NEW JERSEY.—In no State of the Union has the subject received a more thorough investigation than in New Jersey.

The first case of importance is that of Arnold *vs.* Munday, 1 Halstead Rep., 1. It was decided that the patents granted by the king to the Duke of York carried the right to navigable rivers as a royalty appurtenant to the government and sovereignty, and not as an estate or right to property in fee. The grants of the Duke to the proprietors on the shore had the same, and no greater, operation.

When the proprietors surrendered the right of government to Queen Anne, this right of sovereignty went with it. No estate or property was retained. The State succeeded to the power of both king and parliament, and become invested with this royalty. Therefore, the assigns of the proprietors had no exclusive right of fishing or oystering in these waters, unless by grant from the State; which not appearing, the privilege remained in common.

The Chief Justice observed, upon the trial, that a grant bounded on a navigable river extended to the edge of the water—to high water when the tide was up, and to low water when it was down—and that the intermediate space might be appropriated by the owner of the adjacent land to the building of wharves, &c. But when the case was argued before the full bench, he said "that a grant of land, bounded upon a river or other water, which is navigable, and where the tide ebbs and flows, extends to the edge of the water only, that is to say, to high water mark only."

The next case is Gough *vs.* Bell (1 Zabriskie's Rep., 156). In that it was held—

1. That the title in the country, which vested in the British nation, was that of discovery, and was held by the king in trust for the public. Such matters as were part of the sovereignty or regalia were subject to the restrictions then imposed on their alienation by the law of England.

2. The crown could not grant a several fishery in navigable rivers, or arms of the sea; and, consequently, could not grant the soil under water; a grant which would involve the destruction of the fishery.

3. The right to navigable rivers and arms of the sea was included in the surrender to Queen Anne, by the proprietors of East Jersey, as a part of the sovereignty, and at the revolution vested in the State.

4. The shores of navigable rivers and arms of the sea, where the tide ebbs and flows, which includes all between high and low water mark, is part of the sovereignty, and belongs to the State, not to riparian owners.

5. A riparian owner, by filling up in front of his premises, does not become entitled to the land so filled up.

6. A boundary to or along a navigable river, bay, &c., extends to high water mark only; but a grant of land, in a question of jurisdiction, to low water.*

* In Palmer *vs.* Smith, 6 John. Rep., 133, it was decided, that where an act extended the boundaries of a town over navigable waters, it was to be

7. The land under navigable waters, bays, and arms of the sea, are part of the public domain, and the legislature may grant and alien them. However expedient and proper it might be to make such a grant to the riparian owner, it was not obligatory on the State to do so.

The same case of Gough *vs.* Bell came again before the court, under some additional facts. The important one was, that the place of the trepass had been occupied, filled in, and improved by the owner of the adjacent upland before the grant was made by the State.

Gough *vs.* Bell, 2 Zabriskie, 441.

In this it was decided, C. J. Green :

1. That no title to land under water could be made under the proprietors of East Jersey. They had no right. This was definitely settled in Arnold *vs.* Munday, and Martin *vs.* Waddell.

The *locus in quo* was originally between high and low water. But, at the time of the alleged trespass, it had been filled up and occupied as a meadow by the owners of the adjoining shore.

2. " The ancient rule of the common law was, that the title of owners of land bounded by the sea or by navigable rivers, where the tide ebbs and flows, extends to ordinary high water mark only. The title to the shore, between ordinary high and low water mark, as well as the title to the soil under water, belongs *prima facie* to the sovereign." Citing various cases.

3. This title, which by the common law of England is vested in the king, upon the revolution became vested in

---

intended as only made for the purpose of jurisdiction, and did not give the property in the soil under water. The town of Flushing had not, therefore, the right to prohibit the catching of clams below low water.

people. In the State the rule of the common law, as to the limit of the right, remains unaltered. High water mark constitutes the boundary between the proprietors and the title of the sovereign.

The point is fully settled in Arnold *vs.* Munday and Martin *vs.* Waddell.

4. The title to the shore of navigable rivers, between ordinary high and low water mark, being vested in the State, may be granted to individuals by the legislature, as by parliament in England.

5. The views expressed upon this power of the legislature in the same case, when formerly before the court, are reaffirmed. The Chief Justice says he concurred in the views of Justice Randolph.

6. Although the authorities are not uniform, yet the better opinion appears to be, that since Magna Charta, the English sovereign has no power to alien the public domain.

7. A grant of the waters, to the utter destruction of navigation and fishery, would not only be a grievance, but an infringement upon the Constitution of the United States.

8. The plaintiffs made title under a grant from the State in 1836.

It appeared that the owners of the upland adjoining the place in question had filled in the premises, and raised them above the level of the tide prior to the grant.

9. The Chief Justice then enters into a full and elaborate argument, leading to the conclusion, that this occupation and improvement of such soil under water, before and without the intervention of the State on behalf of the public right, was by the custom and common law of New Jersey (sanctioned impliedly by many statutes) sufficient to vest the title in the upland owner.

Justice Carpenter inclines strongly to the opinion that the title to the strip between high and low water mark, as matter of law in New Jersey, vested in the adjoining owners.

Justice Randolph delivered a dissenting opinion. See also the case of Martin *vs.* Waddell, 16 Peters, 307.

PENNSYLVANIA.—The positions established by the Courts of Pennsylvania may be collected from the following cases: Randall *vs.* The Delaware and Raritan Canal Company, Wallace's Rep., 290; Bennett *vs.* Boggs, 1 Baldwin's Rep., 72; Naglee *vs.* Ingersoll, 7 Barr, 194.

They appear to determine—

That previous to the revolution, the channel and waters of the Delaware, below Trenton, so far as the same were navigable, in the common law sense of the term, were vested in the King of England.

That the rights of the shore proprietors on the Delaware river, to low water mark, existed in colonial times, and had been recognized by New Jersey, Pennsylvania, and in various States. But below this, the State is the owner of the river in full sovereignty, and no one can acquire a right in it but by grant or prescription.

The statement of the learned judge, in Naglee *vs.* Ingersoll, 7 Barr, 94, that in England and this country the space between high and low water mark, on navigable rivers, belongs to the owners of the adjacent soil, is certainly an error. But as applied to the bed of the stream, the true rule of the English law cannot be better expressed than in this opinion. The bed of the navigable river is there vested in the crown, and here in the Commonwealth, for the use of the whole community; and no private man can challenge an individual interest therein.

He cites Bennett *vs.* Boggs, Baldwin's Rep., 72, upon the question of encroachments.

MASSACHUSETTS AND MAINE.—In Arundel *vs.* McCullock, 10 Mass. Rep., 75, the law is laid down thus: It is a settled principle of the English and American law that the right of soil of owners of land bounded on the sea or navigable rivers, where the tide ebbs and flows, extends to high water mark, and the shore belongs, in common, to the public; and the people may grant it to private persons, or it may be the property of an individual by prescription, which presupposes a grant.

Inhabitants of Charlestown *vs.* County Commissioners, 3 Metcalf, 202. "It cannot be doubted that a navigable stream may cease to be such, by the application of the soil, under legislative authority, to other purposes; as if the legislature were to authorize the erection of a solid dam over a navigable creek, and permit the land to be filled up, and converted into house lots." State *vs.* Pratt, 19 Pickering, 191.

MARYLAND.—The cases of Broome *vs.* Kennedy, 5 Harris & Johnson, 195; and Wilson *vs.* ——, 11 Gill. & John., 353, refer to this subject.

It was stated by one of the judges, in the first case, that the proprietors under the Bridge grant had the right to grant the land covered by a navigable river, without interfering with or affecting the public or common right of navigation and fishing, and that the grantee, whose grant bounded on the river, would hold land left by the recession of the water, or by alluvion, or filling in. The State of Maryland was invested with all the rights which the King of Great Britain enjoyed.

Buchanan, J., held that, at the common law, the right to the soil under navigable rivers was in the king of England; and it was equally clear that he had the capacity to dispose of it, *sub modo.* "The subject has *de communi jure* an interest in a navigable stream, such as a right of fishing and navigation, which cannot be abridged or restrained by any charter or grant of the soil or fishery, since Magna Charta, at least.

Where the State had not granted the right, all the soil under water belonged to it.

In Wilson *vs.* ——, *ante,* it is declared that in Broome *vs.* Kennedy the court had settled the principle that the State had the right to grant the soil covered by navigable waters, subject to the public or common right of fishing and navigation; and, for the purpose of protecting such public right of navigation from infringement, the legislature passed the law of 1783, appointing wardens of the port of Baltimore. The right to improve, which had been given to the owners of the lot by the act of 1745, was made subject to the jurisdiction of the Board of Wardens, whose permission was necessary before any wharf could be made into the harbor.

It is clear, from the statutes cited in this case, that the language of Judge Buchanan must be modified. He puts the King and the State, as to the power of granting the soil, upon the same footing. And these acts of the legislature plainly authorize an improvement, by docking, &c., which would change, abridge, and perhaps somewhat impair navigation. We come back to the great principle of the English cases. Is it so serious an obstruction as to be a nuisance?

DELAWARE.—Bates *vs.* The Railroad Company, 4 Harrington, 389. The Wilmington and Susquehanna Railroad were incorporated by an act of the legislature of Delaware, in 1832, with power to lay out a road from the Pennsylvania to the Maryland line, to enter upon and take lands, &c., the damages to be ascertained by five persons, appointed in the manner prescribed.

By the 16th section, "if it was found necessary to pass over any navigable river or creek by a bridge, or other edifice, the company was to constitute and keep in repair a sufficient pass or draw over the channel, or deepest part of said river or creek, for the purpose of letting vessels pass and repass."

An act of 1837 authorized the company to convert the drawbridge, erected by it over White Clay Creek, into a permanent bridge, and to keep the draw closed, or dispense with it altogether.

By another act of 1839, the company was authorized to keep a permanent bridge over Boat Creek, at place where a bridge was then erected; but the owners of the land adjoining could sue out a writ *ad quod damnum* to ascertain the damages which they would sustain by reason of the bridge being without a draw.

All these acts were passed, upon the company's application, and were accepted by it.

In 1845 an act was passed, extending the benefits of the act of 1839 to the owners of the land on White Clay Creek, or Red Clay Creek, to enable them to recover damages theretofore sustained in consequence of any act or obstruction theretofore done or constructed, or thereafter to be so, by the company.

This act was not accepted by the company.

The plaintiff was owner of a mill-seat above the bridge

over White Clay Creek, and sued for damages under this last statute. The bridge had been made in 1835, without a draw; and was made a permanent bridge in 1837. In 1839, it being partially injured, a new pier was built, occupying about four feet more of the stream of the creek.

The creek was within the State of Delaware, navigable to vessels with masts, up to the mills, before the bridge was erected; and the tide ebbed and flowed up to and above the bridge.

It was decided—

That the State Legislature could not pass an act impairing the obligation of the contract, under the Constitution of the United States. That the State courts, as well as those of the United States, were bound to treat any such act as a nullity.

That the charter and amendments, giving the power to make the bridge over the creek a close bridge, was a contract with the company; that it was made in 1837, without any provision for allowing damages to owners; that the act of 1845, compelling the payment of such damages, was an infringement of vested rights, and a violation of the contract.

That the Legislature of Delaware had the right to authorize the obstruction of such a water-course as that in question, which, so far as navigable, was wholly within the State of Delaware. The case of Wilson *vs.* Black Bird Creek, 2 Peters, 251, settled this.

The shore owners had no greater rights to the stream than the public at large.

CONNECTICUT.—East Haven *vs.* West Haven, 7 Connecticut Reports, 196.

The premises in question were the soil, with the wharf

and shore thereon, built between high and low water, on the east side of Dragon river. The river was an arm of the sea, where the tide ebbs and flows, and was navigable for large vessels adjoining the premises.

The plaintiffs claimed title, first under a charter from Charles II., and an act of the assembly of 1685.

Ch. J. Hosmer said: "There is no doubt concerning the competency of Charles II. to convey the land in question to the colony of Connecticut. A river, where the tide ebbs and flows, is an arm of the sea; and the shore is that space of ground which is between ordinary high water and low water mark. (Hale, p. 1, § 4.) The title of the king, *prima facie,* to all parts and arms of the sea to high water mark, and to the soil thereof, has long been established law; and, as an undoubted consequence, it is settled that he may grant the property of the soil between high and low water mark to a subject or a corporation," citing the usual authorities.

The court then decide, that the right had not passed to the plaintiffs, under a certain grant of the General Assembly of Connecticut.

The title of the defendants was made out to the adjoining upland lots from the general assembly, and the court then proceed to determine that, by the custom and common law of Connecticut, they had not precisely a title or estate in, but a right or franchise to dock out and occupy the soil between high and low water in the front of their possessions.

This, indeed, was subject to the paramount right of the public, that navigation should not be impaired.

See also, Trinck *vs.* Lawrence, 20 Conn., 120.

North Carolina.—Tagan *vs.* Armistead, 11th Iredell's

Law Reports, 433, affirming Wilson *vs.* Forbes, 2 Dev., 30; and Collins *vs.* Benbury, 3 Iredell, 277; and 5 Iredell, 118. "All waters which are actually navigable for sea vessels, are to be considered as navigable rivers, without regard to the ebb and flow of the tide.

"No one is entitled to the exclusive right of fishing in any navigable water, unless such right be derived from an express grant by the sovereign power, or, perhaps, such a length and kind of possession as will cause a presumption of such grant."

Note 50.—Page 240.

Statutes as to ordering of Wharves, Piers, and Slips.

Act of October 3, 1691. (1 S. & L., 8.)

This statute was the law of the Colony and the State until the 16th of April, 1787. The latter act was, in its provisions, in the present matter, almost identical with the former.

Act of April 16, 1787. (1 Gr., 441.)

"Whereas, for the encouragement of the trade and commerce of this State, it is necessary that the buildings, streets, wharves, and slips, in the city of New York, should be regulated with uniformity, for the accommodation of inhabitants and shipping, wherefore, to remove all impediments that may retard so necessary a work,

Be it, &c., That it shall and may be lawful to and for

the Mayor, &c., in Common Council convened, from time to time, to make such by-laws, ordinances, rules, and orders, for the better arranging and regulating, with uniformity, such new buildings, as after the passage of this act shall be erected for habitations, or for the purposes of trade and commerce; and also, for *regulating and altering* the streets, *wharves* and *slips*, in such manner as shall be most commodious for shipping and transportation. Also, from time to time, to nominate and appoint two or more discreet persons to be the surveyors of the buildings, streets, wharves, and slips of the said city, whose office and duty it shall be to direct and see that all buildings, wharves, streets, and slips to be laid out or altered in the said city, be regulated with uniformity, &c.

By the second section, if in *laying out, for the future, any streets, or wharves, or slips*, the Common Council should require for such purposes the ground of any person, they shall give notice, and a jury shall be empanneled, &c.

These two sections were re-enacted almost verbatim, in the act of the 3d of April, 1801. Sections 1 and 2.

And by the 219th section of the act to reduce, &c., April 9, 1813, the substance of these provisions is thus enacted:

It shall be lawful for the Mayor, Aldermen, and Commonalty of the city of New York, in Common Council convened, to lay out wharves and slips in the said city, whenever and wherever they shall deem it expedient; and if, in so doing, they shall require, for such purposes, the ground of any person or persons, they shall give notice thereof to the owner, or parties interested in such ground, or his, or her, or their agent or legal representative. And, to the end that reasonable satisfaction may be made for all such ground as shall be necessary for the uses aforesaid, the said Common Council shall and may treat with the owners, or persons interested therein, or his, or her, or their agent or legal representative, and if any such owner or owners shall refuse to treat in manner aforesaid, then, and in such cases, it shall and may be lawful to and for the Mayor or Recorder, and any two or more Aldermen, by virtue of this act, by a precept under their hands and seals, to command the Sheriff of the said city and county of New York, to empannel and return a jury to appear before the Mayor's Court of the said city, at any term thereof, not less than three weeks from the date of such precept, to inquire of and assess the damages and recompense due to the owner or owners of such ground, or his, or her, or their agent or legal representative; and at the same time to summon the owner or owners of such ground, or his, her, or their agent, or legal representative, by notice, to be left at his, her, or their most usual place of abode, to appear before such Mayor's Court, on the day and at the place in such precept to be specified; which jury being first duly sworn, faithfully and impartially to inquire into and assess the premises, shall inquire of and assess such damages and recompense as they shall, under all the circumstances, judge fit to be awarded to the owner or owners of such ground, for their respective losses, according to their several interests and estates therein. And the verdict of such jury, and the judgment of the said Mayor's Court thereupon, and the payment of the sum or sums of money so awarded and adjudged to the owner or owners thereof, or tender and refusal thereof, shall be final and conclusive for all intents and purposes, against the said owner and owners, his, her or their respective heirs, executors, administrators, and assigns, claiming any estate or interest of, in, or to the same ground; and it shall thereupon be lawful to and for the said Mayor, Aldermen, and Commonalty of the city of New York, and their successors, to cause the same ground to be converted to and used for the purposes aforesaid.

Piers, Slips, and Wharves.

The provisions as to the laying out the wharves or streets, called South street and West street, in the act of 1798, are before transcribed. They were contained in the first four sections.

In relation to piers and slips, I shall first state each section of the law as it now exists, and then its history.

The 224th section of the act of 1813 is as follows:

It shall and may be lawful for the said Mayor, &c., to direct piers *to be sunk and completed,* at such distance and in such manner as they, in their discretion, shall think proper, in front of the said streets or wharves so adjoining and extending along the said rivers, and the said piers to be connected with the same by bridges, at the expense of the proprietors of the lots lying opposite to the places where said piers shall be directed to be sunk, and by such days and times as the said Mayor, &c., may, for that purpose, limit and appoint; and if the said proprietors shall neglect or refuse to sink or make the said piers or bridges, according to the direction of the said Mayor, &c., it shall be lawful for the said Mayor, &c., to sink and make the said piers and bridges, at their own expense, and to receive to their use wharfage for all vessels that may at any time or times lie or be fastened to the said piers, or bridges, which they shall so make as aforesaid [or it shall be lawful for the said Mayor, Aldermen, &c., to grant the right of making such piers and bridges, and the right of receiving the profits thereof, to any person or persons, in fee or otherwise, upon such terms as they shall think proper].

This provision, down to the last passage between brackets, was the fifty-fifth section of the act of 1798, and the seventh section of the act of April 3d, 1801, with slight verbal changes. The clause between brackets was first enacted in the statute of 1806, being the third section of that statute.

The 225*th* (two hundred and twenty-fifth) *section of the act of* 1813, is as follows:

"It shall be lawful for the Mayor, Aldermen, and Commonalty to grant to the owners of lots fronting on any of the said streets, of seventy feet, their heirs and assigns, a common interest in the piers to be sunk in front of such streets, in proportion to the breadth of their respective lots, under such restrictions and regulations, and within such limits as the said Mayor, Aldermen, &c., shall deem just and proper."

This provision was first enacted in the eighth (8) section of the act of 3d April, 1801, in exactly the same words. (2 Webster, 129.)

The 226*th section of the act of the year* 1813 provides:

"That every clause, covenant and condition in the several grants of the Mayor, Aldermen, and Commonalty of the city, to the said proprietors respectively, or those under whom they claim, to be kept, observed, or performed by the grantees respectively, and their respective heirs, executors, administrators, and assigns, shall, notwithstanding this act, retain their full force and validity, and shall be in no manner affected by the same, or by any thing to be done or performed in consequence thereof; and the said Mayor, Aldermen, &c., shall have, possess, and be entitled to the like payments, rights, and remedies, by virtue of the said grants, as they might or could have had, or would have been entitled to, if this act had not been passed; and shall not, by the performance of anything herein contained, be deemed to have broken or infringed any of the covenants or conditions on their part, contained in the said grants."

This was a re-enactment of the 5th section of the act of 1788, and the 9th of that of April 3, 1801.

Section 227*th of the act of* 1813. "No building, of any kind or description whatever, other than the said piers and bridges, shall at any time hereafter be erected upon the said streets or wharves, or between them respectively, and the river to which they, respectively, shall front and adjoin."

This was the 7th section of the act of 1798, and the 10th of that of April, 1801.

Section 228*th of the act of* 1813. "It shall and may be lawful for the said Mayor, Aldermen, and Commonalty, at their own expense, to cause piers and bridges to be sunk and completed in such places and manner as they shall think eligible, between the Whitehall slip and the east side of the Exchange slip (Broad street), of the said city, so as to form a basin for the safety and accommodation of sloops and other vessels using the trade of the said city;

"*And, also at their own expense*, to cause such and so many other public basins to be formed and completed in the said city, as they may deem necessary for the trade thereof, and to take to their own use the slippage or wharfage arising from the same; any law, usage, or custom to the contrary notwithstanding.

"*Provided always*, that nothing herein contained shall be construed to deprive any persons who may have made piers by the direction of the said Mayor, &c., in pursuance of the act entitled 'An act for regulating the buildings, streets, wharves, and slips in the city of New York' (act of April 3, 1801), of any legal right which they thereby may have acquired, or to interfere with any private property, or right, or privilege, held under grants of the said Mayor, Aldermen, and Commonalty, or otherwise."

This provision is almost verbatim in the first section of the act of the 2d of April, 1806. (1 Webster and Sk., 514.) The preamble to that act recited, that from the great extension and increase of the said city, its trade and inhabitants, it had become necessary to provide additional walls, piers, slips, and basins in the said city, for the accommodation and safety of vessels of different descriptions.

Section 229 *of the act of* 1813. "It shall and may be lawful for the Mayor, Aldermen, and Commonalty of the city of New York to reserve all that part of the water adjacent to the wharves of the said city, from the east side of Coenties slip to the west side of Whitehall slip, for the sole accommodation of sloops and other market vessels, using the trade of the said city, from the 20th day of March to the 20th day of December, in each and every year, and that during the time aforesaid, no registered or sea vessel shall be suffered to use the slips or wharves, within the above described limits, without special permission, any law, usage, or custom to the contrary notwithstanding."

This enactment was first made on the 26th of January, 1808 (5 Web., 250), in an act entitled "An act to amend the act for the better government of the city," &c.

Section 230 *of the act of* 1813. "In all cases where the said Mayor, Aldermen, and Commonalty shall think fit, for the public good, to enlarge any of the slips in the said city, they shall be at liberty and have full power so to do; and, upon paying one third of the expense of the necessary piers and bridges, shall be entitled not only to the slippage on that side of said piers which shall be adjacent to such slips, respectively, but also to one half of the wharfage to arise from the outermost end of the said piers."

This is identically the second section of the act of 1806, when it was first enacted.

Section 231 *of act of* 1813. "In all cases where any of the proprietors of lots lying opposite to the places or streets where piers shall have been or may be directed to be sunk, pursuant to the powers contained in the act last aforesaid (the acts last referred to were those of April 3, 1801, and of the 16th April, 1787), or in this act, shall neglect or refuse to join with the other proprietors in sinking and making such piers and bridges thereunto appertaining, or to pay his, her or their proportion of the expense thereof, then, and in every such case, the said Mayor, Aldermen, and Commonalty may, at their election, join with the other proprietors in making and finishing the said piers and bridges; and shall become entitled to the proportion of wharfage which the said proprietors, so refusing or neglecting, would have been entitled to, if they had joined in making the said piers and bridges."

This was first enacted in the fourth section of the act of April 2, 1806.

Section 232 *of act of* 1813. "In all cases a notice to the proprietors of lots, inserted in two of the public newspapers printed in the said city, for six weeks successively, shall be sufficient notice to all the said proprietors of the said directions of the said Mayor, &c., for sinking and completing such piers and bridges, without specifying therein the name of the said proprietors; and an affidavit, made before a Judge of the Supreme Court or Master in Chancery, of the due publication of such notice in manner aforesaid, shall at all times thereafter be deemed *prima facie* evidence thereof; and every such proprietor, who shall not begin the making of such piers and bridges by the period for that purpose appointed, or who shall not contribute his proportion of the expenses thereof, as the same shall accrue, shall be deemed and taken to have neglected and refused to comply with the said directions, according to the intent and meaning of the last-mentioned act."

This was first enacted in the fifth section of the act of April, 1806.

The 233d, 234th and 235th sections of the act of 1813 empower the Corporation to make regulations in certain particular cases, or give certain remedies and penalties which do not properly belong to the branch of the subject now considered.

The 236th section is as follows: "It shall be lawful for the said Mayor, Aldermen, and Commonalty, in Common Council convened, to make such by-laws and ordinances as they shall, from time to time, think proper, for regulating wharves, piers and slips in the said city."

The 269th section of the act of 1813 must also be adverted to. "In all cases where the said by-laws and ordinances (of the Corporation) shall require any thing to be done by, or with respect to the property of several persons, or in relation to the filling up, altering or amending any of the public slips in the said city, the said Mayor, Aldermen, and Commonalty, in Common Council convened, shall cause the expense of such works to be estimated and assessed in the same manner as is directed in and by this act, with respect to the paving and regulating the public streets in the said city; and where the same shall relate to the filling up, altering or amending the public slips, as aforesaid, one-third of the expense attending the same shall be borne by the said Mayor, Aldermen, and Commonalty, and the residue by the said persons in the vicinity, who may be benefited thereby, and in other cases such expenses shall be borne by the persons, respectively, upon whom the same may be assessed, as aforesaid."

This enactment was made in a statute of the 2d of April, 1803, entitled "An act to invest the Mayor, &c., with adequate powers in relation to certain objects of importance to the police and health of the said city." (3 Webster, p. 229, § 4.)

This act was originally limited to three years. By the statute of 2d April, 1806, the above clause was made permanent, and finally embodied in the 269th section of the act of 1813.

A statute passed April 10, 1830 (Sess. Laws, 1830, p. 342), authorizing the Mayor, Aldermen, and Commonalty to make such by-laws and ordinances as to them should appear fit, to designate and appropriate such of the public wharves, piers and slips of the said city as they may deem expedient, and such private wharves and piers in the said city, as the owners thereof, respectively, may apply to have so designated, or appropriated for the exclusive use of steamboats or of any other class or description of ships or vessels; and to restrain and prohibit any ship or water craft whatsoever from coming into, or lying, mooring, or anchoring at or within any wharf, pier, or slip of the said city, except such as shall be so designated for their use, respectively, and to impose such penalties as they may think reasonable.

Another statute connected with this subject was passed on the 20th of April, 1835. It was provided that "it should be lawful for the Common Council of the city of New York to order and direct that any private wharf, pier, dock, bulkhead, or land, within the limits of the said city, be deepened by excavating or removing the earth and dirt, or sand therefrom, and to cause the same to be done in such places and at such times as are necessary and proper."

"§ 2. The expense of conforming to any such order or direction, or of carrying the same into effect, shall be estimated and assessed upon or among the owner or owners of every dock, pier, wharf, bulkhead, piece of land, water right or privilege, near or adjacent to which any such water may be deepened, and which may in any manner be benefited thereby, in proportion, as nearly as may be, to the advantage which each shall be deemed to acquire."

The third and fourth sections relate to the manner of carrying the provisions into effect.

Statutes respecting Wharfage, Rates, &c.

On the 21st of September, 1744, an act was passed to establish the rates to be taken for wharfage of ships and other vessels, using the three wharfs therein mentioned.

It is recited—

"Whereas, The owners and proprietors of the wharf, called Burnett's Key, in the city of New York, have, by their petition, set forth to the General Assembly that an act, entitled 'An act for regulating the rates to be taken for ships and other vessels using the wharf called Burnett's Key, in the city of New York,' passed in the eighth year of his majesty's reign (22d June, 1734), will expire, by its own limitation, on the first of December next, and praying that the same might be continued, &c.

"And whereas, the owners and proprietors of another free wharf, between the Smith's Fly slip (Maiden lane) and Burling slip, in the East Ward, have prayed that they may be entitled to the like wharfages, and be under the same regulations, as the proprietors of Burnett's Key are now, or shall be entitled to."

The act then established the rates of wharfage, according to the tonnage of the vessels. Other provisions were made; and, by the sixth section, the owners of the three wharves, or the major part of them, might choose a wharfinger or overseer, who should have the ordering and regulating of the wharves, and of the berths of the ships or vessels.

By the eighth section, nothing therein was to impair the right which the Mayor, Aldermen and Commonalty of the city of New York had to the dock, and to the several slips therein beforementioned. On the 1st of May, 1754, this act was continued, being to expire, by its own limitation, on the first of December ensuing.

On the 19th February, 1756, the chief provisions of this act were renewed in another act, and extended to two other wharves, one of them between the slips called Rodman slip and Burling slip.

There was a similar reservation of the rights of the Corporation to the slips and docks. This act was to continue until the 21st of January, 1770. On the 21st of January, 1770, this act was substantially renewed, and on the 21st of February, 1771, was, in some particulars, amended.

And on the 17th of April, 1784, a general act was passed to establish the rates of wharfage and cartage within the city of New York. (1 Greenleaf, 92 ; 2 ibid., 354.)

On the 6th of April, 1795, the statute of 1784 was amended. This statute was renewed and amended on the 3d of April, 1801. Another amendment took place on the 24th March, 1809, and again on the 18th of June, 1812.

And, lastly, all the provisions of these statutes were combined in the general act of 1813 to reduce certain laws, &c., in the 212th and six following sections.

NOTE 51.—PAGE 257.

Abstract Opinion—R. Emmet, Esq.

Document No. 52, B. Ass. Ald., vol. 201.

The learned counsel states, that it was proposed to form a public slip or basin at the foot of Clinton street, on the East river, and for that purpose to build a pier opposite to certain premises granted to Anna Bancker, in 1804, by the Corporation. The parties interested had declined uniting in erecting the pier ; and the question was, if the Corporation could do so at their own expense, without infringing upon any right held under the grant.

The counsel then states the provisions of the grant, observing that it included the space occupied by Front street, down to the river, but no part of Clinton street; that there was no specific grant of wharfage.

He then proceeds to state his reasons for the proposition, that the grantees took, under their grant, the right to wharfage on that part of Front street, co-extensive with their grant; and he proceeds—"The next inquiry is, what impediment does such right offer to the construction of the pier in question by the Corporation? The act of the Legislature makes it lawful for the Corporation to lay out wharves and slips in the city, whenever and wherever they deem it expedient, and to direct piers to be sunk and completed at such distances and in such manner as they, in their discretion, shall think proper, in front of the streets and wharves adjoining and extending along the rivers. The reason and propriety of vesting this power in the Municipal Government of a great commercial city must be obvious; nor would it be going too far to say, that many private rights must be held and enjoyed in reference and subordinate to its exercise. Of such a character, I conceive the right of wharfage, in the present instance, to be."

Note 52.—Page 277.

Petition of 1702, *for Ferry Charter.*

To his Excellency, Lord Viscount Cornbury, &c., &c.

The humble petition of the Mayor, Aldermen, and Commonalty of the city of New York, most humbly showeth unto your Excellency:

That your petitioners, by their charter, having a right and interest in the ferry from this city across the river to Nassau Island, and from the said island to the city again, and to all the perquisites, profits and advantages thereof, which your petitioners perceive to fall much short of what they might reasonably expect from the same, if the bounds and limits of the said ferry were somewhat extended on the said island side, whereby to hinder and prevent that privilege and liberty, which divers persons now take, of transporting themselves and goods to and from the said Island of Nassau over the said river, without coming to or landing at the usual and accustomed place, where the said ferry is kept and appointed, to the great loss and damage of your petitioners, whose farmer of the said ferry complains he cannot live upon, nor longer hold the same, though at a moderate and very easy rent; which mischief and inconvenience your petitioners know not better how to remedy than by gaining a further interest on the shore adjoining to the said island, so as to oblige persons to pay the rate and duty of the ferry who pass and repass the said river with themselves or goods, to and from any other part of the said island, within the bounds and compass hereby prayed for, than that where the said ferry is now kept, which being in your Lordship's power alone to enable your petitioners to do.

We, your said petitioners, do most humbly beg of your Excellency, that you would be pleased to grant unto us and our successors, for the use and behoof of this city and Corporation, under the seal of this province, all the vacant land from high water to low water mark, fronting the harbor of this city from the east side of the Red Hook, upon Nassau Island aforesaid to the East side of Wallabout, upon the said island, for the better and more convenient taking in and loading of passengers, corn, and other goods and things bound to and from this city.

And your petioners as in duty bound will ever pray. (Read in Council, 11th March, 1702.)

The Trustees for the town of Brooklyn, in Kings county, on Nassau Island, whose names are hereunder written, for and on behalf of themselves and said town, enter a caveat against the city of New York, or any particular person, for having a patent for any land between high water and low water mark, from Kickout and the Wallabout to Red Hook in said township, till they be heard, &c. March 16, 1702–3.

No further action appears to have been taken.

Note 53.—Page 277.

Petition of C. Sebring, for Ferry Grant, 23d January, 1707.

To his Excellency, Edward Viscount Cornbury, &c.:

The petition of Cornelius Sebring, of Kings county, on the Island of Nassau, showeth. That your petitioner is seized and stands possessed of a certain farm on the Island of Nassau, directly over and against the centre of the city of New York, being a most fit and convenient place for a ferry, to and from the said city, for the transportation of passengers, goods, wares, merchandise, cattle, corn, and other commodities, to the great use and benefit of many of the inhabitants of the said city and island, considering the situation as aforesaid, and which can be of no hurt or damage to the old ferry, it being not as convenient for that ferry to send their boats to the south end and centre of the city, where he purposes to send his.

Your petitioner therefore humbly prays your Excellency to grant unto your petitioner her Majesty's Letters Patent, under the great seal of the province, for establishing a ferry over the East river or Sound, to be limited on the Island of Nassau on the one side by the old ferry, and on the other side by the Red Hook, and on the side of New York, between the slip, at Captain Theobald's, unto the great bridge, for the loading and landing of all persons, goods, wares and merchandise, except cattle, to be landed at or near the slaughter houses (nevertheless, not excluding the old ferry boat from the places aforesaid), under such regulations and such prices for transportation, and small quit rent or acknowledgment, as to your Excellency shall seem meet.

New York, 23d January, 1707–8.

A considerable number of citizens agreed that such a ferry would be of advantage to the city, if the price of transportation was not excessive.

NOTE 54.—PAGE 278.

Petition of 1708, *for land on Nassau Island, for Ferry Grant.*

To his Excellency, &c.:

The humble petition of the Mayor, Aldermen, and Commonalty of the city of New York, most humbly showeth:

That the petitioners having a right and interest in the

ferry from this city to Nassau Island, and from the said island to the city again, and to all the profits and advantages thereof, perceive it to fall far short of what they might reasonably expect from the same, if the bounds and limits of the said ferry were something extended on the said island side, thereby to hinder and prevent that privilege and liberty which divers persons now take of transporting themselves and goods to and from the said Island of Nassau over the said river, without coming to, or landing at the usual and accustomed place where the said ferry boats are kept and appointed, to the great loss and damage of the petitioners (the profits thereof being wholly appropriated for the public service and government of the said city), and it being obvious to your petitioners that some private persons, for their own use and gain, have solicited your Excellency for another ferry on the said island, fronting to this city, which, if granted, would be of great damage to this Corporation, and all the inhabitants thereof, as the petitioners humbly conceive, would in time, not only prove injurious to the trade and commerce of this city, but also be a means to lessen the income of her Majesty's revenue, established upon trade, to the general decay of the province, the improvement thereof employed now in traffic being scarcely able to maintain the inhabitants now in this city, whose livelihood does only rely thereon.

Your Excellency's petitioners therefore most humbly pray that your Lordship will be favorably pleased to take the premises into your prudent consideration, and order her Majesty's grant unto the petitioners and their successors for all the vacant and unappropriated ground on Nassau Island, from high water to low water mark, fronting unto this city from the place called the Wallabout, unto the Red Hook, against Nutten Island, for the better improvement and accommodation of the said ferry; and also that your Excellency would be further pleased to order unto the petitioners and their successors her Majesty's grant of confirmation for the said ferry on both sides of the said river, with power to establish one or more ferries, if there shall be occasion, and to make by-laws for the more orderly regulation thereof, at such reasonable rates and under such moderate quit-rent as your Lordship in your great prudence shall see meet.

And your Excellency's petitioners as in duty bound shall ever pray, &c.

EBENEZER WILLSON,	WILLIAM SMITH,
JOHN TUDER,	CHRISTOPHER DENNE,
D. PROVOST,	JOHN HENDRICK BREVOORT,
RICHARD WILLETT,	PAUL DROILHET,
ALFRED SWOERTS.	E. BLAGGE.

April 8, 1708.—Read, and granted—a warrant to be prepared for the Attorney General to draw a patent or charter.

NOTE 55.—PAGE 281.

Statute of 1732, *as to Ferries.*

The act recites, that whereas the rates and prices of the ferriage of men, horses, &c., and all other goods transported over the ferry, between the city of New York and the Island of Nassau, were heretofore regulated by the Mayor, Aldermen, and Commonalty of the said city, to whom that ferry belongs; and for the avoiding of disputes, the aforesaid ferriage was afterward established for the term of seven years, by an act of the General Assembly, entitled, &c., passed in the fourth year of his late Majesty's reign, and the same having been generally approved of, was, by another act passed in the first year of his present Majesty's reign, continued until the 12th day of June, 1733. And whereas, the rates and prices of the ferriage aforesaid are full well approved, and allowed to be reasonable and moderate.

The first section then prescribes the rates of ferriage. The second fixes the various penalties upon passengers for refusing to pay the rates; and the third upon the ferryman for not landing at the place appointed, and for taking more than is allowed by the act.

The fourth section directs, that it should and might be lawful for the Mayor, Aldermen, and Commonalty of the city of New York to take the rates of ferriage before fixed, "and shall and may establish and keep one or more ferry or ferries between the said city of New York and the Island of Nassau, for the better and more easy transportation of passengers."

The fifth gave liberty to the owners on the water side to transport their own goods or commodities in their own boats or canoes, but not to bring over the goods of other person or persons, with or without hire.

And the sixth section was as follows:

"And forasmuch as the Mayor, Aldermen, and Commonalty of the city of *New York* have been for many years past, and still are legally and solely seized of the ferry aforesaid, and that they have, at their own great cost and charges, not only purchased lands on *Nassau Island*, at the place where the said ferry has always been kept, but likewise erected there houses, stables, and a pen for the accommodation of travelers, passengers, drovers, horses and cattle, and a convenient bridge or landing for boats to come at, and go off from. Be it therefore enacted by the authority aforesaid, that no other person or persons whomsoever, other than the said Mayor, Aldermen, and Commonalty of the city of New York, their successors and assigns, shall presume to erect and keep a ferry between the city of New York and Nassau Island, for carrying or bringing of any passengers, horses, cattle, hogs, sheep, goods, wares, merchandise, or other commodities or things whatsoever, over the said ferry hereby rated and established, for any hire, wages, or reward whatsoever, or without such, under penalty of fifty pounds for every such offense, with full costs of suit; one moiety thereof to his majesty, his heirs and successors, toward the support of his government in this colony, and the other moiety thereof to such person or persons as shall prosecute and sue for the same, to effect, in any court of record within the said colony, wherein no protection or wager of law or more than one imparlance shall be allowed."

The seventh section directed the ferrymen to hang up a table of the rates at some conspicuous place.

Note 56.—Page 283.

Ferry Act of 1813, 2 *R. S.*, 355.

The first section (being the 45th section of the act to reduce into one act the laws concerning the city of New York, vol. 2, R. S., p. 355) prescribed the rates of passage from the city of New York to the Island of Nassau, and from the Island of Nassau to the city. "Whenever a certain rate of ferriage is fixed for any particular quantity or weight of goods, a proportionable rate shall be taken for any greater or less quantity or weight of the same goods.

"If any person shall refuse to pay the rates of ferriage thus established, he shall forfeit and pay the ferryman treble the rate to which he was liable by the act, to be recovered with costs in any court having cognizance thereof. (§ 46.)

"It shall be lawful for the Mayor, Aldermen, and Commonalty of the city of New York to demand and receive the rates and prices of ferriage aforesaid, for the said ferriage from and to the said city as aforesaid, and they may establish and keep one or more ferries between the said city and the Island of Nassau aforesaid." (§ 47.)

The 48th section fixes a penalty of two dollars and fifty cents, for taking any other or greater rates of ferriage than those settled in the act.

The 49th section provides for the mode of giving publicity to the rates, by putting up lists thereof in a conspicuous place at the ferry houses.

The 50th and 51st sections relate to the marking of the boats in a particular manner, and to the hours of running at different seasons of the year.

The 52d section is as follows: "That it shall be lawful for any inhabitants of the town of Brooklyn to transport their own goods in their own boats, from the Island of Nassau to the city of New York, and from the city of New York to the Island of Nassau, without giving any ferriage for the same. *Provided, however*, that if any such inhabitants, under color or pretext of transporting his or her own goods only, shall carry or bring over the said ferry the goods of any other person of what kind soever, with or without hire or reward, every such inhabitant shall for every such offense forfeit and pay to the ferryman of such ferry two dollars aad fifty cents, to be recovered, with costs of suit, before any justice of the peace, or court having cognizance thereof."

53d section is as follows—"That no person other than the said Mayor, Aldermen, and Commonalty shall erect and keep a ferry between the said city and Nassau Island, for carrying or bringing any passengers, horses, cattle, hogs, sheep, goods, merchandise or other things whatsoever over the said ferry hereby rated, with or without any hire or reward, under the penalty of one hundred and twenty-five dollars for every such offense."

The 54th, 55th, and 56th sections prescribed a sufficient number of men to be attached to the barges and other boats, the dimensions of the barges, &c. These regulations, from the introduction of steam ferry-boats, have fallen into disuse.

By the 57th section, the Harbor Masters of the city, for the time being, shall be the persons who shall, on the complaint of any person, determine whether the ferry boats are kept in proper order.

The 58th section regulates the mode of recovering the penalties, and their application.

NOTE 56 CONTINUED.—PAGE 293.

Cases as to rights and property in Ferries.

Mills vs. *The County Commissioners* (3 Scammon's Rep., 55, Illinois). The Legislature of Illinois had by an act authorized St. Clair county to establish a ferry across the river Mississippi. Commissioners had located the ferry and road leading to it. The county court was authorized to cause the land covered by the location to be condemned, and the damages to be paid to the owner, and then to enter upon the land, and establish the ferry. The mode of ascertaining the damages by a jury was then prescribed, and an appeal given.

The appellants were owners of the lands taken, for considerable distance above and below the point, and had enjoyed a former ferry on their land for the space of thirteen years, called St. Lewis Ferry. The question arose on the refusal of the judge, at the trial, to give instructions that these ferry rights should be estimated, in making up the value to be allowed to the appellants.

The court say, "it is a principle of common law that ferries are *publici juris*, and can be granted by the sovereign power. If this be admittted, it follows that riparian proprietors are not thereby entitled to the franchise."

"Has our statute changed this firm principle? The act entitled, &c., gives the owners of land, adjoining to or embracing the water course over which a ferry is proposed to be established, a preference over others, provided the privilege shall not have been granted to any other person; thus clearly recognizing the common law principle, and implying a power in the public to make the grant to persons other than the owners of the land."

The court proceed to notice that the appellants had only shown possession of thirteen years, but no license or grant, and had not therefore proven themselves entitled to the ferry franchise.

We must advert to the fact that the doctrine as to navigable rivers is applied to the Mississippi.

Mills vs. *The County of St. Clair* (2 Gilman's Illinois Rep., 197).

The grant by an act of the Legislature of Illinois, passed in 1819, was as follows: " That S. Wiggins, his heirs and assigns, were authorized to establish a ferry on the waters of the Mississippi, near the town of Illinois, in this State, to run the same from lands at said place that might belong to him. And that no person except those who had ferries then established at that place should establish a ferry of that description aforesaid (viz.: by boats to be propelled by steam, horses, oxen, or other four-footed animals), within one mile of the ferry established under that act."

But by another section it was provided, that if the provisions of the second section should appear to be injurious to the public good, then such section might be repealed.

The ferry was accordingly located at a given point. In 1833, the Legislature repealed the second section of the act of 1819.

In 1839, the Legislature appointed commissioners to locate a road and ferry across the Mississippi river; and the commissioners proceeded to take three hundred feet of the land of Wiggins' assigns, upon the river, no compensation being granted for the damage done to the franchise.

In 1821, a further act was passed, authorizing Wiggins, his heirs, and assigns, to remove his ferry on any lands which might belong to him, or them, on the said Mississippi river, under the same provisions as were prescribed in the act of 1819.

The new ferry, under the act of 1839, was located below the tract first acquired by Wiggins, and on which his ferry was established. He had purchased this tract.

The court stated the following propositions: "That the grant of a ferry franchise by the Legislature of a State, unless limited by some general law, or some restrictive provisions in the grant itself, is necessarily exclusive to the extent of the privilege thus conferred. When a grant has once been made by the legislative authority, to the extent of the rights conferred by it, the power which made it is exhausted, and it cannot be taken back or transferred to another, until the public interests or welfare shall demand its resumption, and provision shall have been made for just compensation to the owner." Such a contract, however, is always subject to an implied reservation in favor of the sovereign power, that whenever the public good requires, or the exigencies of the State demand it, all the rights and privileges may be resumed, upon adequate compensation being made.

The cause went up to the Supreme Court of the United States (8 Howard, 569). The first grant, that of 1819, was held operative, contrary to the opinion of the court below. It was concluded that the Legislature meant to give the same time to the party, eighteen months, for the acquisition of the lands, as he had for running the ferry.

Wiggins was confined in running the ferry, under the act of 1821, to the ground *then* owned by him. He could not afterward go beyond that tract to other land not then owned by him. Whether he could have changed his location within the limits of the tract actually owned, was not a question before the court.

It was also held that the establishment and regulation of ferries across navigable streams is a subject within the control of the government, which may exercise its power by contracting with individuals. This general principle was not open to controversy.

In North Carolina the right to establish ferries is recognized as in the sovereign authority, but the privilege must first be offered to the owner of the bank where it is intended to be fixed. If he refuse, the grant may be made to another, compensating the owner for the use of the soil taken. (Pipkin *vs.* Winns, 2 D. Rep., 402, overruling Raynen *vs.* Dowday, 1 Murphy, 279.) This is also the rule in Kentucky and in Tennessee. (Harvie *vs.* Carmack, 6 Dana, 242 ; Allen *vs.* Fansworth, 5 Yerger, 189.)

In these cases the rule was fully recognized, that a first right of privilege was the result of statutory provision, not a rule of law binding upon the State.

The case of Young *vs.* Hanson (6 Georgia Rep., 130) settled :

1st. That the owner of land on the banks of a river had not, as matter of right, the privilege of keeping a public ferry. This right to do so could only be by grant, actual or implied.

2d. That the State had a right to erect bridges wherever it was deemed necessary for the convenience of the public.

3d. That a bridge might be established, and a keeper appointed, without any regard to ownership of the soil. The franchise or right to keep bridges or ferries should, however, be conferred upon the owners of the soil, rather than on strangers, if practicable and consistent with the public welfare.

The —— Bridge Company had been incorporated by

the Legislature, with ordinary powers to enter upon and take lands for their purposes. The plaintiff had used a ferry from his land for about thirteen years, but without a grant from the State, although the title to his land adjoining was derived from it.

It was decided that he had no right to ferry across the river, and no property therein; and that the act of incorporation of the Bridge Company was lawful, and authorized them to take his land, making compensation as provided for in their charter.

See also the great case of The Canal Co. *vs.* The Railroad Co. (4 Gill and Johnson, 1).

Costar vs. *Brush* (25 Wendell, 628.) The plaintiffs were holders of a lease granted by the Corporation of New York for the establishment of a ferry between Beekman slip and the old ferry at Brooklyn (now called Fulton Ferry), in which the Corporation covenanted that they would not establish or permit any other ferry between New York and Brooklyn, south of the ferry at Catharine slip. The case involved the legality of this covenant.

The court said, "It is insisted that the grant of the right establishing ferries, made to the Corporation, was a franchise to be exercised for the public good, and that any restriction imposed upon itself in the exercise of this power was illegal. The short answer to all which is, that the Corporation possessed the same power in respect to the establishment of ferries across the East River that before belonged to the Crown or Legislature; and the exclusive privileges extended to the lessees of the Fulton Ferry were fully within its municipal authority, and binding both upon the city and the public."

NOTE 57.—PAGE 99, 329 AND OTHERS.

Titles as existing in 1686.

I have found several points connected with this subject so useful, and so troublesome to ascertain, for any particular case, as to induce me to state—

1. The periods of the administration of the several Colonial Governors;

2. The distances on the chief streets or highways, which tend to illustrate the subject; and

3. Measurements of distances useful in locating particular Dutch ground-briefs or transports.

DATES, GOVERNORS, &C.

1623 to 1632, Peter Minuit, Governor and Director General.

1633 to 1638, Wouter Von Twiller, Governor and Director General.

March, 1638, to May, 1647, William Kieft, Governor and Director General.

May, 1647, to August, 1664, Petrus Stuyvesant.

1664, 26th August, surrender to the English.

1664, August, to August, 1668, Richard Nicholls, Governor.

1668, August, to July, 1673, Francis Lovelace, Governor.

1673, August, Dutch Governor, Anthony Colve. Provisional Instructions.

1674, November 10th, Restoration to the English, under the treaty of peace.

1674, November, to August, 1683, Edward Andross, Governor.

1683 to spring of 1689, Thomas Dongan, Governor.

1689 to 1691, Jacob Leisler, under Committee of Safety.

1689, 11th December, Leisler as Lieutenant-Governor.

1691, March to July, ——— Sloughter as Lieutenant-Governor.

1691, July, to August 1692, Richard Ingoldsby, Governor.

1692, August, to April, 1698, Benjamin Fletcher, Governor.

1698, April, to 5th March, 1701, Earl Bellamont, Governor.

1702, May, to 1708, Lord Cornbury, Governor.

1708, December, to 1709, May, Lord Lovelace, Governor.

1710 to 1719, ——— Hunter, Governor.

1720 to 1728, William Burnett, Governor.

1728, April 15th, to July 1st, 1731, John Montgomery, Governor.

1731, July, to 1st of August, 1732, Rip Van Dam, of the Council.

1732, August 1st, to 7th March, 1736, William Cosby, Governor.

1736 to 1743, George Clarke, Lieutenant-Governor.

1743 to October, 1753, Governor Clinton.

1753, two days, Sir Danvers Osborn.

1753 to 1755, James Delancey, Lieutenant-Governor.

1755, Sir Charles Hardy.

1760 to 1761, Lieutenant-Governor Colden, in the absence of Sir Charles Hardy and in that of Governor Monckton.

1761, October, to 1765, Robert Monckton.

1765 to September, 1769, Sir Henry Moore.

1769, Lieutenant-Governor Colden administered the Government.

1771, July to March, 1780, William Tryon.

1780, March, to the peace, Major-General Robertson.

DISTANCES.

On Broadway (*west side*) :

		Ft. In.	
From	Battery place (Marketfield) to Morris street	461.07	
	Morris street	32.04	
"	Morris to Rector street, south side	641.03	
	Rector street	42.06	
"	Rector to Thames street	431.05	
			1609.01
	Thames street	20.00	
"	Thames to Cedar street	101.00	
	Cedar street	34.05	
"	Cedar to Liberty street	126.08	
	Liberty street	36.10	
"	Liberty to Cortlandt street	226.04	
	Cortlandt street	50.02	
"	Cortlandt to Dey street	222.06	
	Dey street	40.00	
"	Dey to Fulton street	153.06	
	Fulton street	57.03	
			1064.08
"	Fulton to Duane street	1817.09	
	Duane street	40.00	
"	Duane to Leonard street	677.10	
	Leonard street	50.00	
"	Leonard to Canal street	1076.00	
	Canal street	101.00	
"	Canal to Prince street	2007.03	
	Prince street	50.00	
"	Prince to Art street	2226.05	

Broadway (east side):

		Ft. In.
From	Walker to Maiden lane........	843.00
	Maiden lane..................	50.00
"	Maiden lane to John street.....	168.00
	John street..................	44.08
"	John to Fulton street..........	200.11
	Fulton street, 54.08 (formerly)..	32.00
"	Fulton to a point 36 feet from Ann street................	31.00
"	Chambers to Duane street.....	455.00
"	Duane to Catharine lane.......	637.00
"	Catharine lane to White street..	579.00
"	White to Howard street......	823.00

On Greenwich street:

From	Marketfield (Battery place) to Fulton street..............	2766.00
	Fulton street.................	61.03
"	Fulton to Duane street.........	1892.00
	Duane street.................	64.00
"	Duane to Canal street..........	2549.00
	Canal street.................	101.00
"	Canal to Charlton (Bestaver's Killitjie) street..............	1000.00
	Charlton street...............	50.00
"	Charlton to Christopher street..	2000.00
	Christopher street............	50.00
"	Christopher to Gansevoort street,	2313.00

Broadway to east side of Greenwich street:

		FT. IN.
At	Marketfield street	165.00
"	Morris street	241.00
"	Rector street	405.00
"	Fulton street	843.00
"	Chambers street	1424.00
"	Duane street	1548.00
"	Walker street	2165.00

Wall street (north side):

From	Broadway to Pearl street	1258.07
	Pearl street	40.03
"	Pearl to north-east side Water (including Water) street	204.08

Maiden lane (north side):

From Wall to Queen (Pearl) street.....1392.00

On Queen (Pearl) street:

From	Wall to Maiden lane	494.00	
	Maiden lane	52.00	
"	Maiden lane to John street	394.00	
	John street	49.00	
"	John street to Fulton.....300 } Fulton street to Beekman..337 }	597.00	
		———	1040.00
	Beekman street	36.00	
"	Beekman to Frankfort street	750.00	
"	Frankfort to Vandewater street	500.00	
"	From Vandewater to Duane st	215.00	
	Thomas (or Duane) street	50.00	

			Ft. In.
From	Duane to Chatham street.......		450.00
	Chatham street................		60.00
"	Chatham street to Broadway...		1390.00

On Chatham street and Bowery (east side):

From	its beginning, say 36 feet from Ann street to N. W. point Times building................	750.00	
"	thence to Frankfort st...	200.00	
			950.00
	Frankfort street..............		50.00
"	Frankfort to Thomas (Duane) st.		680.00
	Duane street, (before late widening)....................		40.00
"	Duane to Pearl street..........		460.00
	Pearl street....................		50.00
"	Pearl to Roosevelt street........		170.00
	Roosevelt street...............		50.00
"	Roosevelt to Oliver street......		530.00
	Oliver street..................		40.00
"	Oliver to Catharine street......		210.00
"	Catharine to Grand street......		1730.00
	Grand street...................		70.00
"	Grand to north side Houston street.......................		2065.00

On Chatham street and Bowery (west side):

From	Tryon Row to Pearl street.....	900.00
	Pearl street..................	100.00
"	Pearl street to a point opposite centre of Roosevelt street....	140.00

		Ft. In.
From	Roosevelt to Mott street........	390.00
	Mott street....................	55.00
"	Mott to Doyers street..........	230.00
	Doyers street..................	55.00
"	Doyers to Walker street........	810.00
	Walker street..................	50.00
"	Walker to Grand street.........	831.00
	Grand street...................	70.00
"	Grand to Prince street.........	1429.00
	Prince street..................	52.00
"	Prince to Art st. (Astor place)..	2688.00

Art street (Astor place):

From	the Bowery to Greenwich lane.	2930.00
"	Greenwich lane to Fitzroy road.	2030.00
"	Fitzroy road (or Gansevoort st.) to high water mark, Hudson River	1450.00

On Cherry street:

From	beginning to Roosevelt street...	400.00
	Roosevelt street................	40.00
"	Roosevelt to James street.......	345.00
	James street....................	40.00
"	James to Catharine street.......	440.00
	Catharine street................	40.00
"	Catharine to Rutgers street....	1818.00
	Rutgers street..................	60.00
"	Rutgers to Corlaers street......	3123.00
	Across Corlaers street..........	60.00
"	that point to Houston street (north)....................	2460.00

Measurements.

A Dutch foot.....11 Dutch inches.
A Dutch foot.....$11\frac{3}{8}$ English inches.
An English foot...12 inches.
A Dutch rod.....Sometimes 11, 12, and 13 Dutch feet.
A Rhineland perch.12 Rhineland feet.
An English rod...16.6 English feet.
A Dutch rod.....$12\frac{246}{1000}$, say $\frac{1}{4}$ or 3 inches.*
A chain English...100 links.
do. ....66 feet.
A link..........$7\frac{92}{100}$ inches.
An acre.........$17\frac{2}{5}$ lots of 25x100, 43,560 feet to an acre.
A pole...........16 feet 6 inches.

Very frequently the number of rods in a Dutch grant, when compared with the actual distances on a street which can be proved to have been the location, requires

* In the Encyclopedia are the following statements: A Rhineland foot (12 whereof make a Rhineland perch), being taken at 696 parts—

An English foot is $675\frac{1}{2}$.

The Amsterdam foot 629.

An English foot 1000 parts 12 inches.

A Rhineland foot 12, 396-1000.

In the Dictionary of Weights and Measures (Baltimore, 1850) the Rhenish rod is stated at 12, 476-1000 English inches.

The Amsterdam old measure at 12, 72-1000.

The proportion of 629 the Amsterdam foot of the Encyclopedia (M. Picard), to 675 1-2 English, is about a sixth, 11 1-6 inches.

From the Amsterdam measure at the City Hall, Mr. Child, Superintendent of the encroachment survey, has estimated the Dutch rod to be 12 246-1000 English feet.

Sometimes the rod is stated at 13 feet, and sometimes at 12 feet, in the Dutch ground briefs and transports. Frequently the measure is Rhineland measure.

Mr. Valentine has computed the Dutch rod to be 12, $7\frac{1}{2}$ or 8 inches.

at least 14 feet to the Dutch rod. This would be a serious embarrassment if a strict survey and definite boundaries were essential, and would then require more critical examination. For my purposes,—to show the Dutch origin of the most of the titles, it is not of moment. Where (as is largely the case) the adjoining owners hold under Dutch grants, the precise limits between them is not of consequence.

Numerous measurements and comparisons have made me conclude to take 12 6 inches as the measure of a rod. This corresponds better than any other with lines which are already located and defined.

Diagram No. 1.

A. 1650. Grant to Jan Martyn. Lot to the east of the strand of the North River, having to the north the house and lot of Martin Cregier; to the east that of the widow of Pieter Cock; to the south a certain wagon way; to the west the strand of the North River; length on east side six (6) rods 3 feet; on the west along the river, six (6) rods; on the south side, four rods seven feet (4.7); on the north side three (3) rods 3 feet.

I have not traced how the title to this parcel came to Pieter Cock, or the derivation from him. I think it is the lot mentioned as that of Thomas Coker, reserved in Dongan's charter. At any rate, it is found to have been vested in Charles Sleigh, in 1729, with another strip.

DIAGRAM No. 1.

The East Line of Greenwich Street is nearly identical with high Water mark of 1699. At Marketfield Street it was about ten feet East of Greenwich Street.

The distance from Battery Place to North Side of Rector is 1177 ft. 2 in.
Strip belonging to Trinity Church ... 81
1258. 2.

The lines on the Diagram 1227. 5.

100 ft. to an inch.

A. 1729. Mortgage by Charles Sleigh to A. De Peyster. Equity of redemption released, and—

1756, August. A. De Peyster to Archibald Kennedy. In the Montgomery charter of 1730, the line of the West Ward runs between the house of Charles Sleigh, and that of Thomas Edes. The front of Sleigh on Broadway was 54 feet; depth 112 feet south side, and 13 north side. He had acquired a grant of 270 feet from high water mark. High water mark was 122 feet from the corner of Broadway.

B. 1648. To Gerrit Dowman.

Gerrit Dowman to Pieter Cock.

1067, February. Confirmation to Anatie, widow of Pieter Cock. Lot on the east side, 4 rods 6 feet; south side, next to the fort (8.7); next to the stand, west side (4.7).

C. 1643. Governor Kieft to Martin Cregier. Lot for a house and garden lying north of the fort, extending from the house about west, 9 rods 2 feet; towards the fort, south, 6 rods 9 feet; again, about east, with a great outpoint, 14 rods 6 feet; further, to the place of beginning, 4 rods 5 feet.

1645. A lot north of the fort, north of Martin Cregier. It extends on the west side, in length, 11 rods 3 feet; on the north side, 7 rods 9 feet (7.9); on the east side, 9 rods 9 feet (9.9); on the south side, next to Martin Cregier, 11 rods 9 feet.

1666. Confirmation by Nicolls to M. Cregier (Lib. 13, Albany Records, for both parcels).

D. 16—. Widow of Jacob Jansen to Francis Broane.
1665, January. Francis Broane to Van Tright.
1668, May 5. Confirmation to him. A lot to the west of Broadway, having to the south the lot of Captain Cregier; to the west the strand; north, the house of C. Van Ruyven; east and west sides 32 feet; in length, from the street to the water side.
1650, January 8. Gerrit Dowman to Peter Stoutenbergh.
1654, December 3. Peter Stoutenbergh to J. H. Steedman.
1655, March 17. J. H. Steedman to Jacobus Backer. House and lot northward of Fort Amsterdam, and the Beaver's path on the North River, and south of the house of Dominie Megapolensis; breadth, east and west sides, 32 feet; in depth same as the adjoining lots.

E. 1643, July 3. Ground-brief, Kieft to J. J. Rooy.
1649, August 13. J. J. Rooy to Abram Verplanck.
1650, April 15. A. Verplanck to Dirck Bensick, for a part.
1656, January 21. Ab. Verplanck to Dominie J. Megapolensis for residue.
1656, August 3. Dirck Bensick to Dominie Megapolensis.
First. Lot, west side of the great highway; south by Jacob Backer; west by the river; north by the other part of Megapolensis' lot; east by the highway; front on the highway, 4 rods 9 feet; depth, south side, 12 rods 9 feet; north side, 9 rods 5 feet (9.5).

Second. Bounded by the common highway; west by the river; north by the lot of ———; south by the lot sold ——— (*Bensick*); on the street, 4 rods 3 feet; length, one side, 12 rods 4 feet; the other 9 rods 5 feet.

F. 1650, May 23, Governor Stuyvesant to ———.

1652, August 18, ——, to Dirck Ness.

1655, " 31, Dirck Ness to Cornelius De Bruyn.

1657, June 2, Cornelius De Bruyn to R. Jansen Hoorn. A house and lot on the great highway, southward of the church-yard, and northward of the lot of Hans Styn. Front on the street or east side, 3 rods less 1 foot. Rear 3 rods 1½ feet; length, north and south sides, 9 rods 4 feet.

Before April, 1672, R. Jansen Hoorn to Judith Stuyvesant.

1672, April. Judith Stuyvesant to Peter Tinkham (Lib. A, p. 132).

1693, December. Peter Tynkham to B. Le Roux (Lib. 16, p. 268). Lot of ground on Broadway, having to the north the old church-yard, to the south the lot of the widow of Luyckers Derickse. Length, north and south sides, 9.4 to the water-side; on Broadway, 3 rods.

G. *The Church-yard.*

1656, January 24. Resolved, that it is necessary to establish a grave-yard at some other suitable place, or put in order where it now is. (Minutes Burgomasters.)

1665, June. Church-yard ordered to be repaired.

G. 1665, November. Resolution, that the old church-yard or burying-ground, in Broadway, be divided into four lots of 25 feet each, and sold at public auction.

1654. —— to Dominie Samuel Drisius. A piece of land on the west of the common wagon-way, in the rear of the burying-ground. In length, on the east side, 12 rods 2 feet; on the west side, 12 rods 3½ feet; in breadth, on the south side, 6 rods, and on the north side, 6 rods 1½ feet.

H. 1649, May 4. Governor Stuyvesant to Paul Leendertse. Lot, west side of the Broadway, south of Hendrick Van Dyck's. Breadth, 6½ rods; toward the strand, 7 rods; length, 14 rods. Confirmed July 13, 1677.

1654, May 4. Brief for an addition, to the south and west, *to the church-yard,* of 1 rod 7 feet, and another strip, on the north side, next to Van Dyck, of 1 rod 1 foot. Confirmed as above.

I. Governor Stuyvesant to Hendrick Van Dyck.

1649, May 4. Lot, west of the Broadway; to the north of P. Leendertse, and to the south of the orchard of the West India Company. Confirmed 26th July, 1677 (Lib. 2, p. 79, Albany). Breadth, 6½ rods.

K. The orchard or garden of the West India Company.

1649. Peter Stuyvesant, Governor, to Nicholas W. Stuyvesant. Lot, west of the great public highway; south, by Hendrick Van Dyck; north, by Baltar N. Stuyvesant. Along the road, 7½ Rhenish rods; in length, on both sides, 20 rods; on the west side, along the river, 7½ rods.

K. 1649. Governor Stuyvesant to Baltar N. Stuyvesant. Lot, west of the great public road, bounded south by N. W. Stuyvesant; in front, on the road, from north of the garden of the Noble Company (having to the north), its breadth is 7½ Rhenish rods; on each side, 20 rods; on the west side, along the river, 7½ rods.

In a series of five grants, set forth in Valentine's Manual for 1860 (25th May, 1656), a conveyance, by Governor Stuyvesant to the Burgomasters of the city, or to Burgomasters by name, of May 9, 1656, is set forth. The premises are, undoubtedly, the same as contained in these grants to the Stuyvesants. The boundary of the southern of the lots is Van Dyck's parcel; and of the northern, the garden. The distances sufficiently correspond. The title must have got back between 1649 and 1656.

L. 1652, April 2, Lubbert Van Drinklagen to Jacob Helleckers.

A house and lot on the North River; north by Hendrich Gerritsen; east by Mr. Drincklagen; south by the Company's Garden; west by the river shore. In length, ten rods; in breadth, eight rods, less one foot.

1654, Nov. 5, Jacob Helleckers to Dominie Samuel Drisius, for same premises.

M. 1649, April 29, Cornelius Groesen to L. Van Dinklagen.

—— L. Von Dinklagen to ———.

—— ——— to Hendrick H. Obe.

1657, August 13, H. H. Obe to Jacobus Vis.

A house and lot on the west side of the great

highway, about the land port; width on the street, four rods; on west side, four rods; depth, seven rods six feet four inches.

O. 1657, July 30. Lubbertus Von Drinklage to Christian Barentzen. A lot on the west side of the highway on the wall; width, on the north side, 8 rods 1 foot 7 inches; on the south, 7 rods 7 feet 9 inches; depth, 12 rods 6 feet 7 inches. Being premises conveyed by Cornelius Groesen to said Lubbertus Von Drinklage, 20th March, 1655.

1657. Nov. 17. Charles Barentsen to Cornelius Pluvier. A house and lot on the west side of the highway, bounded, east and north, by the highway and city wall; westerly by Dominie Drisius, and southerly, by house and lot of Jacobus Vis and the Company's Garden; width, on east side, 3 rods 4 feet 5 inches; depth, north and south sides, 7 rods 5 feet; the west side, in breadth, 8 rods 6 feet. The length on the north side, which is the wall, is 8 rods 7 feet 7 inches; the south side, 7 rods 7 feet 9 inches, being wide in the rear; the west side, 8 rods 1 foot; being premises conveyed to said Barentsen, 17th February, 1654, and 30th July, 1657.

2. Is the boundary on the north of the parcel L, in the deed of April 2, 1652. I have not been able to find the grant to Gerritsen. I invite Mr. Valentine's attention to it.

P. *The Lutheran Church.*

In a petition of this church, made, I judge, in 1684, it is stated that they had first built out of the gate, but had been obliged, by Governor Colve, to tear their building down. That they then got a patent for a piece of ground within the gate, and that the patent was mislaid (Doc. His. N. Y., vol. iii., p. 484).

24th Feb., 1809 (Lib. 8, p. 195). The boundaries of the Lutheran Church parcel are, on Broadway, 82 feet 6 inches; in the rear, 62 feet; north, on Rector street, 97 feet; south, by J. R. Livingston's. See also Deed Book A, p. 204, Albany Records.

R. *The Queen Garden.*

Among the exceptions or reservations in the 16th section of Dongan's charter is, "the piece of ground by the gate, called the Governor's Garden."

1696. Governor Fletcher made, among his other extravagant grants, one to Colonel Heathcote of a portion of the King's Garden, running to low water mark.

1705. Grant by Queen Ann to Trinity Church; "also, all our piece of land, situate on the south side of the church-yard of Trinity Church aforesaid, commonly known by the name of the Queen's Garden, fronting the Broadway on the east, and extending to low water mark, upon the Hudson River, on the west."

The whole line of Trinity Church property is 391 feet on Broadway, to Rector street on the south. As the burial-ground was 310 feet of this front (see Diagram No. 2, *post*), Trinity Church took but 81 feet of garden. Rector street was 42 feet, and, I think, was included in the garden. The depth to the river (high water mark), say Greenwich street, was about 400 feet.

Diagram No. 2.

A. *The New Burial-ground.*

Recognized in Dongan's charter, 1686, as the new burial-ground without the gate of the city, and having been built and appropriated by it. (Section 1.) The second section granted, ratified and confirmed this and other parcels to the Corporation.

1703. Grant by the Corporation of the city to Trinity Church of this parcel of ground. (Deed in possession of Trinity Church.)

1704. June 27. Colonial statute reciting that the church was in possession of "a parcel without the north gate of the city, in or near a street called the Broadway; in breadth, on the east side, as the said street rangeth northward, three hundred and ten feet (310); on the south side by the line of our garden." (Smith & Livingston, vol. 1, p. 60.) The grant to Trinity Church is recognized in this statute.

The northern point on Broadway was 40 feet

DIAGRAM No. 2.

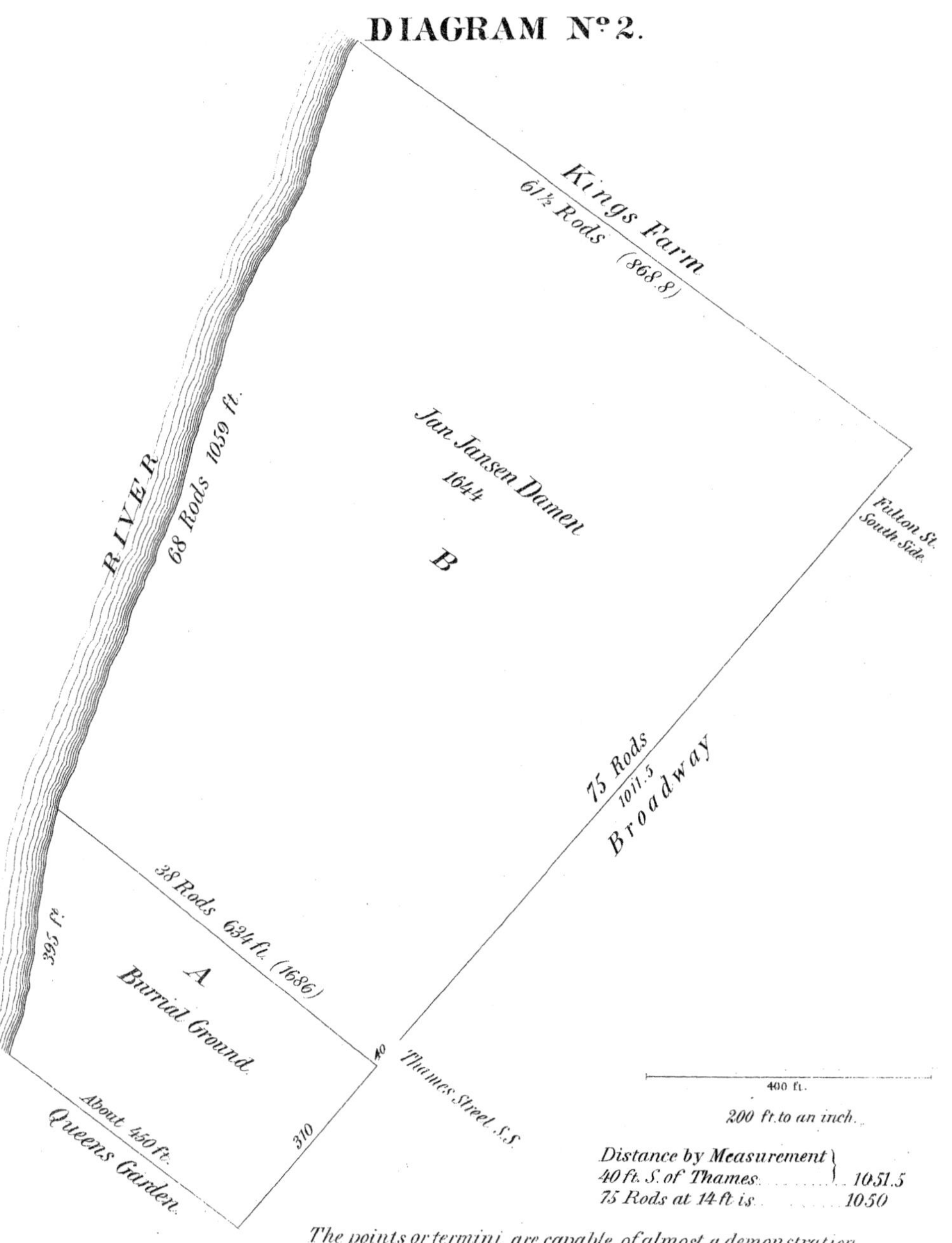

The points or termini are capable of almost a demonstration.
The Rods compared with the actual measurement create some difficulty.

from the south side of Thames street, the present south line of Trinity Buildings. In depth it ran to the Hudson River.

1697. The charter of Trinity Church recited a petition for a grant of a piece of ground without the north gate of the city, in or near a street called the Broadway; in breadth, on the east side, as the street rangeth, 310 feet, until you come to the land of Thomas Lloyd; and from thence toward the west, by the said land, until you come to Hudson River; and thence southward, along Hudson river, 395 feet; and from thence by the line of our garden, eastward, unto the place of the said street or Broadway, where it first began. The charter made no express grant of this piece of land.

The title undoubtedly rests upon the grant from the Corporation of New York.

B. 1644. April 25. Ground brief of Governor Kieft to Jan Jansen Damen. Confirmed by Nicolls, October 3, 1667. (Lib. 2, p. 110, Albany Records, Secretary of State.) A parcel of land lying on both sides of the highway, to the north of the fort.

"The piece that lies between the river and the aforesaid road, extending seventy-five (75) rods north-east; on the northern side, unto the beach, sixty-one rods and a half (61½); on the south side, unto the beach, thirty-eight rods (38); then in an irregular line sixty-eight rods (68). There is a projecting point on the north side."

12

B. 1667. September 18. Records New York, Book A, p. 101, for a part of this parcel.

1662. Deed for another parcel. (*Ibid.*, p. 110.)

1663. March 6. Deed for another parcel. Confirmed September 12, 1667.

1687. February 10th. Christina Capoens to Wm. Dyre. Lot without the land port; east by the highway; south by the church-yard; west by the strand of the North River; north by Lambertse, 65 feet by 36 rods. (Lib. 5, p. 161.)

Mathias Nicolls to Wm. Dyre. Lot bought of Lambertse; west side of the highway, 56 feet by 20 rods. Also, lot adjoining the same, 145 feet wide, extending from the highway to the river. (Lib. 5, p. 237.)

1686. April 23. Wm. Dyre to Thomas Lloyd. Beginning at the corner of the way or passage that leads to the mill of Peter J. Mesier, and running southerly along the highway to the church-yard or burial-place, as the fence of said Dyre now standeth, 468 feet (four hundred and sixty-eight); from thence westerly, as the fence of the said church-yard now standeth, to the water of the Hudson river, six hundred and thirty-six feet (636), and so along the water side four hundred and sixty-eight feet; thence along Mesier's land to the place of beginning. (Lib. 13, p. 202.)

1667. Deed on behalf of heirs of Jan Jansen Damen to Oloff Stevensen Van Cortlandt, for part of this parcel—on the highway or east side 18 $\frac{7}{10}$ rods; in length, from the highway to the strand. (Lib. A, p. 101.)

B. 1791. March 15. Deed from daughters of John Van Cortland to Cornelius Ray, southerly corner Broadway and Thames street. On Broadway, 40 feet; along Thames, 169.6. Easterly, along ground Trinity Church, 106 feet; various courses in rear, about 46 feet. (Lib. 46, p. 436.) This defines the southern point.

1730. October 4. Lib. 31, p. 303. Deed from George Ryerson and Hannah his wife, the widow of Teunis Dey. That Teunis Day was seized of a lot on the west side of the highway, having to the north the farm formerly of his Royal Highness, now called the King's Farm; on the south the land of Oloff Stevenson (*Van Cortlandt*), containing, before and behind, 18 rods and 7-10ths of a rod, and in length from the highway to the water side. Survey by Lodge annexed. On Broadway 309 feet 1 in. N., 51 10. 868 feet 8 inches on the King's Farm; W. and rear, 308 feet 6 inches, on high water mark; south 765.8. High water mark at middling tides.

It is matter of clear proof that the land thus given to Damen in 1644 ran from the point 40 feet south of Thames street to the boundary of the King's Farm, and that is established as either on the south or the north side of Partition (Fulton) street.

Diagram No. 3.

The King's Farm. Dominie's Bowery, Dominie's Hook, &c.

The property of Trinity Church includes several parcels.

In the case of Bogardus *vs.* Trinity Church (4 Sandf. Ch. R., 635), it is deposed to, that the possession and ownership of the Church was as follows: From Partition street, along the North River, to the street now called Christopher; on the east, from Partition street, along Broadway, to a point between Reade and Duane; then the boundary left Broadway, and, crossing Duane at some distance to the west, ran along the estates of Rutgers, Bayard, and Herring, to Christopher street.

The letters patent of 1705 describe the land as follows: Bounded on the east partly by the Broadway, partly by the common, and partly by the swamp; and on the west by Hudson River.

There are four distinct parcels of the Church property traceable. There are others not defined.

1. The southern portion lay between Fulton (Partition) street (south side); high water mark, say Greenwich street, on the west side; a line somewhat north of Warren on the north side; and Broadway on the east side.

2. The southern portion of the Dominie's Bowery.

3. The northern portion of the same.

4. A more northern parcel, acquired from Dirck Decker's heirs.

A large parcel upon Canal street, which must have belonged to Jan Celes, called Old Jans, but which cannot be traced as to the history of the title; and other parcels to the northward.

DIAGRAM No. 3

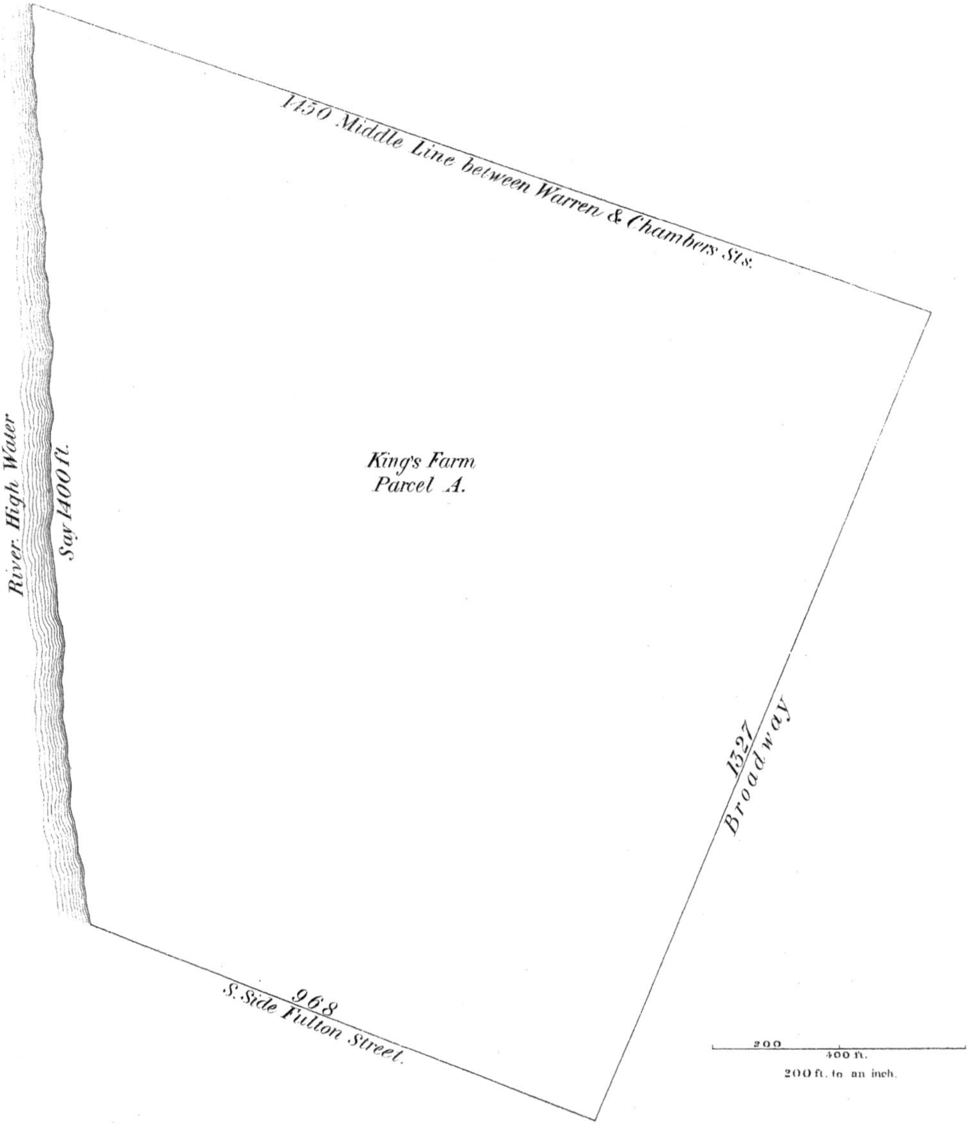

1450 Middle Line between Warren & Chambers Sts.

River High Water

Say 1400 ft.

King's Farm
Parcel A.

1327
Broadway

968
S. Side Fulton Street.

200
400 ft.
200 ft. to an inch.

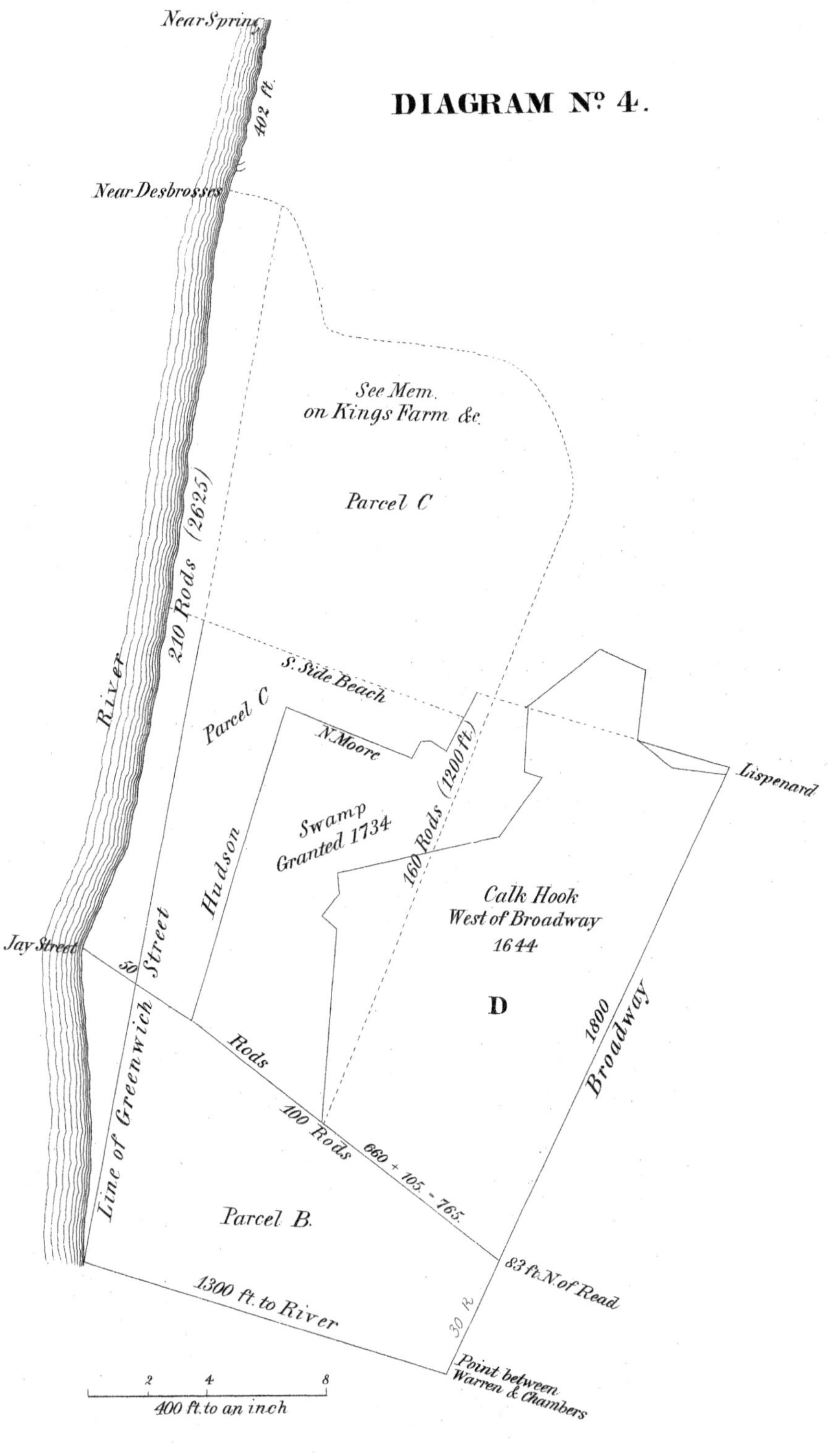
DIAGRAM No. 4.
Near Spring
402 ft.
Near Desbrosses
See Mem. on Kings Farm &c.
Parcel C
210 Rods (2625)
River
S. Side Beach
Parcel C
N. Moore
Lispenard
Swamp Granted 1734
160 Rods (1200 ft.)
Hudson
Calk Hook West of Broadway 1644
Jay Street
50
Street
D
1800
Broadway
Rods
Line of Greenwich
100 Rods
660 + 105. = 765.
Parcel B.
83 ft. N. of Read
30 R
1300 ft. to River
Point between Warren & Chambers
2
4
8
400 ft. to an inch

1. *The Southern Parcel.*

The south line of this parcel was the south side of Partition street. All the evidence in Bogardus *vs.* Trinity Church (4 Sandf. Ch. Rep., 630), the maps of the church property, and the cession of Partition street, show this.

The northern limit of this parcel was about sixty feet north of Warren street. The proof of this is shown in the memorandum upon the next parcel.

The south side was 868 feet 8 inches, according to Lodge's survey (*ante*, Diagram No. 2). On the north side it is about 1,460 feet, bringing it to high water mark.

The title remained ungranted down to the date of the patent to Trinity Church of 1705, and passed by that grant, the annulling act of 1699 being repealed by the act of 1704, which itself was not repealed till 1708. See 22 N. Y. Rep., p. 44, &c.

Within this parcel lies the grant from Trinity Church to Columbia College of land between Barclay and Murray streets, from Church street to the river.

Diagram No. 4.

1654. Sept. 20. Governor Stuyvesant to Annetje Jans, widow of Everardus Bogardus (Lib. 25, No. 14).

Parcel C. A piece of land lying on the Island Manhattan, along the North River, beginning at the palisades (fence) near the house at the river side, and running north by east to the division line of old Jans' land; it is in length 210 rods; then, going along the fence of the said old Jans' land south-east, it reacheth to a certain swamp, and is in breadth 100 rods; and striking along the swamp south-west, it is in length 160 rods, and from the swamp to the river side, extending west, in breadth 50 rods.

Parcel B. The land which lies southerly of the house, and east of the division line of the Company's land, begins at the Palisades, and runs south to the post and rail fence of the Company's land without obstruction to the road, is in breadth sixty rods; in length, on the south side, along post and rails, 160 rods; on the east side, to the gate of the Kalch Hook, in breadth 30 rods; and in length on the north side, along the Kalch Hook to the division line of the aforesaid piece of land, running west, in length 100 rods, containing together 31 morgen (62 acres).

1670, March 9. H. Johannis Van Brugh, in right of Catrina Roeloff, his wife, and attorney of Peter Hartgers, William Bogardus for himself and his brothers Roelson and Jonas Bogardus, and Cornelius Van Bursum, in right of Sarah Roeloff his wife, and by assignment of Peter Bogardus, all children and lawful heirs of Annetzie Roeloff, late widow of Dominie Bogardus, deceased, for a valuable consideration transported and made over to the Right Honorable Colonel Francis Lovelace, his heirs and assigns, their farm or bowery, called the Dominie's Bowery, lying and being on Manhattan Island, towards the North River, the quantity of the land amounting to about sixty-two acres, as in the former ground brief from Governor

Stuyvesant, bearing date the 4th of July, 1651, and the confirmation thereupon from Governor P. Nicolls, bearing date the 27th of March, 1667, is more particularly set forth. (Lib. A, N. Y. Records, p. 122.)

This granted all the shares, except that of Cornelius Bogardus, one sixth. (See 4 Sandford's Ch. Rep., 635.)

Lease from Sir Edward Andross, Governor, 25th March, 1677, to Derck Seckers, for the Duke's Bowery or Farm, for sixty-three acres of land. (4 Sandf., Ch. Rep., 646.)

Lease, 19th August, 1697, Governor Fletcher to the Corporation of Trinity Church, of "our farm, called and known as the King's Farm, on the Island of Manhattan," for a term of years. Annulled by act of Assembly May 12, 1699.

Lease, May 9, 1700, "for our farm, called and known as the King's Farm, for so long as Lord Cornbury should continue Governor."

Lease, 24th January, 1704, from Corporation of Trinity Church to George Ryerse, of the land called "the Queen's Farm," for five years.

Letters patent, under the Great Seal of the Province, from Viscount Cornbury, dated 23d November, 1705, in the name of Queen Ann, to the Corporation of Trinity Church for those several parcels of land, formerly called the Duke's Farm and the King's Farm, and then known by the name of the Queen's Farm, as the same were then in the occupation of George Ryerse, bounded on the east, partly by the Broadway, partly by the Common, and partly by the Swamp, and on the west by Hudson River (Book of Patents, No. 7, p. 338).

From the leases, and other sources, it appears, that the transport to Lovelace, by the heirs of Bogardus, was not treated as to him individually, but was held on behalf of the Crown.

For the further history of the title and present position, see Bogardus *vs.* Trinity Church, 4 Sandf. Ch. Rep., 635, &c., and The People *vs.* Trinity Church, 22 N. Y. Rep., 44.

The northern line is defined in some particulars with entire accuracy by the map in possession of Trinity Church; by a map in possession of Mr. E. Smith, Surveyor, copied from a map of Marschalk, of the farm and meadow of Catherine Rutgers, dated Oct. 1, 1763, and from a survey in the office of the Secretary of State, made to adjust the lines between Rutgers and Trinity Church (Book 19, p. 332). Howell's map of the Calk Hook of 1689 (tin case, office of Register, N. Y., No. 16), and the map on the conveyance of the Hospital grounds by Rutgers (Register's office, N. Y.) may also be referred to usefully.

The southerly line of the Calk Hook and the northerly line of this part of the King's Farm correspond. The point on Broadway is 83 feet 3 inches north of Reade street; about 95 feet from the southerly side of Duane. The south-easterly part of the four parts into which the Calk Hook was divided, ran 105 feet west of Broadway at this point; then the southern line of the south-west part (which came by conveyances to Rutgers) ran as follows: Along the King's Farm, north 59 west, 3 chains 74 links; then north 50 west, 1 chain 53 links; then north 41.30 west, 2 chains 70 links; then north 46.30 west, 1 chain; then north 25 west, 1 chain 40 links, to the meadow; then north 74 west, 80 links; then north 38.15 west, 1 chain 60 links; then north 51 west, 4 chains 90 links; then north 8.15 west, 1 chain 90 links; then north 8.15 east, 2 chains.

We have, then, a distance varying in course but little from a general north-west line, of about 1171 feet, and along the Calk Hook and the meadow. This brings that line a little beyond Hudson street. The line of the northern boundary of this parcel of the Dominie's Bowery is 100 rods, or 1250 feet.

Again, the line in Broadway is stated to be thirty rods to the gate (or entrance) to the Calk Hook. This 375 feet brings it to about sixty feet north of Warren street, and the whole claim and evidence in the Bogardus case (4 Sand. Ch. Rep., 620) show that this was the southern point of the Dominie's Bowery. The Palisades were about this line. (See Hill's map, 1782.) The line on Broadway is ninety-five feet south of Duane, to some point between Warren and Chambers.

Again, one line is sixty rods (750 feet), and plainly meant for the length on the westerly side. The line on Greenwich street, from near Warren to about Duane, is 750 feet.

But then arises a difficulty which I cannot explain. The south line is 160 rods in the ground brief. The line from Broadway to Greenwich street is about 1,500 feet on Chambers, or about one hundred and twenty rods.

I cannot but think that a mistake exists as to the length of this line.

C. *Northerly Parcel of Dominie's Bowery.*

The more northerly parcel of the Dominie's Bowery is described in the ground brief as 210 rods along the strand; then south-east 100 rods, along old Jan's land, to the Swamp; along the Swamp, south-west, 160 rods; then west to the strand, fifty rods. (4 Sandf. Ch. Rep., 699.) The river line may be traced with some certainty. Taking the whole of that line from between Chambers and Warren streets, we have 270 rods (60 and 210); or 3,375 feet. This, following the course of the river, at high water, will reach to about Watts street. The northern boundary was old Jan's land, in 1654, and at the confirmation in 1667.

And on the map made by Marschalk in 1763,* we find old Jan's land laid down on North River, about 231 feet north of the northerly line of Canal street.

On the same map, a straight line along old Jan's land from the river would give twenty-one chains, 1,419 feet. It is, however, extremely irregular. One hundred rods is 1,250 feet. The other line runs 160 rods from old Jan's land south-west.

On the Diagrams four and five, the lines of the 100 rods and 160 rods are dotted out, on the courses and distances, as if the figure was a regular one. The lines thus run include, both at the upper and lower ends, a parcel of the Swamp, granted by patent of the Crown of 1733. This, I think, is easily explained. By Dongan's charter there was reserved to the Crown the King's Farm, with the Swamp, next to the same land, by the "Fresh Water." The patent of 1705 to the church, bounded the King's Farm on the east partly by the Swamp. There can be no doubt that the Swamp was reserved out of this patent, and subsequently passed to Rutgers.

I do not think it a serious objection to this view, that old Jan's land in fact lay north of the Swamp. The ground brief of 1654 carries the line up to old Jan's land; but the Swamp intervened. One of two things is probable—the ground brief did include the part of the

* A most valuable map of Anthony Rutgers' farm and meadow, in the possession of Edwin Smith, Esq., City Surveyor.

Swamp on the river, and some portion of it to the eastward, though not covered by the patent of 1705; or old Jan had the occupation of the Swamp. The former is a very plausible explanation.

1758. May 23. Dirck Dey, heir at law and grandson of Dirck Seckers, to Trinity Church. A lot, &c., bounded west by land belonging to Jan Celes, known by the name of old Jan's land, between said land and a certain swamp; the said swamp having on the east the land of Peter Santome, now belonging to Nicholas Bayard, so stretches to the said swamp next to the land of Jan Celes, *alias* old Jan's land, south-east and by south; it contains five and twenty (25) rods; then going east-south-east, somewhat more southerly, seven and thirty (37) rods; then going east-north-east thirty (30) rods; north, somewhat easterly, eight and forty rods on both sides of the swamp; containing nine acres, two roods, and two perches. (Lib. 54, p. 523, N. Y.)

Christopher Santome's land is mentioned in a ground brief of Dec. 15, 1644. Governor Kieft to Gratian Dangola.

1667. Oct. 19. Confirmation by Nicoll to Christopher Santome and Maria Dangola (Book 2, p. 131); one of the boundary lines runs along old Jan's land; about ten acres.

By reference to the case of Bogardus *vs.* Trinity Church (4 Sand. Ch. Rep., p. 646), it will be seen that Governor Andross leased to Dirck Seckers the Duke's Bowery or Farm for thirty years from 1677. An ejectment was tried against the church in 1760, in which this lease was given in evidence on its behalf. Cornelius Vanderburgh was described as in possession. Korning states that Seckers lived on the premises.

1783. Trinity Church to Abraham Mortier. (Lib. 21, 224–227, Secretary State.)

Ratzell's map shows this parcel quite distinctly. It runs about five hundred feet above Bestaver's Killetjie, which is the distance from Charlton street (the Killetjie) to Hamersley street.

1797. May 1. Lease to Aaron Burr for twenty-six acres, three roods, thirty-six perches land, between Spring and Hamersley streets; Greenwich street on the west; and a line four hundred and fifty feet easterly from Hudson street on the east, excepting a block between Vandam, Morton, Greenwich, and Hudson streets.

Lease for lot No. 1 of the Church farm to Cornelia Rutgers and Leonard Lispenard, 26th March, 1758, for 77 acres, three roods, thirty-two perches, excepting three acres twenty-three perches adjoining Broadway and the Palisades.

1750. Lease by Trinity Church to Burnham (4 Sandf. Rep., 651), four acres of ground at the north-

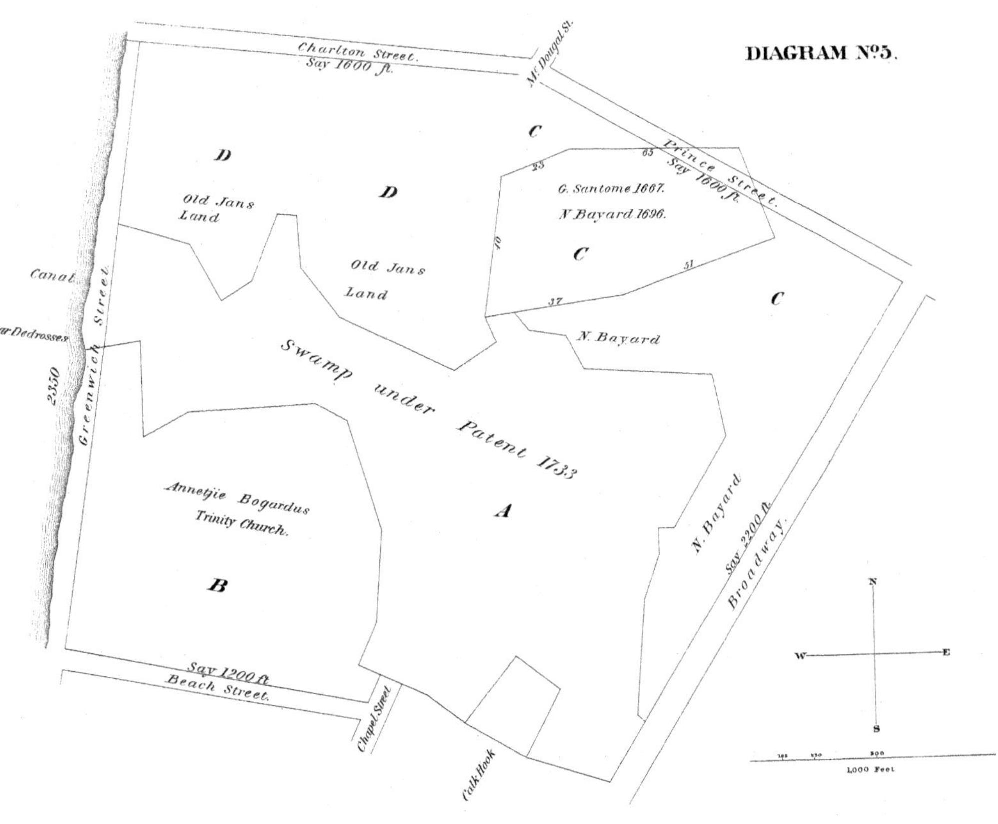
DIAGRAM No. 5.
Charlton Street.
Say 1600 ft.
McDougal St.
Prince Street.
Say 1600 ft.
G. Santome 1667.
N. Bayard 1696.
Old Jans Land
Old Jans Land
D
D
C
C
C
23
63
40
51
37
N. Bayard
Swamp under Patent 1733
A
Canal
Near Dedrosses
Greenwich Street.
2350
Annetjie Bogardus
Trinity Church.
B
Say 1200 ft
Beach Street.
Chapel Street
Calk Hook
N. Bayard
Say 2200 ft.
Broadway.
N
W
E
S
1,000 Feet

> west corner of the Church farm; northerly by land of Sir Peter Warren; easterly by land of Elias and Henry Brevoort; southerly by the Church land; westerly by the Hudson River.

Very extensive searches have proved unavailing to enable me to trace the sources of the title to much of this upper portion of Trinity Church property.

Diagram No. 5.

A. *The Swamp.*

The description, as given in the Colonial act of 1699, and in the Royal Patent of December, 1733, is as follows: (See the account of the title *ante*, vol. i., pp. 121–126.)

Beginning at a stake set in the ground on the south side of the said pond (Fresh Water Pond), and at the north-east corner of the land belonging to William Merritt; thence running along the south side of the said swamp and pond by the upland to the beach on the east side of the Hudson River; so along the beach to the upland; thence crossing a small gut of the said swamp, to the land on the east side thereof; thence by the said land as it runs, to the east side of the Tanyards, and thence to the place where it began, containing in all 70 acres.

This description does not clearly indicate it, but there is no doubt the grant took in the strip west of the Calk Hook, and down to near Duane, east of that part of the Dominie's Bowery. See the map of 1763, before referred to, and the memorandum on the Calk Hook.

By Letters Patent, dated 12th August, 1731, Governor Crosby granted to Anthony Rutgers a parcel of ground called the Swamp and Fresh Pond, by the description above mentioned.

On the 31st of December, 1733, George II. granted a

patent, under the sign manual, to Rutgers, reciting the Colonial act, prohibiting grants by governors for a longer time than their continuing in office, and making the grant himself.

By Dongan's charter of 1686, section 3, all the vacant, unpatented, and unappropriated lands lying and being within the city of New York, with all rivulets, coves, water courses, and ponds in the city and island, were granted to the corporation. By the 37th section of Montgomery's charter, this grant was renewed in similar terms, with the exception of Fort George, the Governor's Garden, and the land called the King's Farm, with the swamp next the same.

Why, under Dongan's charter, this swamp land did not pass to the Corporation, is not clear. Under Montgomery's, it possibly may be comprised in the terms the swamp next the King's Farm, although how this could extend to the swamp adjoining Fresh Water is not very intelligible.

However, the corporation appear to have recognized the title; for, by a grant to Anthony Rutgers, of the 15th of September, 1739, they recite the King's patent to him, and his expenses in draining, and give him a lot on the Hudson River. The Rutgers heirs were before stated, and the partition deeds of 1748 and 1751.

Deed 24th of August, 1790, from Anthony Barclay and executors of Mary Barclay, to John Jay. Beginning on the east side of Ann street, extending along the pond or marsh, and along Fresh Water, bounded by the same, and by land of Nicholas Bayard, and part of land mortgaged to Mary Barclay. (Lib. 46, p. 351.)

Deed 27th June, 1792, by executors of Mary Barclay to Stockholm and Brooks, part of lands mortgaged by Anthony Barclay to Mary Barclay. (Lib. 43, p. 139.)

Deed 27th June, 1792, from executors of Anthony Rutgers to Boyd. Recites that the premises are part of the swamp lands contained in the above patents. (Lib. 47, p. 429.)

B. See Mem. on Diagram No. 4.

C. N. Bayard. See Mem. on Diagram No. 11 and 12.

D. I have been unable to find how Jan Celes, called Old Jans, got his title, or the extent of his possession. We see that his land constituted a boundary in the Bogardus transport of 1659, in Santome's of 1667, and in the deed from Dirck Dey to Trinity Church, of 1758. I have no doubt this description is from an old deed. Certainly Trinity Church owned the ground at that time. It can scarcely be doubted that Dirck Seckers (whom Dirck Dey represented) got his title from Old Jans, and I have no doubt that the parcel granted to Trinity Church in 1758 lies on the parcel marked D. 2 on this diagram.

Diagram No. 6.

1701. Nov. 13. Bastian Elliss, of the Bowery, in the county of New York, husbandman, to John Hendrickse Brievort, of the Bowery aforesaid. All that ffarm or bowery, situate, lying and being in the Bowery, within the county of New York aforesaid, bounded on the east by the King's highway leading from the city of New York to the town of Harlaem, north to the land now in the possession of Ryne, the brickmaker, to the west by the land of Gerrett Dowe, and to the south by the land of John Clapp, and doth contain in quantity, as by four severall patents, the one granted from Richard Nicolls, Governor, to Manuell Sanders, upon the 16th day of October, 1667, which said parcell was since granted and sold by Mary Van Angola, widdow of Manuell Sanders, deceased, to the said Bastian Ellise, by deed bearing date the 15th day of Aprill, 1684, also one patent granted from Richard Nicolls, Governor, to Ffrancisco Negro, upon the 16th day of October, 1667, which said parcell was granted and sold by the said Ffrancisco Negro to the said Bastian Ellise, by deed bearing date the 15th day of April, 1684; alsoe, one patent granted from Richard Nicolls, Governor, to Egbert Wouters, upon the 15th June, 1664, which said parcell was granted and sold by the heirs of Egbert Wouters, after his decease, to the said Bastian Ellise, as by deed bearing date the 20th of May, 1683, more at large will appeare. Alsoe, one patent granted from Richard Nicolls, Governor, to him, the said Bastian Ellise, upon the 18th December, 1667; as also one certain parcell of land containing twelve acres, more or less, as may appear by the patent of Gerrett Dowe, lying on the common way yt leads from the Bowery lane to the Bass Bowery, and is bounded to the land of Egbert Wouters and Hendrick Van Schayck, as also one certain parcell of salt meadow, situate, lying and being upon the west side of Hudson's River, and is joyning to the south to Theunis Ides, and on the north of Jacob Kowenhoven.

Deed in possession of E. Dewitt, Esq.

1664. April 7. Governor Stuyvesant to Peter Stoutenburgh. A piece of ground near unto the Bowery, belonging to Governor Peter Stuyvesant, to the west of the great highway; to the north of Cosyne Gerritse; and to the south of Dirck Michaels; in breadth 24 rods; then a line running N. W. and by W. and W. N. W., and between both in length one hundred (100) rods, and the other side, N. W. and by W., one hundred and thirteen (113) rods. About eight acres

1667. Sept. 3. Confirmation by Nicolls. Stated to be 13 acres instead of 8, which was a mistake.

1608. May 26. Governor Nicolls to Cosyne Gerritse. Land lying near Mynheer Stuyvesant's Bowery, on the west side of the great highway; on the north side of the Negroes' lot; on the south side of Peter Stoutenburgh; abutting on the west with a way that is by a certain swamp; a line running on both sides N. W. and by W. and W. N. W., between both, it containing in breadth 16 rods, and in length 100 rods, being about five acres, or two morgen and four hundred. Together with a house and garden.

Before 1736, this, or a part of this property became vested in Richard Perro.

1736. July. Will of Richard Perro.

1754. Jan. 19. Deed from John Perro, and others, heirs of Richard Perro, to Jellis Mandeville. (Lib. 37, p. 66.)

Land on the west side of the Bowery, between lands formerly granted to Solomon Peters, now of Elbert Herring, and the land granted to Francisca Cartagena; on the north side, adjoining Solomon Peters (now Herring), 46 rods; on the north to Francisca Cartagena, 44 rods; breadth on the Bowery, 27 1-2 rods; rear to other land of Herring, 18 rods, as the same was formerly granted to Otto Grim.

1767. August 18. Deed from John Perro, and others, heirs and devisees of Richard Perro, to Andrew Elliott. E. by land of Asie Ryckman; N. by land of Andrew Elliott; west by the Minetta water; S. by the road leading to Greenwich. (Lib. 38.)

1767. Oct. 10. John Perro, and others, devisees of Richard Perro, to A. Ryckman and Rachel, his wife, a daughter and devisee. Recites that the parties were seized of the lot of ground on both sides of the lane leading to Greenwich, from the highway, and a partition.

John Hendrick Brevoort died in 1718, and left John, Abraham and Ann, by one wife; Elias and Hendrick by another.*

* I am indebted to Mr. J. Carson Brevoort for these particulars of the pedigree. He states that Hendrick Sansom Van Brevoort, from Bridevoort, in Gueldersland, was the first settler; was born in 1630, and John Hendricksen Brevoort was his son or grandson.

1755. Hendrick Brevoort and Elias Brevoort to Elbert Herring. (Lib. 41, p. 125.) A piece of ground of 40 acres, 2 roods, 14 perches, bounded southerly partly by land of Nicholas Bayard, and partly by land in the possession of Adam Vanderbergh; westerly by the King's Farm; northerly and easterly by land of Sir Peter Warren.

(See map of Herring's farm, No. 46, Record office. The above comprises lots 12 to 19.)

The Free Negroes.

In October, 1667, Governor Nicolls prefaced a series of confirmations of ground briefs thus: "Whereas, there was heretofore, that is to say, in the years 1659 and 1660, several grants made by the Dutch Governor, Petrus Stuyvesant, unto certain free negroes, for several small parcels of land lying upon the Island Manhattans, along the highway, near unto the said Governor's Bowery." (Lib. 2, pp. 119–132.) The confirmations are then entered.

A plot marked No. 1. *To C. Santome.*

Along the wagon path, 32 rods, the length on the south side 46 rods, on the west side 39, and on the north side 38 rods. Bounded south by land of Anthonie Sopie; north by Manuel De Ross.

(Santome to Bastiani. Bastiani to Hermanus Rutgers. Lib. 30, 58.)

No. 2.—*Manuel De Ross.*

Along the wagon path 19 rods; south side by C. Santome, 19 rods; north side, along land of Lucyas Pieters, 19 rods.

No. 3.—*Lucyas Pieters.*

Along the wagon path 17 rods; south side 32 rods; west side 17 rods; north side, along land of Solomon Pieters the Negro, 31.

No. 4.—*Solomon Pieters.*

Along the wagon path, 22 rods; south side, 63 rods; west side 19 rods; north by Otto Grim, 46 rods.

No. 5.—*Otto Grim,* 15 May, 1664; confirmed 24 December, 1667.

Along the wagon way, length on the south side next to Solomon Pieters, 46 rods; north side, adjoining Francisco Cartagena, 44 rods; by the highway, 27 rods; behind 18 rods.

No. 6.—*Francisco Cartagena.*

Containing in breadth, along the wagon path, 11 rods and 1-2; in length, on the south side, along the land of Otto Grim, 44 rods; behind, on the west side, 14 rods; and on the north side, along the land of Assento, 40 rods.

No. 7. —— *Assento*

In breadth, along the wagon path, 15 rods; on the south side, along the land of Francisco Cartegena, 40 rods; behind, on the west side, 15 rods; and on the north side, by the land of Manuel Pieters, 28 rods.

No. 8.—*Domingo Angola.*

A lot near Stuyvesant's bowery; in breadth, along the wagon path, 13 rods; in length, on the south-west side, 15 1-2 rods; along Assiento's land, 11 rods; and along Wm. Anthony Portuges, 14 rods.

No. 9.—*Anthony Portuges.*

In breadth, along the wagon path, 34 rods; on the south side, along by the land of Domingo Angola and Christina, 70 rods; behind, on the west side, 31 rods; and on the north side, along the gardens of Groot Manuel, Manuel Sanders, and Claes De Nesser, 70 rods.

1644. Dec. 15. Kieft to Gratian Dangola, a free Negro, confirmed to Christofel Santome and Maria Dangola, 19 Oct., 1667. (Book 2, p. 131.) A parcel, &c., stretching from the land of Cleyn Manuell to that of Maryche, E. and E. by S., then further, to the land of Peter Tumbeer, S., somewhat more easterly, it containing 20 rods, on both sides; along by the land of Jan Francisco and Peter Tombeer, 41 rod; also stretching west, and somewhat to the south, to a certain valley, or piece of meadow ground, it makes 37 rods; then going along to old Jem's land, N. W., somewhat more northerly, 40 rods, to the land of Cleyn Anthony; and along by the said Anthony's land, E. and by N., somewhat more northerly, 23 rods; then E. and by N. and E. N. E., to the first descent, 65 rods; in all ten (10) acres, or 5 morgen, 595 rods.

Recites original brief to Gratian Dangola, that the title had devolved on Maria, his wife, who had since married Christoffel Santome.

The only information I have obtained, as to these free Negroes, is the following:

By the Charter of Privileges and Exemptions, the West India Company was to supply the colonists with as many blacks as they conveniently could.

In Secretary Van Tienhoven's answer to the remonstrance from New Netherlands, he says: "In regard to the letters of manumission, which the Director was so good as to grant to the Negroes who had been the Company's slaves, they were set free in return for their long service, on condition that their children remain slaves."

1659. Stuyvesant to C. Santome.

1667, Oct. 16. Nicoll's confirmation to C. Santome.

Before 1679, Nov. 1. Santome to Sigusmund Lucas.

1679, Nov. 1. S. Lucas to Henry Bastiansen. Henry Bastiansen left Mary, his widow, who married Jacob Stille.

1696, April 23. Jacob Stille and Mary, his wife, widow of Henry Bastiansen, to Richard Ashfield. (Lib. 21, p. 143.)

1697, January 12. Richard Ashfield to Jacob Stille. (Lib. 21, 261.) Certain parcels on the island Manhattan, at the Bowery, beyond the Fresh Water. One parcel lying along the highway, marked No. 1, containing in breadth, along the wagon way, 32 rods; in length on the south side, by the land of Anthony Sopy, 46 rods; behind, on the west side, 39 rods, and on the north side, along the land of Manuel De Ross, 38 rods.

1659. Stuyvesant to Gratian D'Angola.

1667, October 19. Confirmation to Christopher Santome and Maria D'Angola, his wife.

Before 1679. Santome to S. Lucas.

1679, November 1. Lucas to H. Bastiansen. (Book 6, 154.)

1696, April 23. Jacob Stille and Mary, his wife, widow of Henry Bastiansen, to Richard Ashfield. (Lib. 21, p. 143, N. Y.)

Richard Ashfield to Jacob Stille. (Lib. 21, p. 261.)

All land at said Bowery, stretching from the land of Cleyne Manuel to that of Marycke, east and east and by south, then further to the land of Peter Tamboer, south, somewhat more easterly, containing twenty rods on both sides of the land of Jan Francisco and Peter Tamboer, one and fifty rods; then stretching west and somewhat to the south to a certain valley or piece of meadow, seven and thirty rods; then going along to Old Jan's land, north-west, somewhat more northerly, forty rods to the land of Cleyne Anthony, and along his land, east and by north, somewhat more northerly, three and twenty rods, and east and by north and east-north-east to the first descent, sixty-five rods—in all amounting unto about ten acres or five morgen five hundred and ninety rods, as in both the aforenamed patents of confirmation is particularly set forth.

1679, May 16. Phillip Phillipson to Henry Bastiansen—a parcel of ground, lying in the negroes' plantation, between Wolfert Webber's and said Henry Bastiansen, containing about four morgen.

Henry Bastiansen to Jacob Stille.

1667, Oct. 19. Claus Manuel, attorney, to Ana, a free negrine, widow of Andrew D'Angola, to Jacob Stille, a parcel; before, Peter Tamboer; and behind it, Johan De Witt, in said negroes' plantation—east and by north, 51 rods; north, 30 rods; north-north-west, 54 rods; north-east, and north-east and by east, 41 rods; 6 acres, 3 rods;—granted to Ana Negrina, by confirmation, 19th October, 1667.

1681, April 11. Michael Manuelson, and heir of Manuel De Spingler to Jacob Stille, land in negroes' plantation, to east of Henry Kierstede, beginning at Jolyns Bradly's land, stretching to other negroes' land, containing, as it lies, east and by south, to the wagon way, 83 rods; along the wagon way towards the west, 32 rods; then northerly, to a mark on the corner or nook of J. Briell's land, 72 rods.

Patent of confirmation, 19 Oct., 1667.

DIAGRAM Nº 7

Great Hill Road (Gansevoort Street)
1485
Strand of Hudson River
2840
Sir Peter Warren 1773
Say 91 Acres
Became vested in Richard Amos John Ireland
& Abijah Hammond Chiefly under Lord Willoughby
who married a daughter of Sir Peter Warren.
Old Greenwich Road
2068
2310
Skinner's Road
(Christopher Street)
E. Herring
Sir Peter Warren.
Church Land
2
4
6
8
10
12

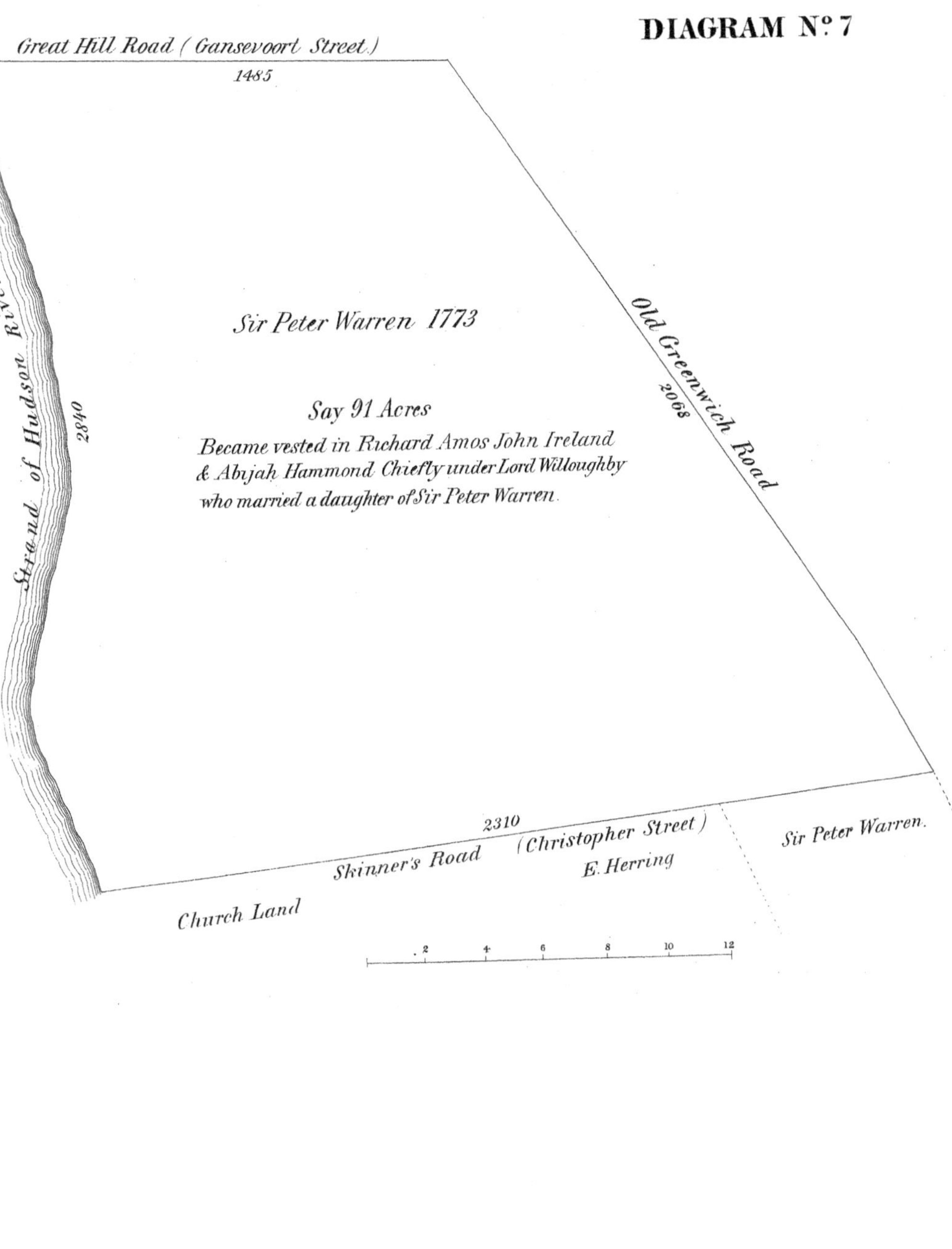

1667, Oct. 16. Confirmation to Anthony Anthony.

Vested in the Deacons.

The Deacons to Jacob Stille.

1696, April 22. A parcel along the highway, between Christopher Santome's and Manuel De Spangui's, in breadth before, towards the wagon path, 16 rods; behind, 30 rods; length on each side, 55 rods.

D.

I have been unable to find how Jan Celes, called Old Jans, got his title, or the extent of his possession. We see that his land constituted a boundary in the Bogardus transport of 1639; in Santome's of 1667; and in the deed from Dirck Dey to Trinity Church, of 1758. I have no doubt this description is from an old deed. Certainly Trinity Church owned the ground at that time. It can scarcely be doubted that Dirck Seckers (whom Dirck Dey represented) got title from Old Jans; and I have no doubt that the parcel granted to Trinity Church in 1758 lies in the parcel marked D. 2, on this diagram.

Whoever will find out who Old Jans was and the land owned by him, and how he got and parted with it, will deserve the thanks of every New York antiquarian.

Diagram No. 7.

The map from which this diagram is taken shows that the property was vested in Sir Peter Warren, in 1773. He was a naval officer in command at New York, and received from the Corporation of the city a grant for about ten acres of ground, situate on the Bowery lane, at the corner of Abingdon road, near Twenty-first street, with the land of Peter Horne on the north. His whole property amounted to 266 acres.

A copy of this map is in the possession of Edwin Smith, Esq., City Surveyor.*

Oloff Stephen Van Cortlandt died before 1683. Left Stephen, Jacob, John, Maria, married to Van Renssalaer, Catharine, wife of John Delavall, and afterwards of Frederick Phillips, Cornelia, wife of Barent S. Schuyler, and Sophia, wife of Andrew Zetter.

Stephen Delancey married a daughter of Stephen Van Cortlandt. (Deed, April 12, 1700, to S. Delancey.)

Sir Peter Warren married a daughter of Stephen Delancey. This must have been before 1747.

In 1768, Ann, one of Sir Peter Warren's daughters, was married to the Earl of Abingdon. (See deed, Lib. 53, p. 1.)

The Earl of Willoughby married another daughter.

1646. Governor Kieft to Oloff Stevensen Van Cortlandt. Land north of the plantation of Leesbore; extending up from the strand east by

* I take this occasion to say that, as I believe, the most valuable collection of maps and surveys, to be found in the city, is in the possession of Mr. Smith. It is the result of the labors of an old and most valuable officer, his father, George B. Smith, and of his own researches. It would be of great service if this collection could be procured for public use.

south one hundred (100) rods till to the wagon road from Saponikan; then eighty (80) rods along the road; then all the way through the valley to Saponikan at the strand; and thence along the strand to the place of beginning.

1711. Sept. 1. Volkert Van Borsum to Dirck Benson, of Saponikan, alias Baassen Bowery (Greenwich). Land within the village aforesaid, bounded south by land of Johannes Thomason; north by land of Bastian Ellison; eastward by the highway that leads to the Baassen Bowery; and west by the Hudson River, being 23 morgen or 46 acres. Also, another parcel of land at the Baassen Bowery, butted to the south by the highway aforesaid; to the north by the land of Jellis Mandeville; to the east by the highway that leads to the Great Kills; and west by the Hudson River; being 8 morgen or 16 acres. (Lib. 30, p. 228.)

1686. Nov. 2. The Mayor, Aldermen and Commonalty of New York to Arian Cornelissen. A parcel of ground in the outward in Baassen Bowery, containing sixteen (16) acres of ground; bounded north-west by Mandeville; north-east by Solomon Pieters; south-east by the highway; and south-west by Garrett Basse Johnson. (Grant, Comptroller's office.)

1691. April 2. Arian Cornelissen Van Schaick and wife to Gerrit Douw. All that dwelling-house and farm situate near the Baassen Bowery;

bounded to the west and north-west by the highway; to the north-east by the land of Peter Jacobson and the land of Solomon Peters; and to the south-west by the highway; thence by the Cripple Bush and the land of Gerritt Basse Johnson; south-westwardly and to the south-eastward by the Cripple Bush; containing 134 acres, as surveyed by Leonard Beckwith Nov. 11, 1690.

1677. Confirmation by Andross, Governor, to Wolfert Webbers, Hendrick Cornelius and Bastian Ellison, for 35 acres of ground near the place called the Sand Hills. Webbers and wife to Gerrit Douw for one-third of such parcel as possessed by him. This deed recites a partition among the owners.

1672. March 11. F. Lovelace to Allard Anthony. Piece of land toward the North River, near the Bowery, called the Bengoe Bowery, also by the Indian name of Sapponikan, otherwise North Wyck or North Wittis; having on the north side 120 rods, on the west 54 rods, on the east 18 rods, in all containing seven morgen and one hundred and twenty rods, or about 14 acres and one-half. (Vol. 3, p. 105.)

N
E
S
Pearl St.
Kalk Hook.
Duane St.
A. Colve Governor to Cornelius Van Bursum 1673.
Reade St.
A
Negroes Burial Ground
Chambers St.
Corporation of New York
Land Claimed by Janeway
Reade St.
Cross Street.
Magazine (Pearl) Street.
B
Augustus Street.
Corporation
Chatham Street.
Chambers St.

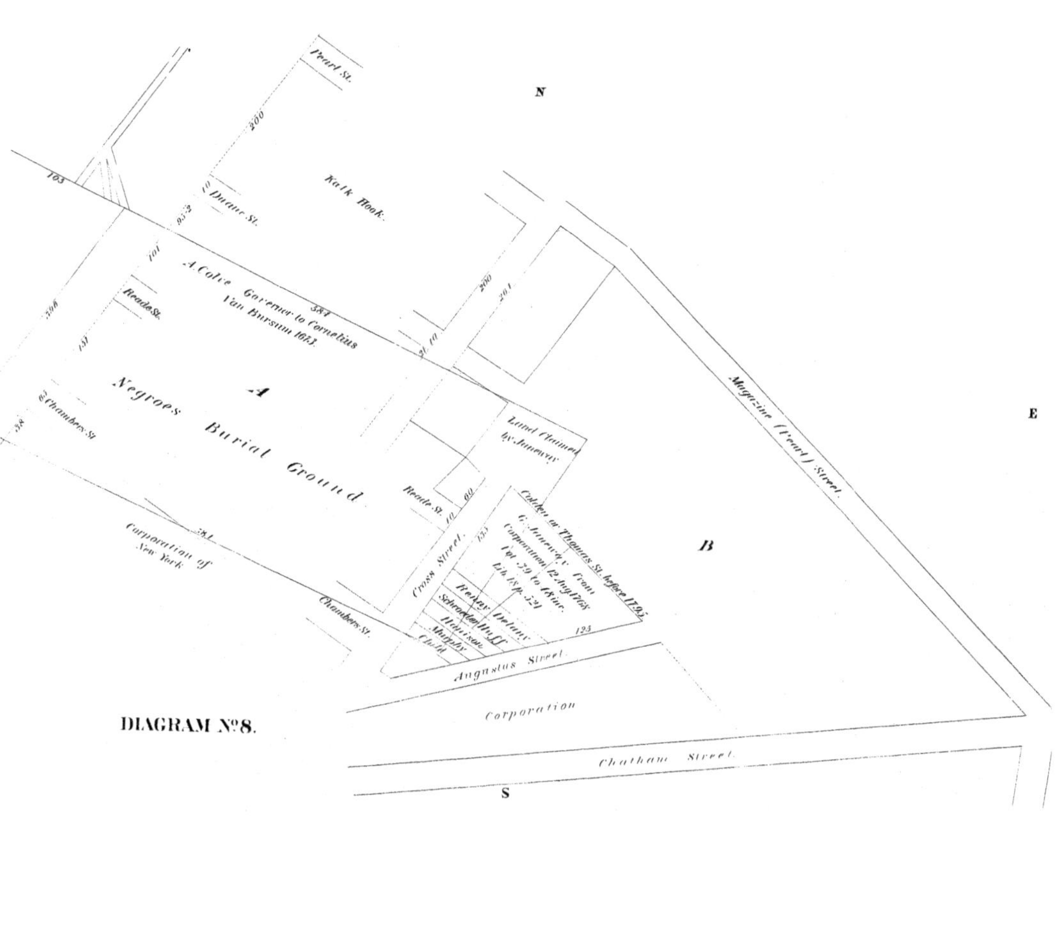

DIAGRAM No. 8.

Note 57.

Memorandum on Diagram No. 8.

A.

1673, October 14. Dutch Governor Colve to Cornelius Van Borsum. A certain parcel of land lying on Manhattan Island, north-west from the windmill, beginning at the north end of the highway leading to the Calk Hook, and containing in breadth, fronting on the west side the highway, 24 rods; in the rear, on the east side, likewise 24 rods; in length on both sides, as well along the Calk Hook as on the south side, 44 rods.

1680, June 16. Will of Cornelius Van Borsum, making his wife, Sarah, his universal heir.

1693, July 29. Will of Sarah Roeloff, demising the property to her children.

1696, April 10. Confirmation by Governor Fletcher to Johannis Kip, Abrm. J. Van Vleeck, and William Teller.

They took as Trustees.

See Smith *vs.* Teller, 10 John. Rep., 347.

1795, January 9. Deed of partition between W. W. Kip, Abraham J. Van Vleeck, John and Samuel Kip, and others (Albany Records).

Map annexed, made by Goerck and Bancker, May 7th, 1795.

1796, October 6. Deed from Kip, Breese, Van Vleeck and Denniston to the Corporation of New York, for the triangular piece on Broadway, south side of Chambers street, being 38 feet on Broadway. Release of lots in exchange on Augustus street.

The road that leads to the Calk Hook was afterwards Broadway. See the diagram by D. Grim, made 1742; Valentine's Manual for 1856, p. 426, and Minutes of the Common Council, 1760, of Marschalk's survey (*Ibid.*, p. 429).

B.

Richard Nicolls, Esq., &c. Whereas there was a patent or ground briefe heretofore granted by ye Dutch Governor, Petrus Stuyvesant, unto Paulus Schrick, for a certain lott of land, lying and being upon this island Manhattan, on ye south-west syde of ye Fresh Water, and on ye east-south-east syde of ye Chalkie Hook, conteining in breadth on ye south-east syde fowre rod in length, on ye south-west syde fowre and twenty rod, so going forward south-south-west, it is more eighteen rod, and on ye west-south-west syde, two and twenty rod, then a line running, neare said Hook, east and by north, it makes seventeen rod, and so north-north-east, somewhat more easterly, twenty rods, then againe forward, east-south-east to ye said Hook, it is eighteen rod, and amounteth in all to about fower acres, or two morgen and five hundred twenty-eight rod, which said patent or ground briefe, so grannted as aforesaid, bearing *date* ye 31st day of January, 1662, was upon ye 19th day of May, 1666, transported and made over unto Jacob Kipp, with all ye title and interest therein, by Maria Teller, ye now wife of William Teller, left widdow and executrix of Paulus Schrick, deceased. Now for a confirmation unto him, ye said Jacob Kipp, &c. The patent is dated September ye 16th, 1667. (Albany Records.)

Before 1695, the property became vested in William Merritt.

1698, October. William Merritt to William Janeway. (Lib. 9, p. 103, New York.)
Map in tin case 111.

1708. Exchange between Janeway and the Corporation of New York, reciting the above ground brief, and conveying various lots to Janeway, and settling boundaries.

It is a demonstration that the property in this deed included the property in the above ground brief; and it is impossible to reconcile all the lines and courses.

Note 57.

Memorandum on Diagram No. 9.

Kolk Hook.

This piece of ground extended from the King's Farm, between Reade and Duane streets on the south, to near Canal street on the north, and about Church street on the west (at the southern side), and along the borders of the Fresh Water, on the eastern side.

Pedigree and Dates.

Jan Jansen Damen received a ground brief from Governor Kieft, dated 15th March, 1646, for this parcel. Left Ariana Cuilyie his sole heiress. She married Gulyn Vinge. Their children were Jan Vinge; Rachel, who married Cornelius Van Tienhoven; Christina, married to Dirck Volkerson; and Maria, married to Abraham Verplanck.

Peter Stoutenburgh, describes himself, in a deed 14th June, 1685, as one of the assigns of Christina, one of the heirs of Ariana Cuilyie, sole heiress of Jan Jansen Damen.

Granted by ground brief of Governor Kieft to Jan Jansen Damen, 15th March, 1646; confirmed to his creditors and heirs by Nicolls, on the 3d of October, 1667. Described in the ground brief as "the land heretofore, ten years ago, leased to said Jan Jansen Damen, in size, according to the map of the same, twenty morgens, three hundred

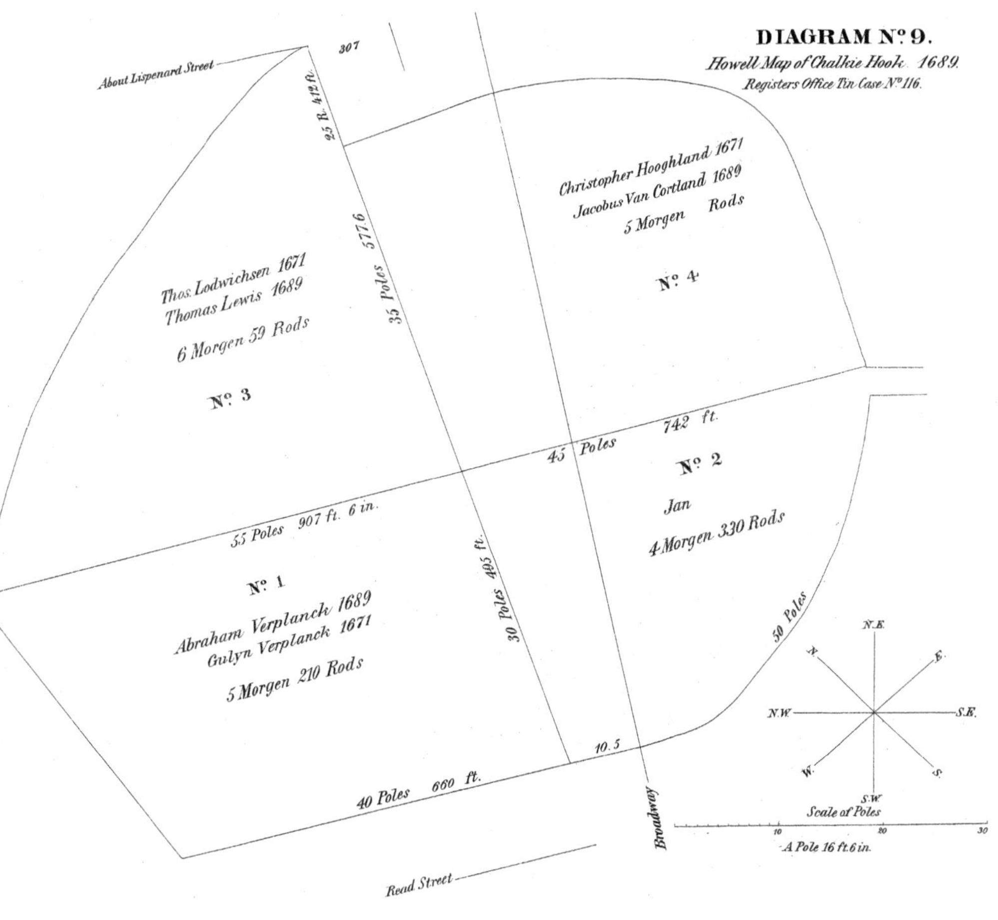
DIAGRAM No. 9.
Howell Map of Chalkie Hook 1689.
Registers Office Tin Case No. 116.
About Lispenard Street
307
25 R. 412 ft.
35 Poles 577.6
Thos. Lodwichsen 1671
Thomas Lewis 1689
6 Morgen 59 Rods
No. 3
Christopher Hooghland 1671
Jacobus Van Cortland 1689
5 Morgen Rods
No. 4
45 Poles 742 ft.
No. 2
Jan
4 Morgen 330 Rods
55 Poles 907 ft. 6 in.
No. 1
Abraham Verplanck 1689
Gulyn Verplanck 1671
5 Morgen 210 Rods
30 Poles 495 ft.
50 Poles
10.5
40 Poles 660 ft.
Broadway
Read Street
N.E.
N.
E.
N.W.
S.E.
W.
S.
S.W.
Scale of Poles
10
20
30
A Pole 16 ft. 6 in.

and eighty-six rods." This is marked in the deed as Chalk Hook. (Book of Patents, Secretary's office.)

It appears that there was a partition made the 17th of April, 1671, between the owners of Chalkie Hook. (Lib. 25, p. 110, Register's office.) They are named as Gulyn Verplanck, John Vangee (no doubt Jan Vinge), Thomas Lodwickson, and Christopher Hooghtland. The deed is stated to be on the records of the city.

There is in the Register's office a map of Chalkie Hook, made by J. Howell, dated April, 1689. (Map No. 116.) On this there appear four lots: No. 1 is the south-westernmost, and is marked Abraham Verplanck; No. 2, the south-eastern, marked Jan Vinge; No. 3, the north-western, marked Thomas Lewis; and No. 4, the north-eastern, marked Jacobus Van Cortlandt.

On the 19th September, 1698, Isaac Verplanck and others, describing themselves as heirs of Abraham Verplanck, executed a power of attorney to John Abeal to convey real estate.

Under that power, 27th February, 1699, J. Abeal conveyed to William Huddlestone "all that tract or lot of ground, in the city of New York, bounded south and west by the King's Farm, north by the land late of Thomas Lodwickson, deceased; and on the east by the land of John Vangee, deceased; containing five morgen and two hundred and ten rods, and called No. 1, being the fourth part of a certain field, called the Calkie Hook, as appears by a deed of partition, &c.

June, 1703. (Lib. 25, p. 114.) Deed from Wm. Huddlestone to Capt. Richard Hill for the same premises.

14th December, 1713 (Lib. 31, p. 115), Richard Hill conveys the same premises to Anthony Rutgers (Jr.), the fourth part of the Calckie Hook.

Map made by Goerck, in 1790, of property late of Anthony Rutgers (map No. 486, Register's office), on this, the northern boundary is Leonard street, and the line continues on Broadway to the Hospital grounds. Behind the Hospital grounds, its southern boundary is Barley (Duane) street; and the ground of the English Church, all along on the west.

Again, the Hospital ground was conveyed by a deed from Anthony Rutgers, dated the 23d June, 1772. (Lib. 45, p. 213.) A survey, made by Bancker, is annexed.

The street is laid down as Broadway, of eighty feet in width.

In January, 1795, there was a division of property at Calckie Hook. (Lib. 27, p. 94.)

It is impossible to doubt that one of the lots of the Chalkie Hook division of 1671 is thus ascertained; and that it ran from the King's Farm, on the south (about Duane street), to Leonard street, on Broadway, and extended on Duane street to the east line of the King's Farm.

This line varied, as the upland varied, which it pursued.

Again, the north-western lot is marked, on the map of 1689, as belonging to Thomas Lewis.

On the seventh day of October, 1669, Petrus Stuyvesant makes a transport to Thomas Lewis, in which is recited the ground brief of Kieft to J. J. Damen, of 15th March, 1646, a transport by Damen's heirs and executors to Augustine Herman, 17th October, 1661, and of Herman to Stuyvesant. Stuyvesant then conveys one quarter of the land called the Kolk Hook to Thomas Lewis. (Lib. A, N. York, p. 102.)

The North-east parcel.

Deed 29th September, 1760 (Lib. 35, p. 382), recites a division of three quarters of the parcel of ground called the Calck Hook, near the Fresh Water and land of Henry Rutgers, deceased, between the children and devisees of the late Jacobus Van Cortlandt. That on such partition lot No. 2 fell to the share of Frederick Van Cortlandt, containing three acres and forty-five perches; lot No. 3, to John Chambers, and lot No. 4, to Peter Jay and Mary, his wife.

Frederick Van Cortlandt devised his lot No. 2 to his two sons, Frederick and Augustus.

Deed from Augustus and Frederick Van Cortlandt to the Corporation, dated in 1774, for an acre of land on Great George street.

Partition deed in 1810 between Peter Jay Monroe and Peter Jay (deed of cessions, p. 160), showing a line on Broadway, beginning 72 feet from White street. Its length on the south side exted to Collect, now Centre street.

NOTE 57.

Mem. on Diagram No. 10.

A.

1697. Governor Fletcher to nine persons.

1774. Partition recited in a deed of this date.

A parcel vested in G. Shaw. See Loss' Map of 1800. (Lib. 101, p. 29.)

B.

1653, Oct. 16. Governor Stuyvesant to Paulus Schrick, a tract of land near Fresh Water, 2 morgen and a half.

1656, June 20. Governor Stuyvesant to William Beekman, tract of land adjoining the above.

1661, April 15. William Beekman to Dominie Megapolensis, for the land granted to him.

1662, September 28. Paulus Schrick to Dominie Megapo-

DIAGRAM Nº 10

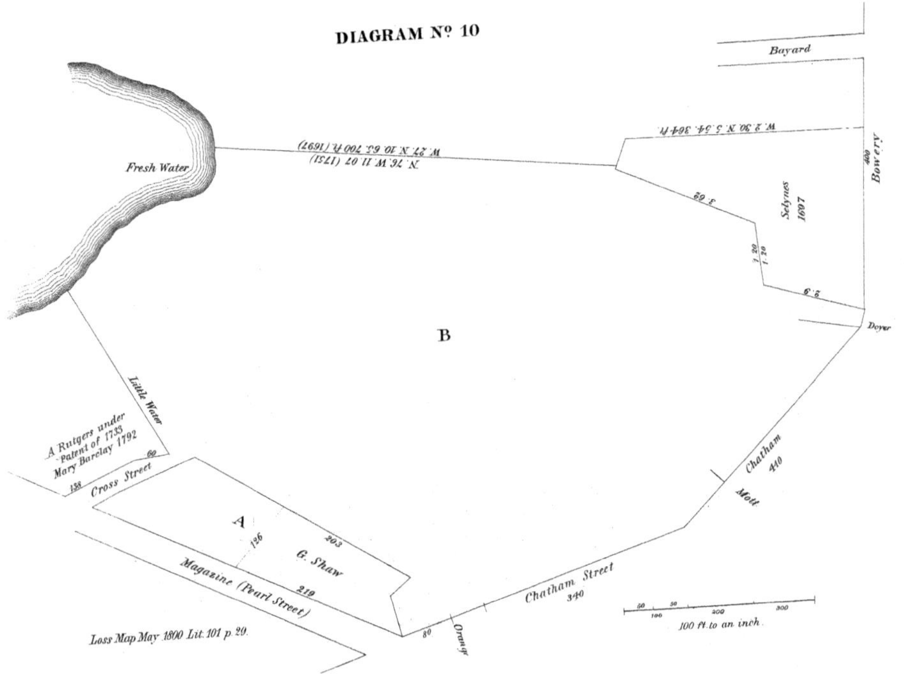

DIAGRAM No. 11.

Bayard's East Farm

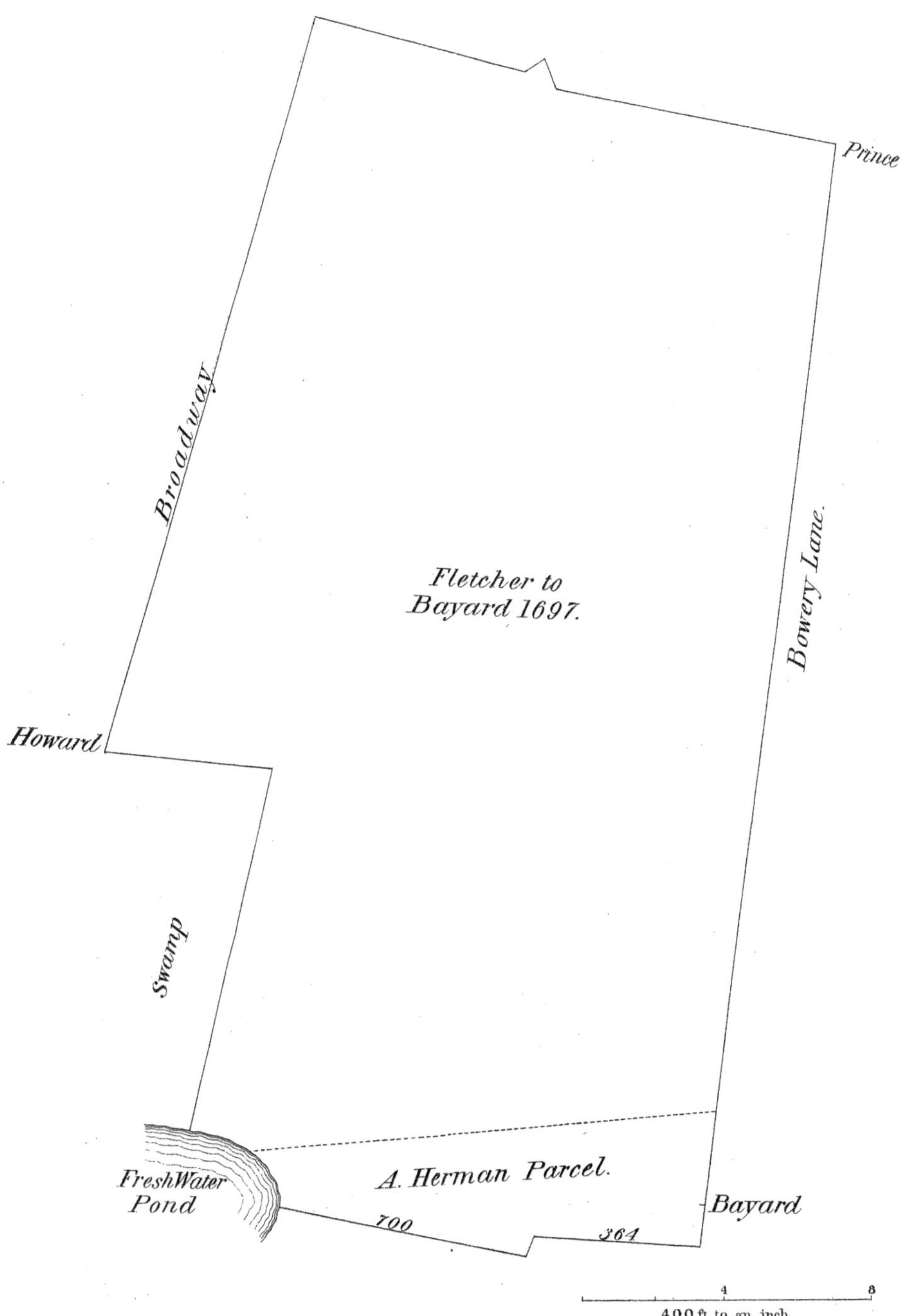

DIAGRAM No. 12

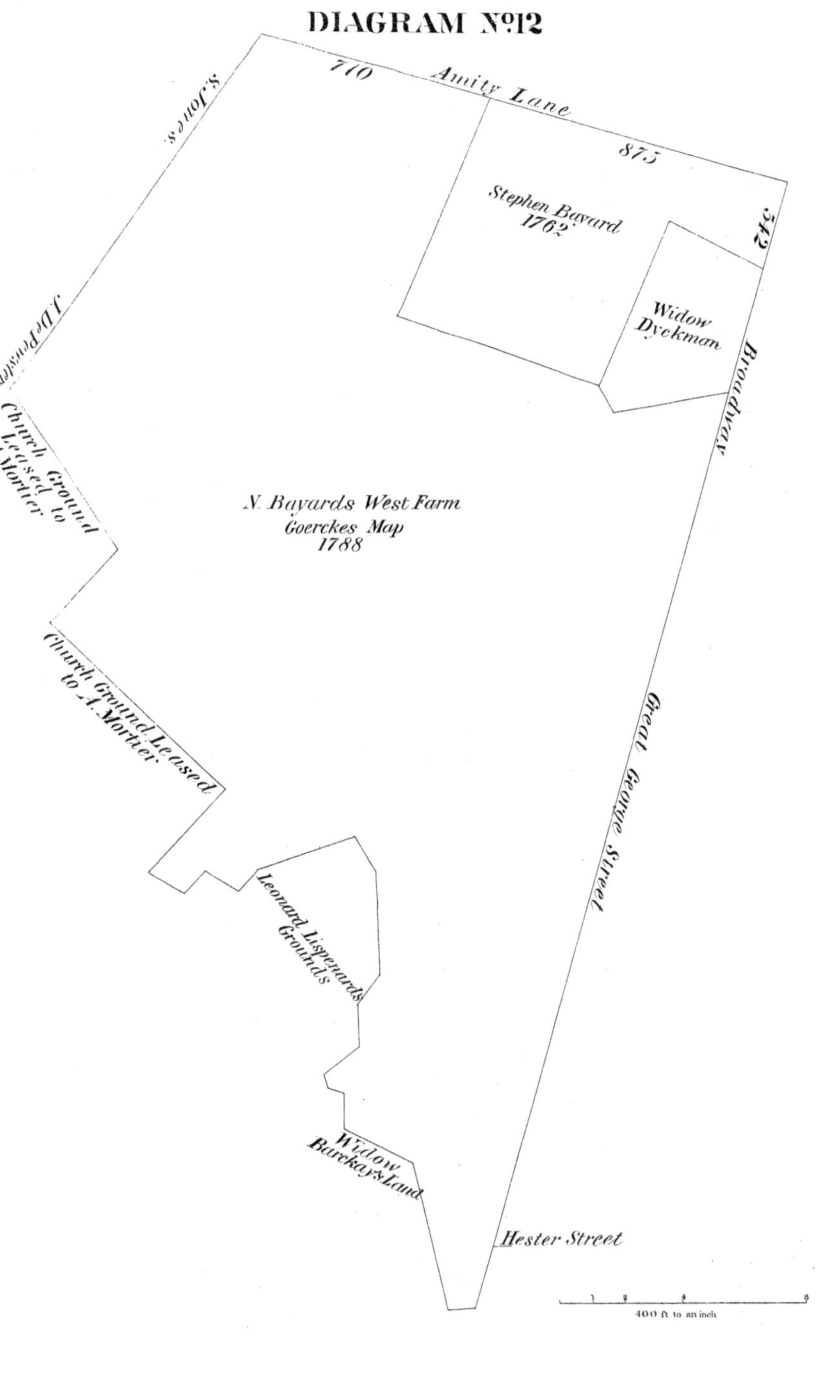

lensis and Ruivens, for the land granted him as above.

1667, January 15. Confirmation by Nicolls of the above parcels.

1673. Became vested in P. Wolfert Webbers.

1699, July 22. P. W. Webbers to Philip Minthorne, for part of the above.

1699. P. W. Webbers to Jacques Fontaine, for part of above.

1713. Webber to P. Minthorne.

1715. Fontaine to P. Minthorne.

All the parcels became thus vested in P. Minthorne.

1749. Will of P. Minthorne—power to sell.

1761, November 21, Jacob Read and others, executors, &c., to John Kingston (Lib. 36, p. 486).

The boundaries in this deed are important.

Bayard's Farm—Diagrams Nos. 11 *and* 12.

Bayard acquired about 9 acres of this farm on the south side from Augustus Herman, which the latter held under a ground brief.

Governor Fletcher to Nicholas Bayard, 21st June, 1697 (Lib. 15, p. 130). Grant and confirmation of a farm called Smith Hill, to the eastward of the Fresh Pond and Swamp: beginning on the highway at the north-east corner of the orchard belonging to Hendr. *Selyns;* thence west 2.30, north 5.54; thence southerly 28 links to the fence of W. Webber; then, by said fence, west 27, north 10.65, to the Fresh Pond; then, by the said pond and swamp, to the free negroes' ground; thence, by their fence, to the land of Jacob Stillie; thence, by his fence, as it runs to the highway; thence, by the highway, to the place of beginning. East by the highway, north by the free negroes, south by W. Webber and Hend. Selyns, west by the swamp—135 acres besides the swamp.

Map of N. Bayard's farm, made by Marschalk, January 15, 1752.

Nicholas Bayard to Stephen Bayard, September 10, 1762. (Lib. Secretary of State, 19, p. 370.)

See maps of Bayard's East and West Farms, in possession of E. Smith, City Surveyor. The division line, Broadway, was arbitrary.

Authorities for Diagram No. 13.

1644, April 25. Ground brief from Governor Kieft to Jan Jansen Damen. Confirmed by Nichols 3d October, 1677. (Lib. 1 Patents.) Under-lease to Damen in 1639.

Description. [Two pieces of land.] The piece on the eastern side extends along the public road 50 rods; on the south side, next to the Company's

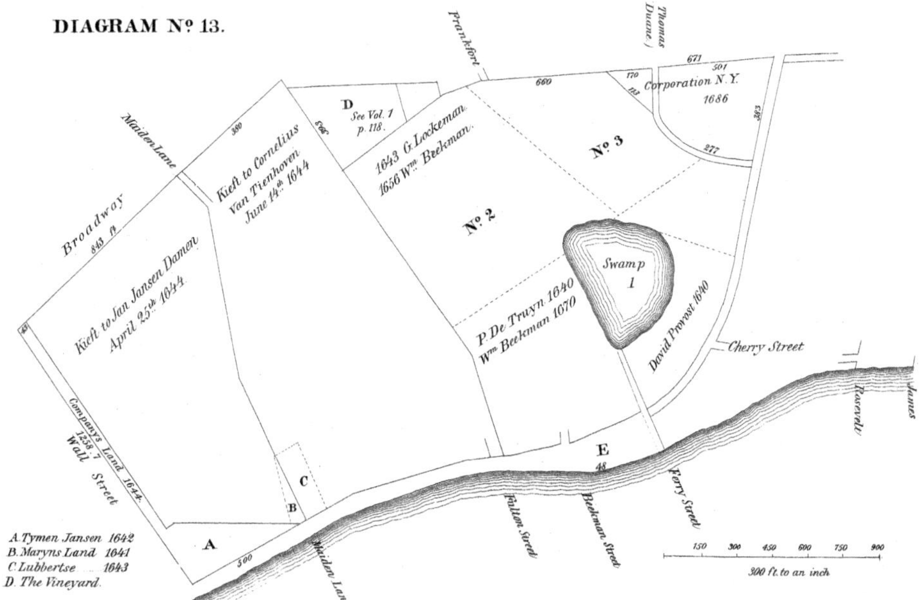
DIAGRAM No. 13.
Maiden Lane
Broadway
843 ft.
Kieft to Jan Jansen Damen
April 25th 1644
Kieft to Cornelius
Van Tienhoven
June 14th 1644
D
See Vol. 1
p. 118.
1643 G. Lockeman
1656 Wm. Beekman
No. 2
No. 3
Frankfort
Thomas
Duane
Corporation N.Y.
1686
Swamp
1
P. De Truyn 1640
Wm. Beekman 1670
David Provost 1640
Cherry Street
Company's Land 1644
1258.7
Wall Street
C
B
A
E
Maiden Lane
Fulton Street
Beekman Street
Ferry Street
Roosevelt
James
A. Tymen Jansen 1642
B. Maryns Land 1641
C. Lubbertse 1643
D. The Vineyard.
150 300 450 600 750 900
300 ft. to an inch

land, south-east a little easterly, 72 rods, 9 feet, 5 inches, to the land of Tymen Jansen ; then 52 feet and two-thirds next to the land of Jansen, till by the beach east by south and east-south-east 37 rods, 3 feet, along by the aforesaid land, to the lot of Maryn 17 rods, 8 feet, and extends further from the north end on the east side of Maryn's land, next to the road running between the Secretary Van Tienhoven, and the said land of Jan Damen, throughout, till to the starting-point at the common highway.

See translation in the Confirmation and Manual of 1840.

A series of deeds from Peter Stoutenbergh, Abraham Verplanck, Lucas Tienhoven, John Vangee (Vinge), and Jacob Kip and wife, to John Knight, dated 14th December, 1685, for 908 feet on Wall street, by 80 feet in depth. (Lib. 13, various pages.) Recital of the grant to Damen as the source of title.

Confirmation by Nichols to Peter Stoutenbergh, 22d Sept., 1667. (Lib. 21, p. 176.)

Series of deeds from Gerrit J. Roose and Lucas Van Tienhoven, Executors of Jan Vinge, for property on Tienhoven street (Pine), generally in 1691. (Lib. 18, N. York.)

Deed to Jonas Bartelf by Jan Vinge, and others, 1st May, 1671 (A., page 24, N. Y.), 229 feet on Broadway.

Rachel Van Tienhoven to E. J. Van Tammerer,

1662 (Lib. 5, p. 225, Secretary State), "west by the highway, 6 rods."

Jan Vinge, &c., to Peter Stoutenbergh, west by the highway 40 feet, 139 depth. (Book 2, Albany, 116.) Peter Stoutenbergh to Dutch Church, 7th Nov., 1700 (Lib. 25, N. York), west by Broadway. Gerrit Roose and Lucas Van Tienhoven, Executors of Jan Vinge, to Morris & Jones, 29th July, 1693, northerly to a street called Maadge Paadge; easterly by South street (William), southerly by Little Queen. (Lib. 18, N. Y., p. 252.)

Jan Vinge and Peter Stoutenbergh, "Trustees of Rachel Van Tienhoven, one of the right heirs of Jan Jansen Damen," to John Andrianzien, 23d October, 1665. (Lib. A., p. 13, N. York.)

Jan Vinge to Van Niss and others, 16th October, 1684 (Lib. 13, p. 43, N. Y.), on Maadge Paadge, recites ground brief of April 25, 1644.

A. *of Diagram* 13.

1640. Governor Kieft to Tymen Jansen, for land in Smith's valley. (Lib. 1, 13.)

1641, August 26. Hendrick Jansen to Maryn Andriasen. (Book 1, p. 20, Albany Dutch Translations.)

B.

1642, April 27. Maryn Andriasen to Jan Jansen Damen, land in Smith's valley. (Ibid., p. 270.)

1644, June 14. Kieft to Cornelius Van Tienhoven.

1667, Oct. 3. Confirmation by Nicolls.

A certain parcel of ground upon the island Manhattan, towards the East river, between the said river and the common highway, on the north side of the land belonging to Jan Damen, being separated by the wagon way and the lot of Frederick Lubbertse; then going to that of Lawrence Cornelius, it stretcheth along the strand of the East river, east and by north, somewhat more easterly, and contains forty-six rods one foot; then along by the land of Philip De Truyn, north, somewhat westerly, thirty (30) rods; so further to the aforementioned highway, north sixteen, and north-west and by north one hundred and two rods, four feet; along the same way, south-west, somewhat more westerly, thirty-eight rods two feet; further along the wagon path, south-south-west, twenty rods; south and by west, eighty rods; south and by east, five rods; south-south-east, thirty rods; south-east, twenty-nine rods four feet; and further to the first descent, ten rods five feet; being twenty-four acres, or 12 morgen 234 rods.

The confirmation recites that portions had been transported.

1656, Aug. 16. Cornelius Van Tienhoven to Wilhelm Beekman—house and lot on the East river, in the Smith's valley, south by the river, east, west, and north by land of Van Tienhoven. With front and rear 80 Rhineland feet; depth on west side,

10 rods 2 feet; on east side, 12 rods 7 feet, of premises patented to said Van Tienhoven 14th June, 1644.

1656, Oct. 16. Van Tienhoven to Henry Breser for another parcel east of the above lot, to Beekman. South, the river, width, front, and rear, 30 Rhineland feet; depth, 121½ feet one side, 13 rods 1½ feet east side; part of premises patented 14th June, 1644.

1649, Aug. 4. Transport of a parcel to A. S. Hanks (Lib. 2, p. 108).

1650, Jan. 29. Transport of another part to John Laurens (Lib. 2, p. 13).

1649, August. Transport to Dirck Volkerson. Confirmed Sept., 1667.

Before 1658, a parcel came to be vested in Oloff S. Van Cortlandt.

The bulk of this property came to be known as "The Shoemaker's Field," derived from Van Tienhoven, as follows:

Nicoll's confirmation of October 3d, 1647, was to the heirs and creditors of C. Van Tienhoven.

1671, July 1. Lucius Van Tienhoven, Jan Vinge, and Peter Stoutenbergh to John Smedes, for the farm or bowery heretofore belonging to Cornelius Van Tienhoven. (Lib. 1, Albany.)

1675, March 20. John Smedes to Conrad Ten Eyck, Aarsen Laren, Jacob Abramse, and John Harpending, for about seventeen acres. (Lib. 1, p. 126, Albany.)

1674. Orloff Stevens Van Cortlandt to Cornelius Clopper, for an adjoining parcel. (Lib. 5,152.)

677. Cornelius Clopper to Ten Eyck, Leersen, Abramse, and Harpending. (Lib. 6, p. 135.)

1596, Sept. 14. Partition deed among the same. (Lib. 28, p. 128, N. Y.) A map is annexed. The general description is between Broadway and G. Van Clift's land, and Maiden lane and Beekman's farm. The north-eastern limit was about 117 feet north of Fair (Fulton) street.

The description of one parcel is important. It is—north-west by the street called Broadway, and along said fence, as it was then fenced in, 580 feet (by the ground brief, 38 rods 2 feet), on the north-east by the ground commonly called the Governor's Garden, and some part of the Commons, being along said Garden and Commons 160 feet; on the south-west by Maiden lane.

Lubbertse's land. C. of Diagram, No. 13.

1643, June 26. L. C. Vandewell to Frederick Lubbertse, for lot next described, with probably another parcel.

1658, Jan'y 10. Frederick Lubbertse to Jan Peeck, lot in Smith's Valley. East, by house of L. C. Vanderwell; south, by the shore of the East river; west, by the Maiden lane, and north by the meadow of Oloff Stevensen. South side, 7 feet 4 inches; north side, 7 rods 7 feet; depth, east and west sides, 17 rods 4 feet 3 inches.

1677, Feb. 18. John Smedes to Henry Rankin. (Lib. 12, p. 11.)

1681, Aug. 11. Henry Rankin to Dirck Vandercliff, (Book 12, p. 61.)

1640. Governor Kieft to Philip De Truyn. (Book G. G. Dutch Records.) A piece of land near the Smith's Valley, having C. Van Tienhoven on the south-west, and David Provost on the east-north-east, extending in breadth from Van Tienhoven's land to Bestaver's Cripple Swamp 40 rods, at 12 feet to the rod, west-south-west, and east-north-east, in length along to the strand, 68 rods; north by west, and south by east, by the land of David Provost; in breadth, along the strand in the Smith's Valley, to the fence of David Provost, 48 rods.

Before August 27, 1654, became vested in Isaac De Forest.

1654, Aug. 27. Isaac De Forest to Thomas Hall, for the same parcel, by the same description.

1667, April 15. Confirmation by Nicolls to Ana Hall.

1670. Anna Hall, widow of Thomas Hall, to William Beekman. (Lib. A., p. 115.)

In 1671, a boundary of the adjacent lot to the eastward, belonging to Balthazar Bayard, is "land of William Beekman."

1647, April 10. Philip De Truyn to Isaac Ollerton. (Lib. 4, p. 92, Albany.) Transport, out of the within-mentioned land, unto Isaac Ollerton, a certain parcel thereof, stretching north from the strand to the highway, being in breadth 1 rod and $\frac{1}{17}$th, and in length, along the said way to the lot of William Goulder, 46 rods; and so back again from the way to the strand.

1692, March 15. William Beekman to Thomas Hoock, a parcel of ground on the eastward, near the Ferry House, beginning at a certain great tree, extending thence northerly to the highway, 108 feet; thence westerly along the highway, 103 feet; thence southerly to the shore side, 68 feet; then easterly along the shore side, 100 feet, all English measure, to the Great Stone.

(1.) *Bestaver's* Cripple Bush, or Swamp — Beekman's Swamp.

Vested in the Corporation by the Charter of 1686.

1733, July 20. Granted by the Mayor, Aldermen, and Commonalty, to Jacobus Roosevelt.

1734, February 27. Partition deed of that parcel of land known as The Cripple Bush, containing 4 acres and a half. Bounded on the south by land lately of William Beekman; on the west-north-west and northerly by land lately claimed by Jacob Leister and Margaret Vandewater; easterly, by land claimed by Cornelius Clopper, and the heirs and devisees of Theophilus Elsworth. (Lib. 32, p. 482.) A map accompanies the deed. Queen street lies to the south-east, from 190 to 220 feet distant.

The boundaries of this piece of ground can, from the map and deed, be laid down with accuracy. They are given very roughly in the diagram. The outline is all that is required for present purposes.

2 and 3 of Diagram 13.

1642, March 10. Governor Kieft to Govert Lockerman and T. Vandergriest. A house and lot of land on the East River, as the same is fenced in by David Provost; which fencing begins at a brook of fresh water emptying into the East River, up till to the land of Cornelius Van Tienhoven, whose palisades extend from the long highway towards the East River, as may be seen by the marks made by him; then bordering on the aforesaid land (Van Tienhoven's), from the fence to the great tree, which is on the right division line between Philip De Truyn and Van Tienhoven, the said Philip's palisades extending from said tree north-east by east, and east-north-east to Bestaver's Cripple Bush ; and from the East River north-west and north-north-west, between both, up to the said swamp. And since, from old time till now, there has been a wagon-way running to the great highway, betwixt the land which we sell to Lockerman and Vandergriest, and the farm of the said Tienhoven, it is ordered that, until the land hereby conveyed shall be enclosed, Tienhoven may use the road as it is; afterwards to be used as a private road between the parties.

Some facts are of moment in locating this parcel. Elsie Leisler, wife of Jacob Leisler, was a daughter of Govert Lockerman. In 1682, Govert Lockerman and Maatje, his wife, and Jacob Lockerman conveyed to Jacob Leisler all the estate of their father and mother, and of Cornelius Dircksen, in the city of New York. (Lib. 23, p. 75.)

A map of Leisler's property is referred to in a conveyance of Peter Delancy to William Croilius, 1749. (Lib. 57, p. 636.) A copy of this map is in the possession of Edwin Smith, Esq., city surveyor. It shows a line on Chatham street of 660 feet, commencing about 100 feet south of Frankfort street. It came within 170 feet of Thomas, now Duane street. It ran on the line of Frankfort street 840 feet, then north-east about 462 feet, then 250, and 298 feet to Chatham street.

The valuable map of the Corporation lands, compiled by Bancker, in 1773, shows that the

Corporation property extended from the south-west corner of Pearl, for about 671 feet on Chatham street; then touching Leisler's land.

The parcel marked No. 2 in the diagram was certainly vested in William Beekman before 1685. I am inclined to think it belonged to him as early as 1656.

The description of the Vineyard, according to the survey of 1685, bounds it on the south-east by William Beekman's land.

In 1656 William Beekman petitioned the burgomasters and schepens, stating that certain persons claimed a right of way through his farm, and requested that they might be called upon to show their title. The claimants stated that they and their neighbors had for many years herded their cattle on the commons, and that there had been a right of way there before that time. (Dutch Records, New York, 1656.)

I think this explains the clause in the ground brief of Kieft to Lockerman of 1642, of a wagon way, running between the land of Tienhoven and that granted to Lockerman; and this wagon way must, I think, have run about the line of Ann street. An examination of Line's map, supposed to be of 1728, will strongly corroborate this view. Following Ann street down to Gold street, and then along Gold street, we will get the line of Tienhoven on the south-west, and of De Truyn to the Cripple Bush, on the south-east.

Again, the map of Beekman's pasture (vol. 28, p. 382, N. Y. Records) shows about 635 feet on Kip street (Nassau). That carries it close to the Leisler line. The line of the same map on Queen street is 572 feet. That corresponds nearly with the De Truyn line.

No reasonable doubt can be entertained, of the fact, that this part of Beekman's property, marked No. 1, was part of the ground brief to Lockerman, of 1642. We get Van Tienhoven's fence palisades extending from the long highway, (clearly Broadway,) on one side. Certainly, this was the northern line of the grant to Van Tienhoven, of 1644; running over that line, we reach De Truyn's line, and run along his line to the Swamp. Thus far, there is very little obscurity, and no room for doubt, upon a careful examination.

Parcel marked 3 on Diagram No. 13.

This belonged to Jacob Leisler, and his connection with Lockerman makes it nearly certain that it came from the latter. It must, then, have been part of the grant of 1642 to him.

1640. David Provost.

1671, June 10. Purchase by Balthazar Bayard, at public auction, parcel of ground described as No 1; 3 morgen 45 rods—6 acres 34 perches. (Lib. 32, p. 235.) All that lot, &c., in the Smith's Vly or Valley, called Lot No. 1, east of the lot of William Beekman, stopping with the south-east side, with the land of Beekman ; north-west and west-north-west side to the Cripple Bush Swamp, and to the lot No. 2, being the separation line between the two ; from the point of the Cripple Bush to the fence, south-south-east ; with the south-south-east and south-east side to the highway, and with the north-east side to the fence ; being 3 morgen 45 rods.

1683, January 25. Conveyed by Balthazar Bayard to Creetjie, widow of H. Vandewater, Theophilus Elsworth, and Harman Jansen (Lib. 13, p. 38), 3 morgen 45 rods.

1697, July 17. Partition deed and map, Lib. 12, p. 235. Divided into three parcels.

Boundary of parcel 3, the northerly lot. Beginning at the south-east corner of Leisler's fence, on the north side of the Swamp ; thence by the said fence north, 21, east 5 chains 80 links, to the highway ; then east 9.30, south, 3 chains ; then southerly by the highway to the Clopper division (Jansen House), so to the Swamp, and then to the place of beginning.

The line of front, on Queen street, of the whole parcel, is 1,008 feet.

The southern parcel has its south-west boundary on Beekman's land.

NOTE 57.—DIAGRAM NO. 14.

East side of Chatham and Bowery.

The outlet of the Fresh Water forms a natural point of

DIAGRAM No. 14.

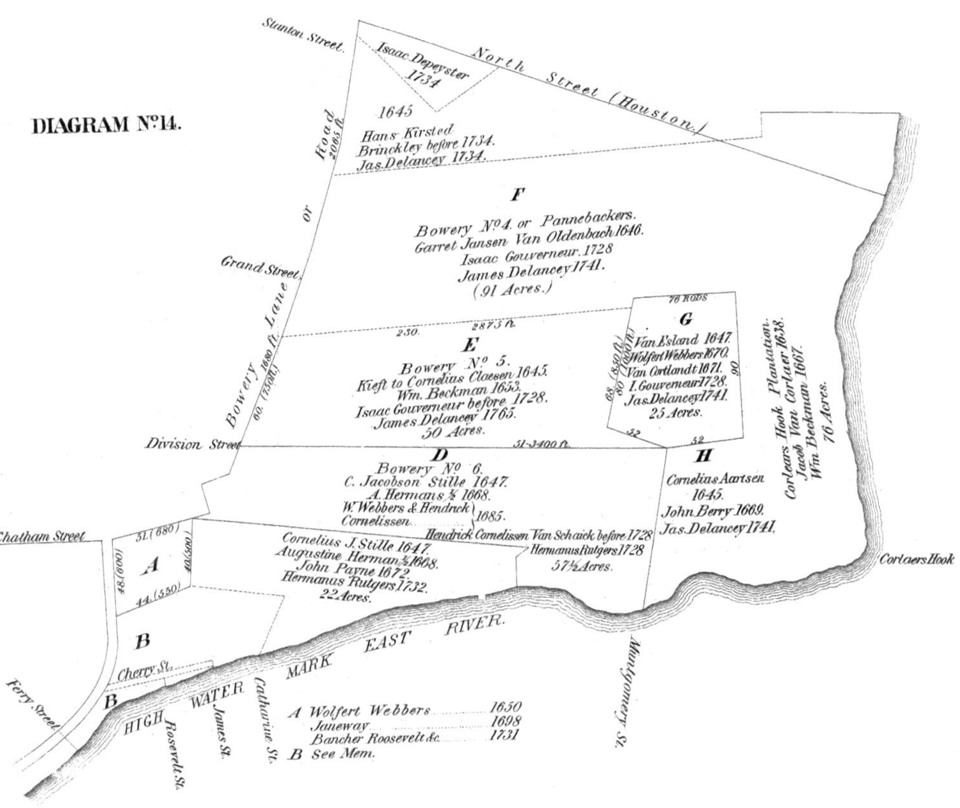

starting, with the location of the grants in this vicinity. It was called the Ould Kill, the outlet of Fresh Water, the rivulet from Fresh Water. At what point it flowed out of the pond is not very clear. From the map of Lines, of 1728, from the shape of the ground, even yet apparent, and from Ratzell's map, this must have been between Pearl and Orange streets. It crossed Chatham street about one hundred feet above the junction of Queen street (Pearl). This is shown on Lines' map of 1728, distinctly; and there was the bridge.

Its course to the East River, from this point, is defined in Montgomerie's charter of 1730, giving the boundary of the Montgomerie ward, which runs "through the middle of South street to the rivulet which runs from Fresh Water into the East River; from thence along the said rivulet, so far as it goes, till it empties itself into the East River.

The map of Lieutenant Ratzell, of 1764, shows this line to be Roosevelt street until near Cherry, and then a variation to the north-east to James street, where it enters the river.

The line of the Montgomerie ward, on this map, runs through William street up to Frankfort, where William ended, and then was continued in precisely the same direction till it struck the Fresh Water.

But the stream flowed through a considerable expanse of swamp or meadow land, as is shown on Lines' map. This was known as Wolfert's meadows, and the low ground as Wolfert's valley.

By an act of the Legislature of April 1, 1792, commissioners were appointed to fill up the tract called the meadows, bounded northerly by Chatham street, southerly by the rear of the lots on the northerly side of Cherry street, westerly by the rear of the lots on the easterly side of Queen street, and easterly by Catharine street.

The Fresh Water Pond had another outlet on its western side, running into the Hudson River. It is possible, however, that this side was only the draining of the swampy ground and did not actually connect. I have heard my father say that he has often skated from river to river, walking across Chatham street at the bridge.

A.

1650, April 2. Governor Stuyvesant to Wolfert Webbers.

A piece of land lying beyond Fresh Water, between the land of Cornelius Jacobson Stille and the valley or meadow ground, being in length from the beginning of the Kill, along the highway to the mark which divides Cornelius Jacobson's land, 51 rods, stretching north-east further in length along said Stille's land 40 rods, south and by west; along the valley to the Hook 66 rods (north*) west; then along the hills to the beginning, 48 rods northerly.

1670, June 18. Confirmation by Nicolls to Annette, widow of Wolfert Webbers.

1670, Nov. 11. Annette Webbers, widow, to A. L. Mott.

A. L. Mott to Arnoult Webbers.

Arnoult Webbers to Lawrence Colvell.

---

* An error—should be west.

1680, May 4. Lawrence Colvell to William Merritt. (Lib. 6, p. 170.)

1698, May 10. William Merritt, Mayor, &c., to William Janeway. (Lib. 9, p. 462, Albany.) A further confirmation by Governor Dongan is also recited.

Mortgage by Janeway to Noy Willy.

1699, March 15. Release by Janeway. Recital of an act of Parliament and virtual foreclosure.

1731, July 31. Noy Willy to Christopher Bancker.

A lot of land beyond Fresh Water, between land late of Jacob Stille, now of Harmanus Rutgers, and the valley or meadow ground. Beginning at a certain creek that cometh out of the Fresh Water where it crosses the present high road; thence along the high road, 51 rods, to the mark dividing the land of Stille; along said Stille's land 40 rods to the meadow; along the meadow, on a direct line westwardly, 44 rods; thence northwardly to the place where it began, 48 rods; excepting a lot sold Price, and another sold Gomez, on the 17th December, 1729.

1792. Arian Bancker to Isaac Roosevelt. (Lib. 48, p. 6.) Refers to a map of a division between Jacobus Roosevelt, John Roosevelt, Christopher Bancker, and executors of Anthony Rutgers. West by Queen street.

1765. Leonard Lispenard to John Hutchings (37, 804). East in front by Roosevelt street, northerly by road leading to Boston.

1771. William Bancker to Jacobus Roosevelt, for various lots on St. James street. (Lib. 54, p. 223.)

The map of the Corporation lands, compiled by Marshall in 1766, from various surveys, puts down on the east side of Pearl street, on Chatham, "Lands purchased by Roosevelt, Bancker, and others."

It must be that the grant to Webbers of 1650 came down to the present Pearl street, although the beginning is from the kill or creek running from Fresh Water, which was, by Montgomerie's charter and Ratzell's map, Roosevelt street.

B.

It may be satisfactorily proven that the parcels I have marked B on this diagram were derived under the ground briefs and Dutch transports next specified; but I have not been able to locate the division boundaries with anything like accuracy. The whole land was undoubtedly covered by one or the other of them.

1642, March 10. Kieft to Govert Lockerman. See description in Mem. on Diagram No. 13.

1653, July 28. Govert Lockerman to Thomas Stevenson. A parcel of land, with houses, on Manhattan Island, situate at the East River, on the point at the west side of the Fresh Water Little Creek, bounded north, along the valley called Wolfert's Valley; on the west by the lot of Harry Bresar; breadth on the west side 14 rods; on the north side, in length, unto the end of said point, 31½ rods.

1654, October 6. Thomas Stevensen to William De Groot and Jan Peck.

1657. Wm. De Groot to Dirck Claesen Van Luwerden.

1680, September 4. Dirck Claesen Van Luwerden to John Ewouts and Claesen. (Lib. 12, p. 485.)

1654, July 3. Governor Kieft to Tymen Jansen. A parcel of land on the Island Manhattan, beginning at the creek where the Fresh Water runs into the East River, and extends to Bestaver's Swamp. (Lib. 2, p. 13.)

Govert Lockerman married the widow of Tymen Jansen. Balthazar Bayard married a daughter of G. Lockerman.

1671, August 10. Maritjie Jans, widow of Govert Lockerman, Balthazar Bayard, Hans Kiersted and Jacob Lockerman to Thomas Delavall.

Lot of ground at the ferry, formerly belonging to Egbert Boerum (*Quere* the *Ferry*), and a parcel of meadow, with a strip of upland, abutting upon the south-west side, with the lot of Henry Brasier; with the north-east side upon the Ould Kill; with the south-east side upon the highway along the East River, and with the north-west side upon the highway, being 3 morgen 85 rods. Recited to have been sold at public outcry.

1672, May 20. Delavall to Elias Puddington.

1672, July 10. E. Puddington to John Payne, reserving the orchard from the north end thereof, at the furthermost point of the cherry-trees; and so from thence to the river, as comprehended between the cherry-trees and the lot of Henry Bresier.

1708. Robert Puddington to Richard Sackett. (Lib. 26, p. 314.)

1713, May 22. Robert Puddington to Thomas Huth. (Lib. 28, 23.)

1769, May 2. Jacobus Rosevelt, Evert Bancker, Anthony Rutgers and wife, and others, including the executors of John Rosevelt, to Hendrick Rutgers.

Parcel of meadow ground at Hughsen's Point in the outward part of the meadow ground belonging to said Jacob Rosevelt and others, to the eastward of a street laid out on Hendrick Rutgers' plan as Catharine street, beginning at the corner part of the south boundary of said Rutgers' land at the East River, running northerly along said Catharine street 508 feet, then easterly along the upland of H. Rutgers' land 50 feet, then south-easterly 110 feet along said upland, then south-westerly along said upland 396 feet to the said corner part; containing ten lots, as laid down on a plan of such meadow, all fronting westerly on Catharine street, excepting two lots left for streets, and lot 203, being property of the heirs of Henry Barclay, they not being party to the instrument. (Lib. 18, p. 228, Albany.)

1765, Oct. 30. Andrew Barclay and others, executors of Rev. Henry Barclay, to Anthony Rutgers. (Lib. 38, 117.) Lot of land lying on the south along the

East River, east by the Ould Kill and land late of Harman Rutgers, north along the highway or road, and on the west by the road or Queen street, referred to, in part at least, in deed of Augustine Herman to Wolfert Webbers of January 10, 1685.

The act of the Legislature of April 1, 1792 (Sess. Laws, ch. 69) defines these meadows. It appoints commissioners to fill up the track called the Meadows, bounded northerly by Chatham street, southerly by the rear of the lots on the northerly side of Cherry street, westerly by the rear of the lots on the easterly side of Queen street, and easterly by Catharine street.

C.

1647. Kieft to Cornelius Jacobsen Stille.

Before 1668. Transport of one half to Augustine Herman.

1672, July 9. Augustine Herman to John Payne. A parcel of upland (without the marsh), heretofore belonging to C. J. Stille, being one half of 22 morgen of upland of said Stille, beyond Fresh Water, near Corlaer's Hook, having to the east (*west*) the Fresh Marsh or Meadow; to the south the river and Scheppen Louw's point; to the west (*east*) the lot of Cornelius Jacobsen Stille, and to the north the land of the said Stille, 11 morgen or 22 acres (Lib. A., N. Y. Records, 141), as in patents as to length and breadth is set forth.

1732, June 20. Thomas Fayerweather, grandson and heir-at-law of John Payne, to Hermanus Rutgers

(Lib. 23, p. 28). A certain piece of land lying over the Fresh Water, near Corlaer's Hook, along the East River, and which was mortgaged by John Payne, of Boston, to Augustine Hermans.

1750, June 20. Will of Hermanus Rutgers (Surrogate's office, N. Y., Lib. 18, p. 347). Devises (*part of*) the land bought of Thomas Fayerweather to certain persons, beginning at the corner post, and running eastward 1,700 feet; northward 200 feet; then westward 1,700 feet, and then southward to beginning 200 feet ($7\frac{80}{100}$ acres).

D.

Bowery No. 6.

1647, March 18. Governor Kieft to Cornelius Jacobson Stille. Land, &c., known as the Bowery No. 6, heretofore in the possession of Wolfert Gerritse, containing, according to the surveyor's certificate, about 57 acres, or 28 morgen and a half.

Before 1668. Cornelius Jacobson Stille to Augustine Hermans for one half of such premises.

1668, August 10. Confirmation by Governor Nicoll to Francisca Hermans. Recites the ground brief to Stille, and, "Now said Cornelius Jacobson Stille having transported one half to Augustine Hermans, it is confirmed."

1685, January 10. Francisca Hermans, as attorney for her father, Augustine Hermans, to Wolfert Webbers and Hendrick Cornelissen. One half of a certain farm or Bowery, upon the Island Manhattan, near Fresh Water, being the Bowery No. 6, heretofore granted to Cornelius Jacobson Stille, containing about 57 acres, or 28 morgen and a half, as more at large appears by the patent of confirmation, dated 10th of August, 1668, excepting the lot of salt meadow belonging to said farm (Lib. 9, p. 132, Albany).

1728, June 9. Neltjie Van Schaick, widow, and Jacob Van Schaick and others, heirs of Hendrick Cornelissen Van Schaick, to Harmanus Rutgers (Lib. 33, p. 21). A farm near Fresh Water Hill, on the east side of the Bowery Lane; beginning at the north-west corner of the barn, and running along the fence east 51 chains and a half to the north-east corner of the land; then south 1.16, along the fence 23 chains to high water mark; then along high water mark south 83.30 west 6 chains to the point of rocks; then north 50 west 7 chains; then north 74.30 west 6 chains 35 links, ranging with the fence in the meadow; then from high water mark north 7 west 3 chains 45 links; then north 74 east 3 chains to the division fence between Janeway and Van Schaick; then north 85 west along the fence 38 chains to the north-east corner of the Jews' Burying-ground; then north 16.30 west 4.70; then north 61.30 east 4.25; then north 18 east 1.80 to the place of beginning. Bounded north by land of Governeur & Company, east by land of Gouverneur, south by the river and Janeway's land, west by the wagon road or highway, containing 28 morgen.

Also a piece of meadow land adjoining Steenwyck and Van Cortlandt, and F. Herman, conveyed to Hendrick C. Van Schaick by the Mayor, Aldermen, &c., 1st September, 1687.

E.

Bowery No. 5.

1645, December 13. Governor Kieft to Cornelius Clasen.

1653, March 22. Cornelius Clasen to William Beekman.

1667, August 10. Confirmation by Nicolls to William Beekman. (Lib. 2, p. 91, Albany.)

Beginning at the north end of Cornelius Jacobson (*Stille*) land, or the Bowery No. 6 ; stretching along the said land east by south 242 rods ; then north-east 68 rods to the Pannebacker Bowery ; then next to the same west and west and by north 230 rods ; then south-south-west by the wagon path, 60 rods ; containing 50 acres, 25 morgen.

Before 1728, became vested in Isaac Gouverneur.

Before 1741, became vested in James Delancey.

1765, October 31. Agreement between Hendrick Rutgers and James Delancey, for settling a division line between them. (Lib. 48, p. 304.) Two roads to be laid out (see Ratzer's Map). Roads were Division and Little Division streets, now Montgomery.

F.

Pannebacker Bowery, or No. 4.

1646, February 17. Governor Kieft to Garret Jansen Van Oldenbach. A piece of land formerly known by the name of the Pannebacker's (Tile Baker's) Bowery, extending (*from*) next the land of Cornelius Claesen, along the wagon road till to Hans Kierstede's plantation, and further on straight through the woods to the division line of Laendert Aerden; (*then*) till the place where three ways meet of the inside wagon-road; containing forty-five and a half morgen and 125 rods. (About 91 acres.)

1715. Garritt Van Oldenbach to Mathys Hope (Lib. 31, 211), for fifteen acres of ground, at the Bowery in the outwards; being bounded on the south side by the land of Giles Silly; on the east by a certain swamp and land of Jan Pierters; having to the north side the land of Mrs. Van Cortlandt and Maritjie Solomons; which have been for twenty-two years in the peaceable possession of Marian Van Schaick, measuring fifteen acres.

G.

Before 1647. Governor Kieft to Claes Van Esland; Claes Van Esland to Jan Cornelissen.

1647. Jan Cornelissen to Wolfert Webbers.

1670, June 17. Confirmation by Lovelace to Anecke

Webbers, widow of Wolfert Webbers :

" A certain piece of land upon the Island Manhattan, lying and being at the east end of Cornelius Claes (*Claesen*), and stretching from the land of Cornelius Jacobsen to the wagon-way, north and by east 80 rods; along the wagon-way east and half a point northerly, 76 rods; further south and by east, half a point easterly, 90 rods; so west, half a point southerly, to the fence then belonging to Edward Manell, 52 rods; and along the fence unto the land of the aforementioned Cornelius Claes, 52 rods west and by north to the first descent; in all, 25 acres and 152 rods."

1670, Nov. 11. Anna Webbers, widow of Wolfert Webbers, to A. Moll (Lib. A., p. 122):

" Two parcels of ground, the first near Corlaer's Hook, amounting to about 25 acres; and the other lying beyond Fresh Water, between the land of Cornelius Jacobson Stille and the valley, as in the patents will appear."

1671, March 17. A. Moll to Cornelius Steenwyck and Oloff S. Van Cortlandt. A parcel of land near Corlaer's Hook, as described in the ground brief to Claes Van Esland.

Before 1728 became vested in Isaac Gouverneur.

H.

1645. Ground brief to Cornelius Aartsen.

1669. Sept. 16. Confirmation by Lovelace to heirs of Cornelius Aartsen.

1669–70, Jan. 16. Arian Cornelissen, Hendrick Cornelissen, and Lysbèrt Cornelissen, heirs of Cornelius Aartsen, to John Berry. Land on the east end of Cornelius Jacobson (Stille), and west end of Corlaer's plantation. It stretches from the strand through a piece of meadow which reaches to Cornelius Jacobson's land, north and by east 76 rods; from said Jacobson's land to Corlaer's plantation, east and by north 70 rods; nearly west by said Corlaer's land; to the strand of the East River, south and by west a half *strooks (northerly)*, 120 rods; in all, 22 acres, or 11 morgen 200 rods.

Corlaer's Hook.

Before 1658. Wouter Van Twiller and Council to Jacob Van Corlaer.

Jacob Van Corlaer to Cornelius Van Tienhoven.

1645, July. Cornelius Van Tienhoven to Conrad Van Curler.

1667, June 9. Conrad Van Curler to William Beekman.

1667, Aug. 10. Confirmation by Nicolls to W. Beekman (Lib. 2, Patents, p. 90, margin paging, 73).

"A certain parcel of land on the Island Manhattan, commonly known as Corlaer's Hook, bounded by the lands of Cornelius Aartsen and Wolfert Webbers on the west side; on the south and east sides with the East River; on the north side with the highway, stretching along the land of Laendert the Boor, in length 128 rods; containing about 76 acres, or 38 morgen and 496 rods. As also a piece of meadow ground or valley, lying to the north of Corlaer's Hook, over a small creek; having on the west side the land of Laendert the Boor (*Aarden*); on the east side the river, about ten acres or five morgen; with a parcel of fresh meadow where the said Hook goeth out by the Bowery of Cornelius Steenwix and Oloff Stevens Van Cortlandt, being about four acres, or two morgen and 32 rods."

1688, Nov. 6. Jacobus Van Cortlandt to Hendrick Selyns. One half of the farm and tract of land, known as Corlaer's Hook, inherited from his father, Oloff S. Van Cortlandt.

1687, Oct. 21. Release by the Mayor, &c., to Francisca Hermans. Beginning by the bank of the upland, called Corlear's Hook, runs east by south 2.15 easterly 88 rods to the river, then along the river side, but in a straight line south and by west 7.45 west 12 rods; then west and by north 84 rods, to the upland, so northerly to the beginning. Bounded north by land of Stephen Van Cortlandt; east by the river; south by the meadow of Hendrick Cornelissen; west by the upland of

S. Steenwyck and Jacobus Van Cortlandt; 5 acres 3 roods 24 perches, English measure.

1701. Abraham Gouverneur, Recorder of the city. (Manual, 1857, p. 527.)

1741, June 12. Henry Courteen and Mary Gouverneur, Peter De Reimer, son and heir of Isaac De Reimer, jr., Cornelius Low, jr., and Hanna, his wife, late Joanna Gouverneur; Margaretta Gouverneur, John Hall and Magtalina, his wife, late Gouverneur; John Broughton and Alida, his wife, late Gouverneur; Nicholas Gouverneur, son and heir of Isaac Gouverneur, and Lewis Morris, jr., which said Joanna, Magtalina, Margaretta, Alida, Nicholas Gouverneur, and Lewis Morris, jr., are executors of Isaac Gouverneur, deceased—To James Delancey. (Lib. 21, p. 84, Albany.) All that certain tract and parcel of land or farm, situate in the outward of the city of New York, to the northward of Fresh Water, and commonly called the Dominie's farm, containing 269 acres of land, little more or less, according to a certain draft thereof mad by James Howell, surveyor, on the 5th of April, 1689.

(See will of Isaac Gouverneur, Surrogates' office, New York.)

Blyvelt's Bowery.

1645. Ground brief of Governor Kieft to Laendert Aarden. A farm called Blyvelt's Bowery, lying behind Corlaer's plantation, extending from the valley next said plantation to a valley 170 rods; further on west, sixty rods (60), all to the wagon road; further along the wagon road, north by east, a little east, 115 rods—then south, 35 rods, next to the land of the Schout, till to the valley about west.

1653, October 30. Transport by —— ——— to Thomas Hall.

1667, October 30. Thomas Hall to Steenwyck and Oloff Stephen Van Cortlandt.

1734, September 5. Brune Brinkley to James Delancey (Lib. 32, p. 489). Land on the east side of the highway called the Bowery Lane, between the land late of Thomas Ackers, now of Isaac Depeyster, and the land formerly called Dominie Sellyn's pasture, now in possession of James Delancey, about 18 acres of land.

Depeyster's land is shown on Ratzer's map, adjoining James Delancey.

Mr. Smith states the Delancey farm comprised about 339 acres, and the Van Cortlandt piece, 15 acres—making 354. Gouverneur's deed to Delancey conveyed 269 acres. The Corlaer's Hook parcel was 76 acres; the meadow over the creek, 10, and fresh meadow, 4 acres—make 359 acres.

The above located parcels make 50+91+25+22=188 and 76 is 264 acres, which probably were the parcels conveyed by Gouverneur's devisees to Delancey. How he got the residue, I have not traced.

Note 58.—Page 344.

In this note will be found some statements of the action of the Corporation upon closing streets, and the principles which have governed them. Nothing can exceed the equity and sound judgment which has, in general, controlled their course in this matter.

Acts of Corporation on Closing Streets.

A most elaborate report was made upon this subject to the Board of Aldermen, on the 25th of October, 1833 (Documents 1833, No. 32), by the Committee on Laws, &c., of which Judah Hammond, Esq., was chairman.

Some of its leading propositions and facts are of importance. It is observed that the declarations of trust contained in the 178th section of the act of 1813 was intended as a general declaration of trust in the tenure under which the streets are held in the city of New York, and that the enactment is declaratory of the common law, as it was understood, before and at the time of passing that act, in relation to the estate which the Corporation have in the public streets and roads.

After a full statement of the statutory provisions, the report proceeds: "What, then, is the conclusion to which these premises would seem to conduct us, as the fair construction of several statutes, but that the land so acquired by the Corporation, should be offered in payment of the damages awarded to the adjoining proprietors in the case of closing streets and roads, so far as it will go, if the individuals entitled to damage will receive it at the price at which the Commissioners have estimated it. If they will not take the lands, the Corporation is free from any restraint, and may sell them to the highest bidder." "The Corporation have, as a general principle, always regarded the individual proprietors of the adjoining lands as having the pre-emptive right in lands so situated, and have, as a general rule, always conveyed the lands either at the sum assessed for them by the Commissioners, including interest and charges in the case of gores, and generally for the damages in case of discontinued streets and roads. Of late, however, a desire has crept in to obtain a higher price for these lands.

"The Committee infer, that if the Corporation determine to sell these lands, the adjoining owner has the first right of purchase, and may take them, in lieu of money, for his damages, at an equalized valuation, paying or receiving the difference between the amount of his damages, and the value of the land, if there be any."

A number of examples are then stated, in which the Corporation pursued this system.

It appears that, in March, 1832, the Corporation deviated from their ordinary course, and in relation to the Warren, Fitzroy, and Southampton roads, it was determined not to sell at private sale, but at public auction, at a rate equal to the amount assessed, with twenty per cent. added, and charges.

In March, 1833, however, it was resolved to sell such parts of the said closed roads as were contiguous and opposite to the lands of certain petitioners, at prices to be fixed by two appraisers, and an umpire. And a general rule was embodied in a resolution, that in all cases when roads, streets, lanes, or alleys, should be closed by law, the owner of the adjacent land should have the pre-emptive right to such part of the same, to the centre thereof, as may lie opposite and contiguous to his property, at such price as may be determined by appraisers and an umpire; provided he elect to purchase within sixty days after the actual closing.

The report cites another document, made on the 5th of August, 1833, in which the Committee on Finance advert to the proposition whether the price of the land to be fixed by appraisers may not be the actual value at the time of appraisement, or what other rule would be proper.

Note 59.—Page 370.

Cessions of Streets.

A large number of cessions to the Corporation of land for streets are transcribed into a book in the office of the Street Commissioner. I notice some of them.

A cession of Ferry street, in the Swamp or Cripple Brush, 27th March, 1759, twenty feet wide, Lib. 1, p. 1. Other portions were ceded, 5th March, 1759. Ibid., 5. Trinity Church to the Corporation, 9th April, 1761, (Ibid., p. 7), for Lumber street, and First, Second and Third streets, for the length of the Trinity Church adjoining property; part of Thames street; Partition streets Vesey and Barclay, from Broadway to the river; Robinson street to the College ground; Murray, Warren, Chambers and Reade; Chappel street, from the College ground to Reade, and Church street, from Partition to Reade.

On a map annexed to this deed of cession, Broadway is laid down up to Reade street. Spring Garden appears commencing between Fulton and Ann streets, and running beyond the turn on Chatham street. The phraseology of this deed is—That the grantors remise, release, and forever quit-claim to all and every the said streets, as laid down on the several maps or plans annexed, to have and to hold all and singular the respective streets and their right, title and interest therein, unto them, the said Mayor, &c., and their successors; to be and remain forever public streets and ways for the inhabitants of the city, and all others passing and returning through or by the same, in the same manner as the other public streets of the said city now are or lawfully ought to be.

Columbia College, by a deed of June 1, 1791, completed the cessions of the streets, laid out the Trinity Church ground; and N. Bayard on the 9th of January, 1749, perfected the cession of Thames street. See also cessions of Greenwich and Washington streets, 20th June, 1797; and of Hudson, from Barclay to the Pasture fence, at Moore street.

A series of cessions was made by proprietors when Broadway was opened, from Art street to about Sixteenth street. They comprise the whole of the strip in the street, except from Art to between Ninth and Tenth streets, belonging to the Sailors' Snug Harbor.

One of them recites, that Broadway was to be made

from the ground of Captain Randall to a house known by the name of the White House, and then conveys the strip of the owner.

In these deeds of cession, full and sufficient words are used to convey the fee. And the use is thus declared: "In trust, that the same be kept open as a public street, for the use and benefit of the inhabitants of New York, forever," or in similar words.

A map is referred to in many of these grants, as made by Magnin, and dated August 10, 1804. I have not been able to find it. The maps in Atlas No. 8, in the Street Commissioner's office, will supply the loss, to a great extent.

Note 60.—Page 384.

Roads distinguished from Streets.

As early as February 22, 1669, an order was made in Council, as follows (Minutes of Council, 111, 5). The order is: An order for laying out a convenient wagon way between the city of New York and Harlem, made in Council, February 22, 1669. Four Commissioners were appointed, two for New York, and two for Harlem.

(See orders, warrants, &c., II., 336.)

1671, April. Whereas, the road between this city and the village of New Harlem is impassable, it is ordered that the overseers of roads and the magistrates of Harlem lay out a suitable road, and that it be made by the citizens of Harlem in conjunction with those living on the other side of Fresh Water, each within their respective limits.

1672, February. Whereas, the road to Harlem is still unfinished, and many complaints have been made, therefore, overseers are appointed to urge the inhabitants to go on with the work, and to impose fines for neglect. (Extracts from Minutes, Valentine's Manual for 1862, p. 517.)

On the 14th of February, 1679, a Commissioners' return was made as follows:* "In pursuance of an order received from the Governor and Magistrates of this city, bearing date the 5th of May, 1679, unto us underwritten for the staking out the new highway, and apprising the same specified in the said order, we have in obedience thereunto, to the best of our skill, staked out the said highway, and do apprise the land contained in the said way at twenty (20) guilders per rood, Dutch measure, according to each owner's land brief, excepting that part fronting to the street of Roulofe the Butchers, formerly belonging to the widow of Urin Planke, which 28 rods or thereabout sould unto the Carpen. Hogenar, and now taken up in the highway for eight hundred guilders, which we judge ought to be allowed to the said widdow. Humbly offered to the

* I am indebted to Mr. George H. Moore, Librarian of the Historical Society, for these valuable documents.

Gouvernour and Magistrates from whom we received our order.

Under our hands, this 14th of May, 1679, New York.

JOHN LAWRENCE,
JOHANNAS VAN BRUGE.

ADOLP PETERS, SEURT OLFERT, } *Measurers of land for the toune commonly called Roemeestrs.*

I cannot account for the difference of time between the date of the order in Council, and the Commissioners' return, assuming that the return was under that order of 1669.

NOTE 60.—*Continued.*

Act of 1703. The act of the Colonial Assembly, of June 19, 1703, referred to in the text, provided for laying out a public highway in the various counties in the State. The provision as to New York was as follows: "That there be laid out, preserved, and kept forever in good and sufficient repair, one public, common, and general highway, to extend from the now scite of the city of New York, through the city and county of New York, and the county of Westchester, of the width of four rods, English measure, at least, to be continued and remain forever the public, common, general road and highway from the said city of New York to the adjacent colony of Connecticut."

Commissioners for executing the act were named

in it for the several counties. Those for New York were William Anderson, Clement Elsworth, and Peter O'Blenis.

The Commissioners were to lay out the roads within eighteen months. Their office was to last three years. They were empowered to allow and direct the felling, cutting out, carrying away, and consuming any living trees for the clearing of the road or highway; might remove any fence which obstructed such road or highway, giving a reasonable time to the owner to remove the same.

They were to return to the Clerk of the county, respectively, a full and perfect report and description of the manner and extent of every road laid out by them, and the Clerk was to record the same.

At the expiration of the three years, the surveyors of the highways, under the act of the Province to regulate highways, &c., (that of 6th May, 1691,) were to superintend the roads.

The Commissioners appointed under this act for New York laid out a road, or highway, from New York, through Westchester county, to Connecticut. Their survey was made and filed on the 16th of June, seventeen hundred and seven (1707). It is as follows:

"Pursuant to an act of the Assembly, made in the second year of her said Majesty's reign, for laying out, &c., public common highways through this province, and another act made in the fourth year of her Majesty's reign, for enlarging the time, &c., we, being appointed Commissioners for laying out the said roads and highways, through the Island of New York, have viewed and laid out the same as follows:

"To begin from the gate at Spring Garden to Fresh Water, the course east by north. *Also*, from the gate at the end of Queen street, by a small turning northerly, until it meets with the other road at Fresh Water. From thence, by small turning, to the tree in the highway upon the hill; so along the said lane to the furthermost house in the same, the course being about north-north-east.

"From the said last house, the road for Kingsbridge to run along the fence upon the right hand, and so, as the road now lyes, to Kip's Runs. From thence north-north-east to the bridge beyond the hill; from thence by the corner of Turtle Bay farm to the top of the next hill, about east-north-east; from thence to the Sawkill Bridge, north-east, a little northerly. From Sawkill Bridge along Mr. Codrington's fence, taking some of the corner thereof, to the Half-way House, about north-east. From thence along the lane to the next hollow about north; from thence to Meyers, north-east, and thence to the run by Barent Waldron's, north-north-east. From thence along the fence, and so by John Kierse's house on the right hand, two corners of the fence on the left hand being taken in, and so along as the road now lyes to Hendrich Oblimus's, and from thence along the road as it now lyes, leaving the run of water on the left hand until you come to the Deep Bridge ; from thence along the foot of the hill, which is to the left, about half a mile ; then turning to the left and leaving the swamp on the right hand, as the road now is, unto Nagel and Dyckman's Run ; from thence as the way now lyes, leaving the fence on the left hand, through the ground of the said Nagel and Dyckman, by the house where the said Dyckman now lives and over his bridge ; and so forward as the road now is unto Kingsbridge, the main course being north, a little easterly."

"From the Bridge by the Half-way House the road turns to the right hand, and so over the Creek to Harlaem, and from Harlaem by the lane as it now lyes to Johannes Myers, where it meets with the main road."

"From the house at the end of New York lane, there is likewise to lie a road, turning to the left hand, the course being northerly, and so by Great Kills, and forward as the said road now lyes, unto Teunis Edis's, and Captain D'Keys, through the said Edis's land."

"Also, from Rebecca's house in said New York lane, there is to be a road as it now lyes unto Greenwich, the said road running to the leftward of the house late of Captain Douw, deceased."

"All of the aforesaid roads are to be and remain of the breadth of four rods at least. Witness our hands this 16th of June, in the sixth year of her Majesty's reign, in An. Dom. 1707. Will. Anderson, Clement Elsworth, Pieter V. O'Blienis."

By the sixth section of the act of the 7th November, 1741, cited in the text, it was provided, that, "as doubts and scruples have arisen about the course of the road from Spring Garden Gate, at the end of the Broadway, towards Fresh Water, that the said road shall for ever thereafter be on a straight line or course from Spring Garden aforesaid, through the new road lately cut through the hill, by the house of Captain John Brown, where the windmill formerly stood, until it meets with the old road."

In June, 1774, the Corporation ordered that the street, beginning at the house of Andrew Hopper, nearly opposite St. Paul's Churchyard, and leading to Fresh Water, should be called Chatham street (Lib. 7, p. 327 Minutes).

The point of beginning of this road, Spring Garden, is easily located. It was at the northern end of the Shoemaker's field.

The location of the house of Andrew Hopper is defined by a deed from Thomas White to him, of 1775 (Lib. 40, p. 359).

So, on Lines' map of 1728, we find a windmill on a spot about the present line of Duane street, and Lieutenant Ratzer's map shows that the hill stretched across Chatham street. Hill's map of 1782 shows this more distinctly, and such hill was in the line of Chatham street for some distance.

Accordingly, the most ancient road turned from Chatham street, about Duane, and wound round into Pearl street, as is plainly shown on Lines' map of 1728. It pursued, I judge, the course of Thomas street.

The gate at the end of Queen street, mentioned in the act of 1703, is, no doubt, referred to in the resolution of the Common Council of the 15th of September, 1735, directing the surveyor to lay out a public road from the house of Benjamin Peck, in Queen street, to the Fresh Water, as the same was laid out on the 21st June, 1707, by Anderson and others, and appointed by the act of Assembly made in the second year of Queen Anne, 1703, entitled, &c.

The house of Benjamin Peck is ascertained by a deed from William Beekman to him, of the 30th May, 1718, and was about 150 feet easterly from the corner of Beekman and Pearl streets. It was bounded south by high water mark. It was known on the partition deed of 1708 as No. 217.

The Bloomingdale Road appears to have been opened under the act of 1708. In the act of 25th November, 1751, cited in the text, this fact is recited, and it is provided that such road, from the dwelling-house of John Horn, through Bloomendale district to the house of Abraham Hoogland, should be kept in order by the inhabitants of that district, and they were exempted from working on the Post Road leading from New York to King's Bridge.

On Ratzer's map of 1764, the road to Bloomendale is laid down diverging from the Post Road, and plainly just at the point of Twenty-third street, where it left the latter road, until within a few years, upon Madison square being enlarged and opened.

Sir Edmund Andross, in 1670, issued a patent to Solomon Peters, whose widow and heirs conveyed to John Horn and Cornelius Webber. The parcel of ground was close to this point of commencement, and thus the location of John Horn's house is indicated. (Valentine's History of New York, and map, p. 379.)

In a very valuable map, made by G. Bancker, in August, 1773, of Sir Peter Warren's property, in the possession of Edwin Smith, Esq., one parcel of such land is located at the corner of the Bowery and Abingdon road. It was a parcel of ten acres, and was granted to him by the Corporation of New York. On the opposite side of Abingdon road, the property is marked as of John Horn. The location is just above Twenty-first street, on the Bowery.

On the 1st of April, 1760, T. Marschalk, one of

the City Surveyors, presented a survey of the Bloomingdale Road, beginning at the north-east corner of Sir Peter Warren's land; running from the corner of said land north 11.45 east, above 10 chains, thence north 14 chains, to the east side of a large split rock, in the middle of the road, about 10 yards to the north of Peter Van Orden's house.

Approved of, with the addition, that the road there be 4 rods wide, and done at the expense of the Corporation; afterwards, to be kept in repair by the inhabitants of the Bloomingdale division.

1791, May 30. Committee reported, that great benefit would arise from laying open a new road from Bloomingdale to Fort Washington, and, on viewing the road, find it easy to extend the present road, terminating in lands of Nicholas De Peyster, through the lands of said De Peyster and others, and falling in with the present high road to Kingsbridge, somewhere about the lands of Dr. Brodhurst and Widow Watkins. The Committee ask power to have survey made, which is granted, and to be submitted to this Board.

1792, Feb. 17. Petition of Charles Ward Apthorpe and others, that Bloomingdale Road be continued to Morris House. Referred.

1792, March 12. Counter petition of inhabitants of Harlaem. Referred.

1792, October 22. Street Commissioners ordered to cause a survey of the contemplated road from Bloomingdale Road to Heights of Harlem, and report.

We observe that the survey of 1707 includes two roads besides the Post Road.

One of these roads was the Sandy Hill road, and road to Greenwich, with which it connected. On Ratzer's map, 1766, these roads are laid down very distinctly, and also on Hill's map, 1782. On the latter, part of it is called the road to Greenwich. It is described also as running to the left of Captain Douw's house. On diagram No. 6 Gerritt Douw's land is located behind the Brevoort parcel.

And there can be little doubt that the other road was what was subsequently called the Abingdon road.

Ratzer's map shows this road commencing about Twenty-first street, and running about north by west. It is not named on such map.

To a considerable extent we can establish the line of the old road to Harlaem with accuracy.

1. A road ran from about opposite St. Paul's Church over the common as far as Duane street, and on the line of Chatham street. It then turned short to the eastward, and ran on a winding course south-east, east by south, east, and north by east into what is now the line of Pearl street, and came into the present Chatham street on such line, about 100 feet south of the bridge on Roosevelt street. Lines' map of 1728 shows its course plainly.

That this road so far ran over the common lands of the city, is quite clear. Among other proofs, Bancker's compilation of surveys, dated in 1773, shows this as to the line from Chatham street through Thomas or Duane, to the point near the bridge.

That this line of road was used before the ordinance of 1669, is also clear. It may be that it was legally established under such ordinance.

2. The Commissioners under the act of 1703 opened the line of Chatham street, from Spring Garden (near Ann street) to Fresh Water, that is, the bridge about Roosevelt street. From Thomas (Duane) to the bridge, it was entirely new. They also opened a road on the line of Queen street (Pearl), from a point as before shown, 150 feet east from the corner of Beekman and Pearl, up to the present line of Chatham street.

3. From the bridge (Fresh Water), the act of 1703 recognizes that a road was in use, and locates it thus: "From thence by a small turning to the tree in the highway upon the hill; so along the said lane to the furthermost house in the same, the course being about north-north-east.

It can be clearly proven that, as far as the Brevoort property at least, near Eleventh street, the road, adopted in 1703, was the identical highway used and known as early as 1659. The ground briefs referred to in explanation of the Diagrams

6, 9, 10, 11, 12, and the patent to Bayard of 1697, show this plainly.

I have a strong impression that it was also identical as high up as the turn at the present Madison square, a little below Twenty-third street, where the Old Post Road proper commenced, bending to the eastward. This, I think, was "the end of the New York lane" mentioned in the act. It was where Horn's property lay, and where the Abingdon road led to the Great Kills. In part it ran over the line of a pre-existing road.

Middle Road.

1792. Petition to have the road leading to the Powder Magazine repaired.

1791. Committee ordered to view the Middle Road at Inklebergh, and report.

The Committee, on obtaining a profile of the Middle Road, submit a profile of about 1,600 feet between the bridge near the Powder-house and William Ogden's gate, which deserves the first attention.

The Bloomingdale Road was open, and is laid down on Ratzer's map of 1766. The middle road is not, although there is apparently a road on the hill, commencing about Thirty-fifth street, and running northerly. A lane ran down to the Post Road.

NOTE 61.—PAGE 382.

Commissioners on Encroachments.

The reports made under the act of March 30, 1855, and of that of April 16, 1860, are very important and voluminous. One was transmitted in January, 1856 (Senate Doc., No. 3); another in January, 1857 (Senate Doc., No. 40); and the last in January, 1862 (Senate Doc., No. 10). The importance of these reports, and especially of the shore maps, with which the last is accompanied, cannot be too highly estimated. They have been made with the highest skill and care, and will tend greatly to determine rights, and abridge litigation.

Washington square.

From accident, the memorandum upon this parcel of property was omitted at its proper place.

The property consisted of about ninety lots of ground, on the old Sandy Hill lane. It was purchased in 1797 for a potter's field, from the estate of Wm. S. Smith.

In October, 1827, proceedings were had in the Supreme Court, by which the ground was taken for a public square.

ADDENDA.

The case of the People *vs.* Bartholomew, mentioned in the text (vol. I., p. 363), as heard at General Term, has not yet been decided—June, 1862.

www.ingramcontent.com/pod-product-compliance
Lightning Source LLC
LaVergne TN
LVHW010225110826
845151LV00004B/1182

* 9 7 8 1 4 2 5 5 2 7 4 2 6 *